Core Data
by Tutorials

Third Edition

By the raywenderlich.com Tutorial Team

Aaron Douglas, Saul Mora, Matthew Morey and Pietro Rea

Core Data by Tutorials Third Edition

Aaron Douglas, Saul Mora, Matthew Morey and Pietro Rea

Copyright ©2016 Razeware LLC.

Notice of Rights

Notice of Liability

Trademarks

ISBN: 978-1-942878-26-1

Dedications

"To my husband, Mike, and my parents - all whom have inspired me to do my best and keep plugging away throughout the years."

— Aaron Douglas

"To my Family, Friends and the greater Apple Developer Community, without your support and attention, my life and career would not be nearly as awesome as it is with you all."

— Saul Mora

"To my amazing wife Tricia and my parents - Thanks for always supporting me."

— Matthew Morey

"To my wonderful wife Emily and my parents Aldo and Zoraida. Thank you for always supporting me every step of the way."

— Pietro Rea

About the authors

Aaron Douglas was that kid taking apart the mechanical and electrical appliances at five years of age to see how they worked. He never grew out of that core interest - to know how things work. He took an early interest in computer programming, figuring out how to get past security to be able to play games on his dad's computer. He's still that feisty nerd, but at least now he gets paid to do it. Aaron works for Automattic (WordPress.com, Akismet, Simplenote) as a Mobile Maker primarily on the WordPress for iOS app. Find Aaron on Twitter as @astralbodies.

Saul Mora is trained in the mystical and ancient arts of manual memory management, compiler macros and separate header files. Saul is a developer who honors his programming ancestors by using Optional variables in swift on all UIs created from Nib files. Despite being an Objective C neckbeard, Saul has embraced the Swift programming language. Currently, Saul resides in Shanghai, China working at 流利说 (Liulishuo) helping Chinese learn English while he is learning 普通话 (mandarin).

Matthew Morey is an engineer, author, hacker, creator and tinkerer. As an active member of the iOS community and Director of Mobile Engineering at MJD Interactive he has led numerous successful mobile projects worldwide. When not developing apps he enjoys traveling, snowboarding, and surfing. He blogs about technology and business at matthewmorey.com.

Pietro Rea is the founder and CEO of Sweetpea Mobile, a mobile-focused strategy, design and software development agency based just outside Washington D.C. Pietro's work has been featured in Apple's App Stores many times across several different categories: media, e-commerce, lifestyle and more. From Fortune 500 companies, to venture-backed startups to bootstrapped independents, Pietro has a passion for mobile software development done right. You can find Pietro on Twitter as @pietrorea.

:ditors

Ferguson is the technical editor for this book. He is a
Developer, with a passion for mobile development, for a
systems integration provider based out of Northern Virginia in
. metro area. When he's not coding, you can find him
life with his wife and daughter trying to travel as much as

elanger is the editor of this book. Chris Belanger is the Book
ead and Lead Editor for raywenderlich.com. If there are words
gle or a paragraph to ponder, he's on the case. When he kicks
ou can usually find Chris with guitar in hand, looking for the
beach, or exploring the lakes and rivers in his part of the world
oe.

irton is the final pass editor of this book. Rich is an iOS
er for MartianCraft, prolific Stack Overflow participant and
author of a development blog, Command Shift. When he's not in
front of a computer he is usually building Lego horse powered
spaceships (don't ask!) with his daughters.

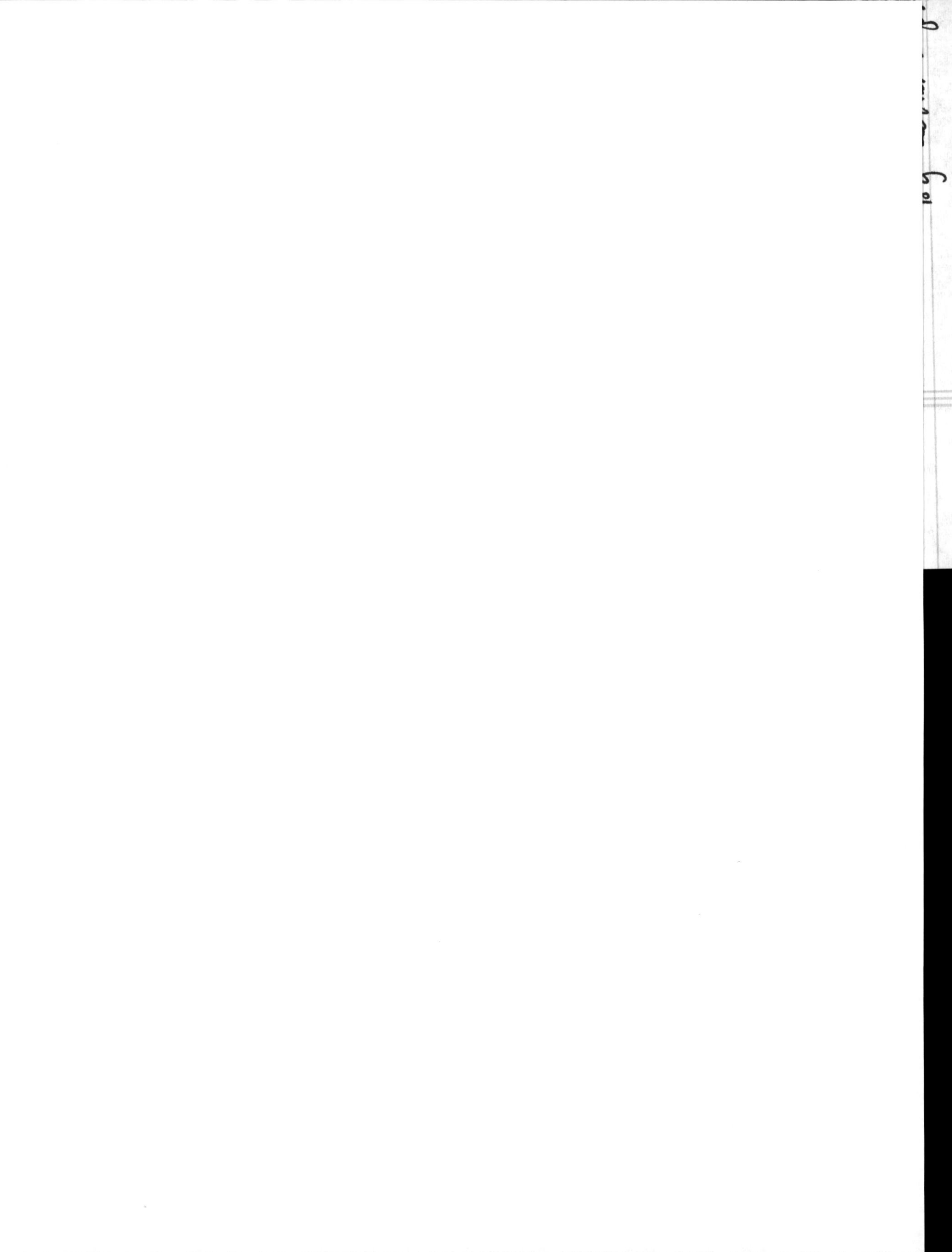

Table of Contents:

Introduction

What is Core Data? You'll hear a variety of answers to this question: It's a database! It's SQLite! It's not a database! And so forth.

Here's the technical answer: Core Data is an object graph management and persistence framework in the OS X and iOS SDKs.

That means Core Data can store and retrieve data, but it isn't a relational database like MySQL or SQLite. Although it can use SQLite as the data store behind the scenes, you don't think about Core Data in terms of tables and rows and primary keys.

Imagine you're writing an app to keep track of dining habits. You have a varied set of objects: restaurant objects, each with properties such as name and address; categories, to organize the restaurants; and visits, to log each visit to a restaurant.

The object graph in memory might look something like this:

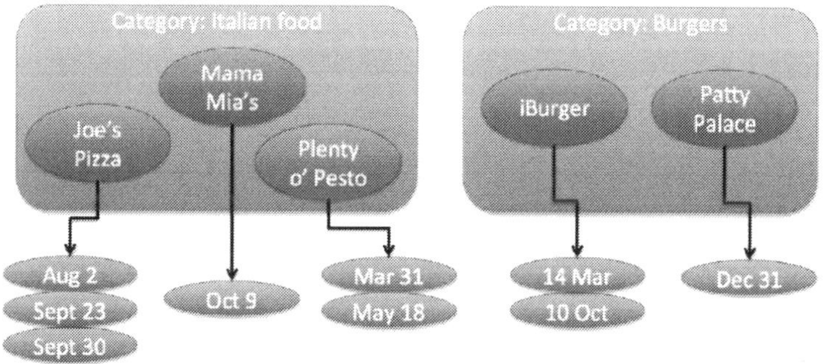

Object graph management means Core Data works with objects that you define, such as the ones in the diagram above. For example, each restaurant (represented by a red bubble) would have a property pointing back to the category object. It would also have a property holding the list of visits.

Since Cocoa is an object-oriented framework, you're probably storing data in objects already. Core Data builds on this to keep track of the objects and their relationships to each other. You can imagine expanding the graph to include what the user ordered, ratings and so on.

Persistence means the data is stored somewhere durable such as the device's flash memory or "the cloud." You point to the entire graph and just say "save."

When your app launches, you just say "load" and the entire object graph pops up in memory again, ready for use. That's Core Data at work!

Maybe your users eat out a lot and have thousands of restaurant visits — rest assured Core Data is smart about lazily loading objects and caching to optimize both memory usage and speed. Core Data has many other features aside from simply storing and fetching data:

You can perform custom filtering with predicates, sort the data and and calculate statistics. You'll learn all about these features and more in this book.

Introducing the third edition

Core Data this year is all about lowering the barrier of entry:

- Say goodbye to screens and screens of code just to set up the Core Data "stack".

- Say goodbye to generating and maintaining managed object subclasses.

- Say goodbye to having to tell Swift what type of managed object you're using.

- Say goodbye to single readers at the persistent store level.

- Say goodbye, sadly, to iCloud. Hey — it can't all be good news. :]

We've updated all the chapters in this book for Swift 3, iOS 10 and Xcode 8.

What you need

To follow along with the tutorials in this book, you'll need the following:

- A Mac running OS X Yosemite (10.11) or later. You'll need this to be able to install the latest version of Xcode.

- Xcode 8.0 or later. Xcode is the main development tool for iOS. You can download the latest version of Xcode for free from the Mac app store here: https://itunes.apple.com/app/xcode/id497799835?mt=12

You can use the iOS 10 Simulator that comes with Xcode for all of the chapters.

Once you have these items in place, you'll be able to follow along with every chapter in this book.

Who this book is for

This book is for iOS developers who already know the basics of iOS and Swift, and want to learn Core Data.

If you're a complete beginner to iOS, we suggest you read through The iOS Apprentice, 5th Edition first. That will give you a solid foundation in building iOS apps from the ground-up.

If you know the basics of iOS development but are new to Swift, we suggest you read Swift Apprentice first. That book has a similar hands-on approach and takes you on a comprehensive tour through the Swift language.

You can find both of these prerequisite books at our store: raywenderlich.com/store

How to use this book

This book will teach you the fundamentals of Core Data by means of hands-on tutorials. You'll jump right into building a Core Data app in Chapter 1, as we think most people learn best by doing. We encourage you to type along with the instructions in the book.

If you're new to Core Data or want to review the basics, we suggest you start with Chapters 1–3. These chapters cover the fundamentals of Core Data and you'll need the knowledge in them to understand the rest of the book.

Otherwise, we suggest a pragmatic approach. Each chapter stands on its own, so you can pick and choose the chapters that interest you the most.

What's in store

Here's a quick summary of what you'll find in each chapter:

1. Chapter 1, Your First Core Data App: You'll click File\New Project and write a Core Data app from scratch! This chapter covers the basics of setting up your data model and then adding and fetching records.

2. Chapter 2, NSManagedObject Subclasses: NSManagedObject is the base data storage class of your Core Data object graphs. This chapter will teach you how you customize your own managed object subclasses to store and validate data.

3. Chapter 3, The Core Data Stack: Under the hood, Core Data is made up of many parts working together. In this chapter, you'll learn about how these parts fit together, and move away from the starter Xcode template to build your own customizable system.

4. Chapter 4, Intermediate Fetching: Your apps will fetch data all the time, and Core Data offers many options for getting the data to you efficiently. This chapter covers more advanced fetch requests, predicates, sorting and asynchronous fetching.

5. Chapter 5, NSFetchedResultsController: Table views are at the core of many iOS apps, and Apple wants to make Core Data play nicely with them! In this chapter, you'll learn how NSFetchedResultsController can save you time and code when your table views are backed by data from Core Data.

6. Chapter 6, Versioning and Migration: As you update and enhance your app, its data model will almost certainly need to change. In this chapter, you'll learn how to create multiple versions of your data model and then migrate your users forward so they can keep their existing data as they upgrade.

7. Chapter 7, Unit Tests: Testing is an important part of the development process, and you shouldn't leave Core Data out of those tests! In this chapter, you'll learn how to set up a separate test environment for Core Data and see examples of how to test your models.

8. Chapter 8, Measuring and Boosting Performance: No one ever complained that an app was too fast, so it's important to be vigilant about tracking performance. In this chapter, you'll learn how to measure your app's performance with various Xcode tools and then pick up some tips for dealing with slow spots in your code.

9. Chapter 9, Multiple Managed Object Contexts: In this final chapter, you'll expand the usual Core Data stack to include multiple managed object contexts. You'll learn how this can improve perceived performance and help make your app architecture less monolithic and more compartmentalized.

Book source code and forums

You can get the source code for the book here:

www.raywenderlich.com/store/core-data-by-tutorials/source-code

You'll find all the code from the chapters, as well as solutions to the challenges for your reference.

We've also set up an official forum for the book at www.raywenderlich.com/forums. This is a great place to ask any questions you have about the book, or to submit any errors you might find.

PDF Version

We also have a PDF version of this book available, which can be handy if you want a soft copy to take with you, or you want to quickly search for a specific term within the book.

Buying the PDF version of the book also has a few extra benefits: free PDF updates each time we update the book, access to older PDF versions of the book, and you can download the PDF from anywhere, at anytime.

Visit the book store page here: https://www.raywenderlich.com/store/core-data-by-tutorials.

License

By purchasing Core Data by Tutorials, you have the following license:

- You are allowed to use and/or modify the source code in Core Data by Tutorials in as many apps as you want, with no attribution required.

- You are allowed to use and/or modify all art, images and designs that are included in Core Data by Tutorials in as many apps as you want, but must include this attribution line somewhere inside your app: "Artwork/images/designs: from Core Data by Tutorials book, available at http://www.raywenderlich.com."

- The source code included in Core Data by Tutorials is for your personal use only. You are NOT allowed to distribute or sell the source code in Core Data by Tutorials without prior authorization.

- This book is for your personal use only. You are NOT allowed to sell this book without prior authorization or distribute it to friends, co-workers or students; they would need to purchase their own copies.

All trademarks and registered trademarks appearing in this book are the property of their respective owners.

About the cover

The North Pacific giant octopus is normally red in color, but can quickly assume the color of its surroundings to blend in and hide from predators. Since it has no internal or external skeleton, it can squeeze into extremely small crevices. Core Data is a lot like that; it's easier than ever to work it into your apps and let its various tentacles weave their way into your persistent data store! :]

Chapter 1: Your First Core Data App

By Pietro Rea

Welcome to Core Data! In this chapter, you'll write your very first Core Data app. You'll see how easy it is to get started with all the resources provided in Xcode, from starter code templates to the Data Model editor.

You're going to hit the ground running right from the start. By the end of the chapter you'll know how to:

- Model data using Xcode's model editor

- Add new records to Core Data

- Fetch a set of records from Core Data

- Display the fetched records using a table view.

You'll also get a sense of what Core Data is doing behind the scenes, and how you can interact with the various moving pieces. This will put you well on your way to understanding the next two chapters, which continue the introduction to Core Data with more advanced models and data validation.

Getting started

Open Xcode and create a new iPhone project based on the **Single View Application** template. Name the app **HitList** and make sure **Use Core Data** is checked.

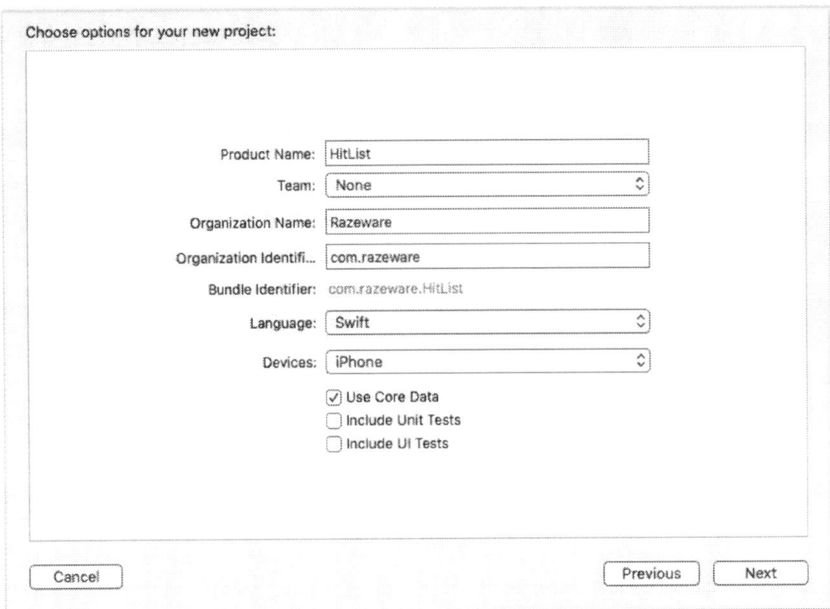

Checking the **Use Core Data** box will cause Xcode to generate boilerplate code for what's known as an `NSPersistentContainer` in **AppDelegate.swift**.

The `NSPersistentContainer` consists of a set of objects that facilitate saving and retrieving information from Core Data. Inside this container is an object to manage the Core Data state as a whole, an object representing the Data Model, and so on.

You'll learn about each of these pieces in the first few chapters. Later, you'll even have the chance to write your own Core Data stack! The standard stack works well for most apps, but depending on your your app and its data requirements, you can customize the stack to be more efficient.

> **Note:** Not all Xcode templates under iOS/Application have the option to start with Core Data. In Xcode 8, only the **Master-Detail Application** and **Single View Application** templates have the **Use Core Data** checkbox.

The idea for this sample app is simple: There will be a table view with a list of names for your very own "hit list". You'll be able to add names to this list and eventually, you'll use Core Data to make sure the data is stored between sessions. We don't condone violence in this book, so you can think of this app as a favorites list to keep track of your friends too, of course! :]

Click on **Main.storyboard** to open it in Interface Builder. Select the view controller on the canvas and embed it inside a navigation controller. From Xcode's **Editor** menu, select **Embed In...\ Navigation Controller**.

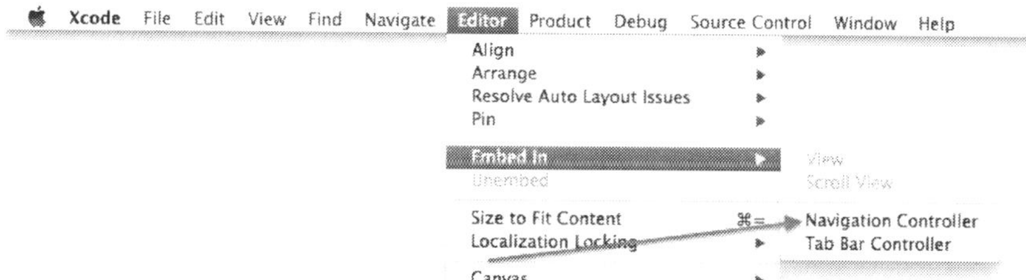

Next, drag a **Table View** from the object library into the view controller, then resize it so it covers the entire view.

If not already open, use the icon located in the lower left corner of your canvas to open Interface Builder's document outline.

Ctrl-drag from the **Table View** in the document outline to its parent view and select the **Leading Space to Container Margin** constraint:

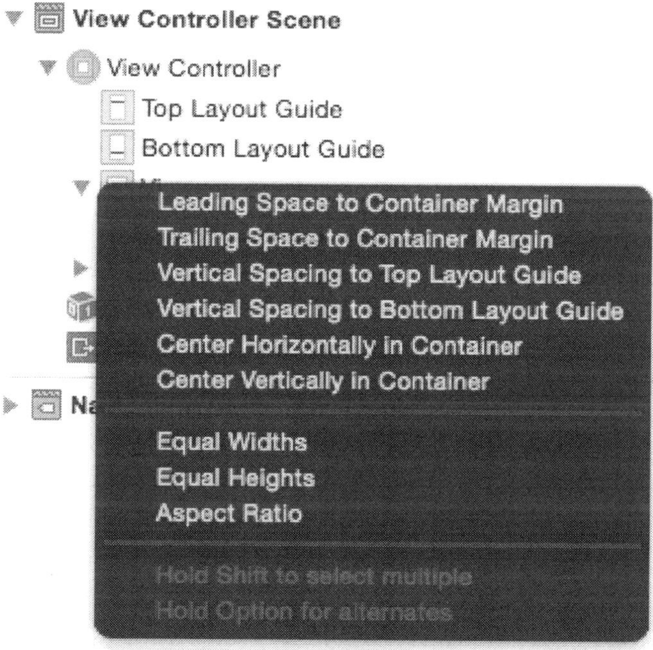

Do this three more times, selecting the constraints **Trailing Space to Container Margin**, **Vertical Spacing to Top Layout Guide** and finally, **Vertical Spacing to Bottom Layout Guide**. Adding those four constraints makes the table view fill its parent view.

Next, drag a **Bar Button Item** and place it on the view controller's navigation bar. Finally, select the bar button item and change its system item to **Add**. Your canvas should look similar to the following screenshot:

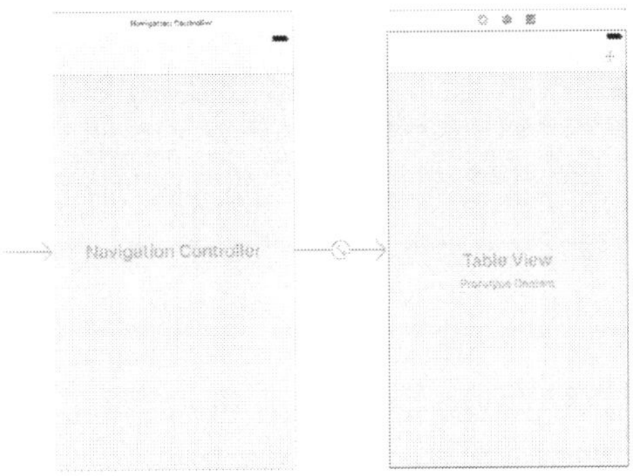

Every time you tap the **Add** button, an alert controller containing a text field will appear. From there you'll be able to type someone's name into the text field. Tapping `Save` will save the name, dismiss the alert controller and refresh the table view, displaying all the `names` you've entered.

But first, you need to make the view controller the table view's data source. In the canvas, Ctrl-drag from the table view to the yellow view controller icon above the navigation bar, as shown below, and click on **dataSource**:

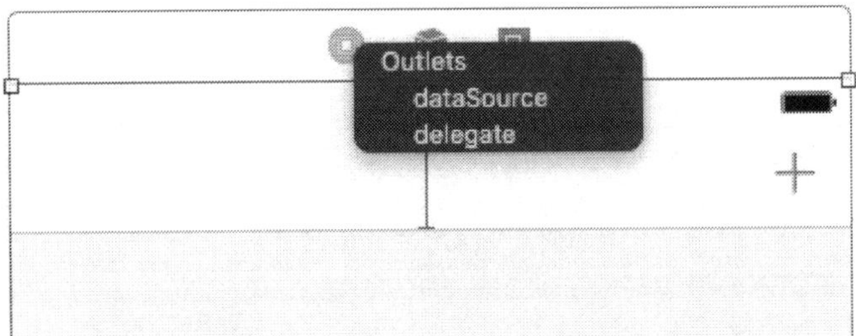

In case you were wondering, you don't need to set up the table view's delegate since tapping on the cells won't trigger any action. It doesn't get simpler than this!

Open the assistant editor by pressing Command-Option-Enter or by selecting the middle button on the Editor toolset on the Xcode bar. Delete the `didReceiveMemoryWarning()` method. Next, Ctrl-drag from the table view onto **ViewController.swift**, inside the class definition to create an `IBOutlet`.

Next, name the new `IBOutlet` property `tableView`, resulting in the following line:

```
@IBOutlet weak var tableView: UITableView!
```

Next, Ctrl-drag from the **Add** button into **ViewController.swift** just below your
`viewDidLoad()` definition. This time, create an action instead of an outlet, naming the
method `addName`, with a type `UIBarButtonItem`:

```
@IBAction func addName(_ sender: UIBarButtonItem) {

}
```

You can now refer to the table view and the bar button item's action in code.

Next, you'll set up the model for the table view. Add the following property to
ViewController.swift below the `tableView IBOutlet`:

```
var names: [String] = []
```

`names` is a mutable array holding string values displayed by the table view. Next, replace
the implementation of `viewDidLoad()` with the following:

```
override func viewDidLoad() {
  super.viewDidLoad()

  title = "The List"
  tableView.register(UITableViewCell.self,
                     forCellReuseIdentifier: "Cell")
}
```

This will set a title on the navigation bar and register the `UITableViewCell` class with
the table view.

> **Note**: `register(_:forCellReuseIdentifier:)` guarantees your table view will return a cell of the correct type when the **Cell** reuseIdentifier is provided to the dequeue method.

Next, still in **ViewController.swift**, add the following `UITableViewDataSource` extension below your class definition for `ViewController`:

```swift
// MARK: - UITableViewDataSource
extension ViewController: UITableViewDataSource {

  func tableView(_ tableView: UITableView,
                 numberOfRowsInSection section: Int) -> Int {
    return names.count
  }

  func tableView(_ tableView: UITableView,
                 cellForRowAt indexPath: IndexPath)
                 -> UITableViewCell {

    let cell =
      tableView.dequeueReusableCell(withIdentifier: "Cell",
                                    for: indexPath)
    cell.textLabel?.text = names[indexPath.row]
    return cell
  }
}
```

If you've ever worked with `UITableView`, this code should look very familiar. First you return the number of rows in the table as the number of items in your `names` array.

Next, `tableView(_:cellForRowAt:)` dequeues table view cells and populates them with the corresponding string from the `names` array.

Next, you need a way to add new names so the table view can display them. Implement the `addName` `IBAction` method you Ctrl-dragged into your code earlier:

```swift
// Implement the addName IBAction
@IBAction func addName(_ sender: AnyObject) {

  let alert = UIAlertController(title: "New Name",
                               message: "Add a new name",
                               preferredStyle: .alert)

  let saveAction = UIAlertAction(title: "Save",
                                 style: .default) {
    [unowned self] action in

    guard let textField = alert.textFields?.first,
```

```
        let nameToSave = textField.text else {
          return
      }

      self.names.append(nameToSave)
      self.tableView.reloadData()
    }

    let cancelAction = UIAlertAction(title: "Cancel",
                                     style: .default)

    alert.addTextField()

    alert.addAction(saveAction)
    alert.addAction(cancelAction)

    present(alert, animated: true)
  }
```

Every time you tap the **Add** button, this method presents a `UIAlertController` with a text field and two buttons, **Save** and **Cancel**.

Save inserts the text fields current text into the `names` array then reloads the table view. Since the `names` array is the model backing the table view, whatever you type into the text field will appear in the table view.

Finally, build and run your app for the first time. Next, tap the **Add** button. The alert controller will look like this:

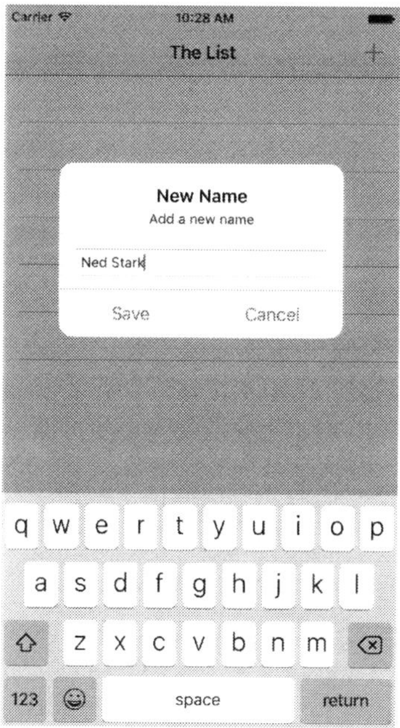

Add four or five names to the list. You should see something similar to below:

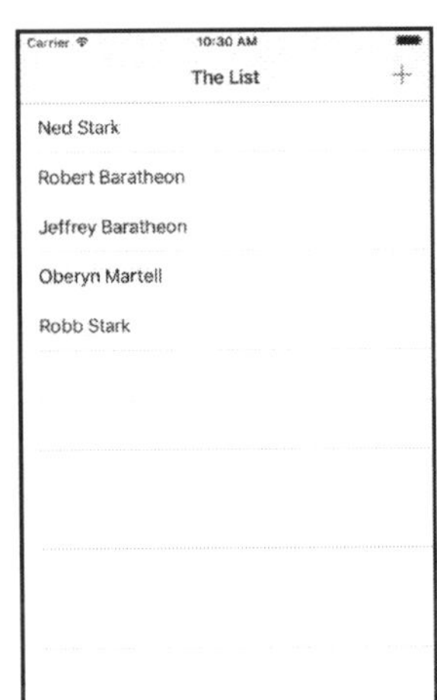

Your table view will display the data and your array will store the names, but the big thing missing here is **persistence**. The array is in memory but if you force quit the app or reboot your device, your hit list will be wiped out.

Core Data provides persistence, meaning it can store data in a more durable state so it can outlive an app re-launch or a device reboot.

You haven't added any Core Data yet, so nothing should persist after you navigate away from the app. Let's test this out. Press the Home button if you're using a physical device or the equivalent (Shift+⌘+H) if you're using the Simulator. This will take you back to the familiar app grid on the home screen:

From the home screen, tap the **HitList** icon to bring the app back to the foreground. The names are still on the screen. What happened?

When you tap the Home button, the app currently in the foreground goes to the background. When this happens, the operating system flash-freezes everything currently in memory, including the strings in the names array. Similarly, when it's time to wake up and return to the foreground, the operating system restores what used to be in memory as if you'd never left.

Apple introduced these advances in multitasking back in iOS 4. They create a seamless experience for iOS users but add a wrinkle to the definition of persistence for iOS developers. Are the names really persisted?

No, not really. If you had completely killed the app in the fast app switcher or turned off your phone, those names would be gone. You can verify this, as well. With the app in the foreground, double tap the Home button to enter the fast app switcher, like so:

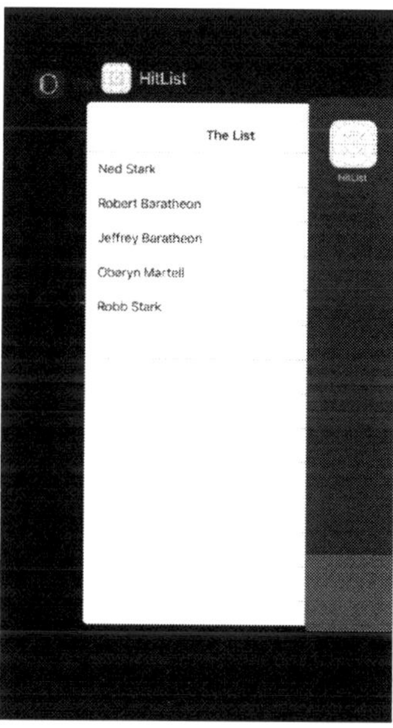

From here, flick the HitList app snapshot upwards to terminate the app. There should be no trace of HitList in living memory (no pun intended). Verify the names are gone by returning to the home screen and tapping on the HitList icon to trigger a fresh launch.

The difference between flash-freezing and persistence may be obvious if you've worked with iOS for some time and are familiar with the way multitasking works. In a user's mind, however, there is no difference. The user doesn't care *why* the names are still there, whether the app went into the background and came back, or because the app saved and reloaded them.

All that matters is the names are still there when the app comes back!

So the real test of persistence, is whether your data is still there after a fresh app launch.

Modeling your data

Now you know how to check for persistence, you can dive into Core Data. Your goal for the HitList app is simple: persist the names you enter so they're available for viewing after a fresh app launch.

Up to this point, you've been using plain old Swift strings to store the names in memory. In this section, you'll replace these strings with Core Data objects.

The first step is to create a **managed object model**, which describes the way Core Data represents data on disk.

By default, Core Data uses a SQLite database as the persistent store, so you can think of the Data Model as the database schema.

> **Note:** You'll come across the word *managed* quite a bit in this book. If you see "managed" in the name of a class, such as in `NSManagedObjectContext`, chances are you are dealing with a Core Data class. "Managed" refers to Core Data's management of the life cycle of Core Data objects.
>
> However, don't assume all Core Data classes contain the word "managed". Actually, most don't. For a comprehensive list of Core Data classes, check out the Core Data framework reference in the documentation browser.

Since you've elected to use Core Data, Xcode automatically created a Data Model file for you and named it **HitList.xcdatamodeld**.

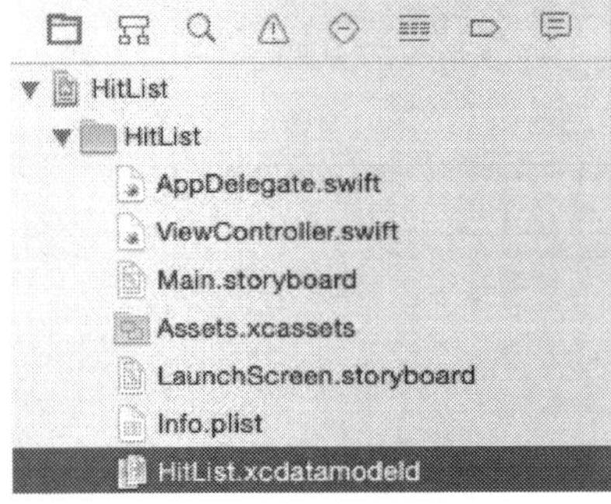

Open **HitList.xcdatamodeld**. As you can see, Xcode has a powerful Data Model editor:

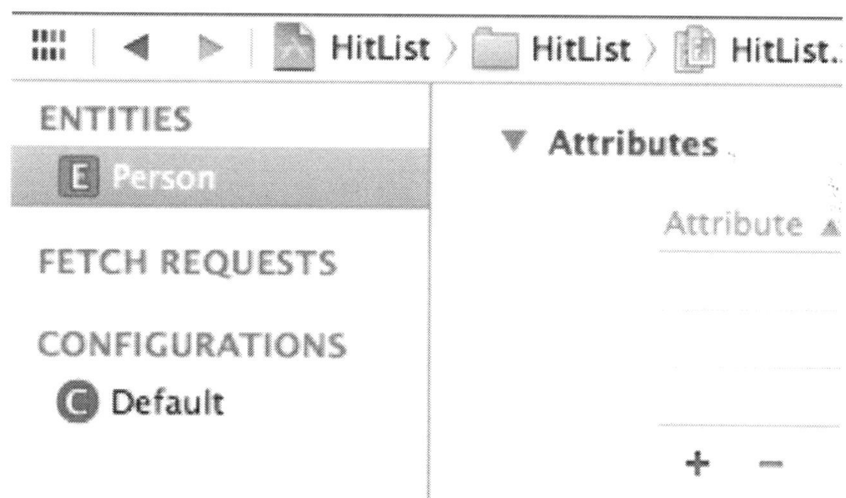

The Data Model editor has a lot of features you'll explore in later chapters. For now, let's focus on creating a single Core Data entity.

Click on **Add Entity** on the lower-left to create a new entity. Double-click the new entity and change its name to **Person**, like so:

You may be wondering why the model editor uses the term `Entity`. Weren't you simply defining a new class? As you'll see shortly, Core Data comes with its own vocabulary. Here's a quick rundown of some terms you'll commonly encounter:

- An **entity** is a class definition in Core Data. The classic example is an `Employee` or a `Company`. In a relational database, an entity corresponds to a table.

- An **attribute** is a piece of information attached to a particular entity. For example, an `Employee` entity could have attributes for the employee's `name`, `position` and `salary`. In a database, an attribute corresponds to a particular field in a table.

- A **relationship** is a link between multiple entities. In Core Data, relationships between two entities are called **to-one relationships**, while those between one and many entities are called **to-many relationships**. For example, a `Manager` can have a **to-many relationship** with a set of employees, whereas an individual `Employee` will usually have a **to-one relationship** with his manager.

> **Note:** You've probably noticed, entities sound a lot like a classes. Likewise, attributes and relationships sound a lot like properties. What's the difference? You can think of a Core Data entity as a class definition and the managed object as an instance of that class.

Now you know what an attribute is, you can add an attribute to `Person` object created earlier. Open **HitList.xcdatamodeld**. Next, select `Person` on the left-hand side and click the plus sign (+) under **Attributes**.

Set the new attribute's name to, er, **name** and change its type to **String**:

▼ Attributes

In Core Data, an attribute can be of one of several data types. You'll learn about these in the next few chapters.

Saving to Core Data

Open **ViewController.swift**, add the following Core Data module import below the UIKit import:

```
import CoreData
```

This import is all you need to start using the Core Data API in your code.

Next, replace the names property definition with the following:

```
var people: [NSManagedObject] = []
```

You'll store Person entities rather than string names, so you rename the array serving as the table view's data model to people. It now holds instances of NSManagedObject rather than simple strings.

NSManagedObject represents a single object stored in Core Data; you must use it to create, edit, save and delete from your Core Data persistent store. As you'll see shortly, NSManagedObject is a shape-shifter. It can take the form of any entity in your Data Model, appropriating whatever attributes and relationships you defined.

Since you're changing the table view's model, you must also replace both data source methods implemented earlier. Replace your UITableViewDataSource extension with the following:

```
// MARK: - UITableViewDataSource
extension ViewController: UITableViewDataSource {
  func tableView(_ tableView: UITableView,
                 numberOfRowsInSection section: Int) -> Int {
    return people.count
  }

  func tableView(_ tableView: UITableView,
                 cellForRowAt indexPath: IndexPath)
                 -> UITableViewCell {

    let person = people[indexPath.row]
    let cell =
      tableView.dequeueReusableCell(withIdentifier: "Cell",
                                    for: indexPath)
    cell.textLabel?.text =
      person.value(forKeyPath: "name") as? String
```

```
        return cell
    }
}
```

The most significant change to these methods occurs in
`tableView(_:cellForRowAt:)`. Instead of matching cells with the corresponding
string in the model array, you now match cells with the corresponding
`NSManagedObject`.

Note how you grab the `name` attribute from the `NSManagedObject`. It happens here:

```
cell.textLabel?.text =
    person.value(forKeyPath: "name") as? String
```

Why do you have to do this? As it turns out, `NSManagedObject` doesn't know about the
name attribute you defined in your Data Model, so there's no way of accessing it directly
with a property. The only way Core Data provides to read the value is **key-value coding**,
commonly referred to as KVC.

> **Note**: If you're new to iOS development, you may not be familiar with KVC.
>
> KVC is a mechanism in Foundation for accessing an object's properties indirectly
> using strings. In this case, KVC makes `NSMangedObject` behave more or less like
> a dictionary at runtime.
>
> Key-value coding is available to all classes inheriting from `NSObject`, including
> `NSManagedObject`. You can't access properties using KVC on a Swift object that
> doesn't descend from `NSObject`.

Next, find `addName()` and replace the `save` `UIAlertAction` with the following:

```
let saveAction = UIAlertAction(title: "Save", style: .default) {
    [unowned self] action in

    guard let textField = alert.textFields?.first,
        let nameToSave = textField.text else {
            return
    }

    self.save(name: nameToSave)
    self.tableView.reloadData()
}
```

This takes the text in the text field and passes it over to a new method named `save(_:)`. Xcode complains because `save(_:)` doesn't exist yet. Add it below `addName(_:)`:

```swift
func save(name: String) {

  guard let appDelegate =
    UIApplication.shared.delegate as? AppDelegate else {
    return
  }

  // 1
  let managedContext =
    appDelegate.persistentContainer.viewContext

  // 2
  let entity =
    NSEntityDescription.entity(forEntityName: "Person",
                               in: managedContext)!

  let person = NSManagedObject(entity: entity,
                               insertInto: managedContext)

  // 3
  person.setValue(name, forKeyPath: "name")

  // 4
  do {
    try managedContext.save()
    people.append(person)
  } catch let error as NSError {
    print("Could not save. \(error), \(error.userInfo)")
  }
}
```

This is where Core Data kicks in! Here's what the code does:

1. Before you can save or retrieve anything from your Core Data store, you first need to get your hands on an `NSManagedObjectContext`. You can consider a managed object context as an in-memory "scratchpad" for working with managed objects.

   Think of saving a new managed object to Core Data as a two-step process: first, you insert a new managed object into a managed object context; then, after you're happy with your shiny new managed object, you "commit" the changes in your managed object context to save it to disk.

   Xcode has already generated a managed object context as part of the new project's template. Remember, this only happens if you check the **Use Core Data** checkbox at the beginning. This default managed object context lives as a property of the `NSPersistentContainer` in the application delegate. To access it, you first get a reference to the app delegate.

2. You create a new managed object and insert it into the managed object context. You can do this in one step with `NSManagedObject`'s static method: `entity(forEntityName:in:)`.

    You may be wondering what an `NSEntityDescription` is all about. Recall earlier, `NSManagedObject` was called a shape-shifter class because it can represent any entity. An entity description is the piece linking the entity definition from your Data Model with an instance of `NSManagedObject` at runtime.

3. With an `NSManagedObject` in hand, you set the `name` attribute using key-value coding. You must spell the KVC key (`name` in this case) **exactly** as it appears in your Data Model, otherwise your app will crash at runtime.

4. You commit your changes to `person` and save to disk by calling `save` on the managed object context. Note `save` can throw an error, which is why you call it using the `try` keyword within a `do-catch` block. Finally, insert the new managed object into the `people` array so it shows up when the table view reloads.

That's a little more complicated than an array of strings, but not too bad. Some of the code here, such as getting the managed object context and entity, could be done just once in your own `init()` or `viewDidLoad()` then reused later. For simplicity, you're doing it all in the same method.

Build and run the app, and add a few names to the table view:

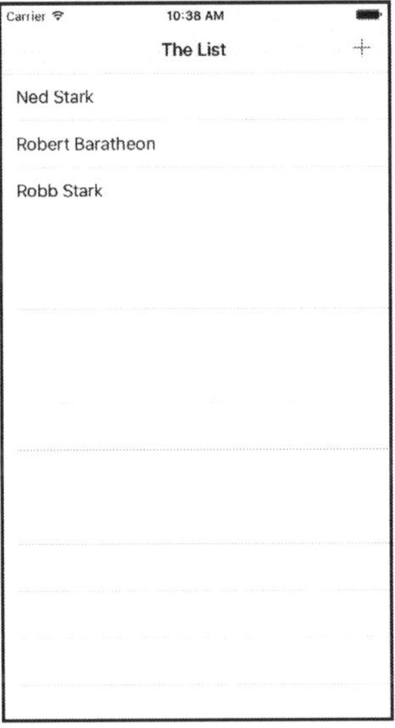

If the names are actually stored in Core Data, the HitList app should pass the persistence test. Double-tap the Home button to bring up the fast app switcher. Terminate the HitList app by flicking it upwards.

From Springboard, tap the HitList app to trigger a fresh launch. Wait, what happened? The table view is empty:

You saved to Core Data, but after a fresh app launch, the `people` array is empty! That's because the data is sitting on disk waiting for you, but you're not showing it yet.

Fetching from Core Data

To get data from your persistent store into the managed object context, you have to **fetch** it. Open **ViewController.swift** and add this code below `viewDidLoad()`:

```swift
override func viewWillAppear(_ animated: Bool) {
  super.viewWillAppear(animated)

  //1
  guard let appDelegate =
    UIApplication.shared.delegate as? AppDelegate else {
      return
  }

  let managedContext =
    appDelegate.persistentContainer.viewContext

  //2
  let fetchRequest =
    NSFetchRequest<NSManagedObject>(entityName: "Person")

  //3
```

```
  do {
    people = try managedContext.fetch(fetchRequest)
  } catch let error as NSError {
    print("Could not fetch. \(error), \(error.userInfo)")
  }
}
```

Step by step, this is what the code does:

1. Before you can do anything with Core Data, you need a managed object context. Fetching is no different! Like before, you pull up the application delegate and grab a reference to its persistent container to get your hands on its `NSManagedObjectContext`.

2. As the name suggests, `NSFetchRequest` is the class responsible for fetching from Core Data. Fetch requests are both powerful and flexible. You can use fetch requests to fetch a set of objects meeting the provided criteria (i.e. give me all employees living in Wisconsin and have been with the company at least three years), individual values (i.e. give me the longest name in the database) and more.

    Fetch requests have several qualifiers used to refine the set of results returned. You'll learn more about these qualifiers in Chapter 4, "Intermediate Fetching"; for now, you should know `NSEntityDescription` is a required one of these qualifiers.

    Setting a fetch request's `entity` property, or alternatively initializing it with `init(entityName:)`, fetches *all* objects of a particular entity. This is what you do here to fetch all `Person` entities. Also note `NSFetchRequest` is a generic type. This use of generics specifies a fetch request's *expected* return type, in this case `NSManagedObject`.

3. You hand the fetch request over to the managed object context to do the heavy lifting. `fetch(_:)` returns an array of managed objects meeting the criteria specified by the fetch request.

> **Note:** Like `save()`, `fetch(_:)` can also throw an error so you have to use it within a do block. If an error occurred during the fetch, you can inspect the error inside the `catch` block and respond appropriately.

Build and run the application. Immediately, you should see the list of names you added earlier:

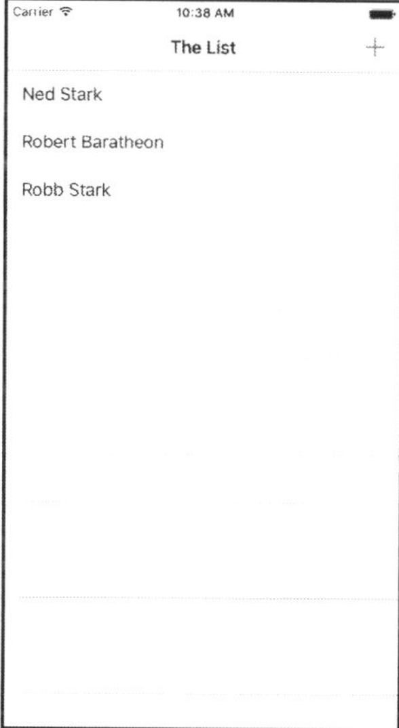

Great! They're back from the dead (pun intended). Add a few more names to the list and restart the app to verify saving and fetching are working. Short of deleting the app, resetting the Simulator or throwing your phone off a tall building, the names will appear in the table view no matter what.

Where to go from here?

In just a few pages, you've already experienced several fundamental Core Data concepts: Data Models, entities, attributes, managed objects, managed object contexts and fetch requests.

There were a few rough edges in HitList: you had to get the managed object context from the app delegate each time, and you used KVC to access the attributes rather than a more natural object-style `person.name`.

The best way to get familiar with Core Data is to play with it, and that's exactly what you'll do in the next chapter! You'll file away some of those rough edges and also work with a more complex Data Model as you learn more about Core Data.

Chapter 2: NSManagedObject Subclasses

By Pietro Rea

You got your feet wet with a simple Core Data app in Chapter 1; now it's time to explore more of what Core Data has to offer!

At the core of this chapter is subclassing `NSManagedObject` to make your own classes for each entity. This creates a direct one-to-one mapping between entities in the data model editor and classes in your code. It means in some parts of your code, you can work with objects and properties without worrying too much about the Core Data side of things.

Along the way, you'll learn about all the data types available in Core Data entities, including a couple that are outside the usual string and number types. And with all the data type options available, you'll also learn about validating data to automatically check values before saving.

Getting started

Head over to the files that accompany this book and open the sample project named **Bow Ties**. Like HitList, this project uses Xcode's Core Data-enabled **Single View Application** template. And like before, this means Xcode generated its own ready-to-use Core Data stack located in **AppDelegate.swift**.

Open **Main.storyboard**. Here you'll find the sample project's single-page UI:

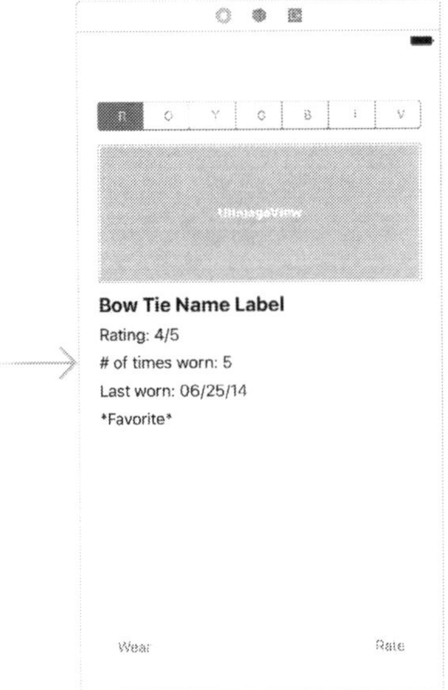

As you can probably guess, Bow Ties is a lightweight bow tie management application. You can switch between the different colors of bow ties you own — the app assumes one of each — using the topmost segmented control. Tap "R" for red, "O" for orange and so on.

Tapping on a particular color pulls up an image of the tie and populates several labels on the screen with specific information about the tie. This includes:

- The name of the bow tie (so you can tell similarly-colored ones apart)

- The number of times you've worn the tie

- The date you last wore the tie

- Whether the tie is a favorite of yours

The **Wear** button on the bottom-left increments the number of times you've worn that particular tie and sets the `last worn` date to today.

Orange is not your color? Not to worry. The **Rate** button on the bottom-right changes a bow tie's rating. This particular rating system uses a scale from 0 to 5, allowing for decimal values.

That's what the application is **supposed** to do in its final state. Open
ViewController.swift to see what it currently does:

```swift
import UIKit

class ViewController: UIViewController {

  // MARK: - IBOutlets
  @IBOutlet weak var segmentedControl: UISegmentedControl!
  @IBOutlet weak var imageView: UIImageView!
  @IBOutlet weak var nameLabel: UILabel!
  @IBOutlet weak var ratingLabel: UILabel!
  @IBOutlet weak var timesWornLabel: UILabel!
  @IBOutlet weak var lastWornLabel: UILabel!
  @IBOutlet weak var favoriteLabel: UILabel!

  // MARK: - View Life Cycle
  override func viewDidLoad() {
    super.viewDidLoad()
  }

  // MARK: - IBActions
  @IBAction func segmentedControl(_ sender: AnyObject) {

  }

  @IBAction func wear(_ sender: AnyObject) {

  }

  @IBAction func rate(_ sender: AnyObject) {

  }
}
```

The bad news is that in its current state, Bow Ties doesn't do anything. The good news is
you don't need to do any Ctrl-dragging! :]

The segmented control and all the labels on the user interface are already connected to
`IBOutlets` in code. In addition, the segmented control, `Wear` and `Rate` button all have
corresponding `IBActions`.

It looks like you have everything you need to get started adding some Core Data — but
wait, what are you going to display onscreen? There's no input method to speak of, so the
app must ship with sample data.

That's exactly right. Bow Ties includes a property list called **SampleData.plist** containing
the information for seven sample ties, one for each color of the rainbow.

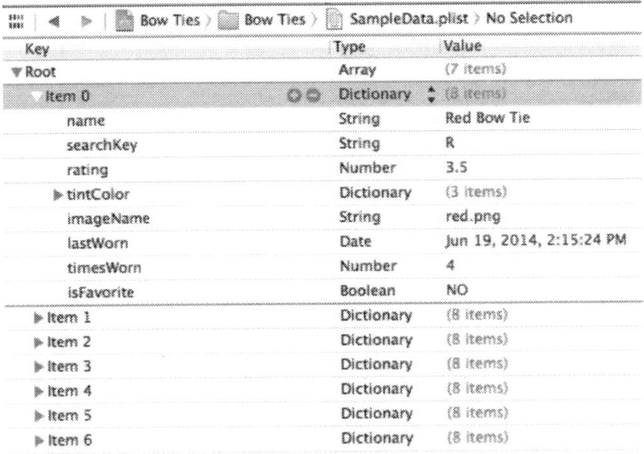

Furthermore, the application's asset catalog **Assets.xcassets** contains seven images corresponding to the seven bow ties in **SampleData.plist**.

What you have to do now is take this sample data, store it in Core Data and use it to implement the bow tie management functionality.

Modeling your data

In the previous chapter, you learned that one of the first things you have to do when starting a new Core Data project is create your data model.

Open **Bow_Ties.xcdatamodeld** and click **Add Entity** on the lower-left to create a new entity. Double-click on the new entity and change its name to **Bowtie**, like so:

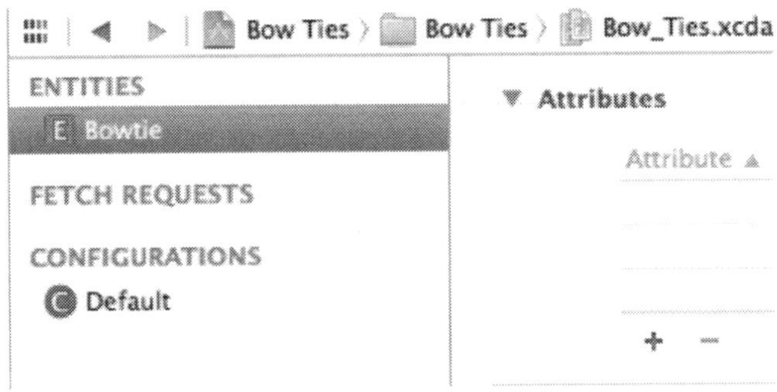

In the previous chapter, you created a simple `Person` entity with a single string attribute to hold the person's name. Core Data supports several other primitive data types, and you'll use most of them for the new `Bowtie` entity.

An attribute's data type determines what kind of data you can store in it and how much space it will occupy on disk. In Core Data, an attribute's data type begins as `Undefined` so you'll have to change it to something else.

If you remember from **SampleData.plist**, each bow tie has eight associated pieces of information. This means the `Bowtie` entity will end up with at least eight attributes in the model editor.

Select `Bowtie` on the left-hand side and click the plus sign (+) under **Attributes**. Change the new attribute's name to **name** and set its type to **String**:

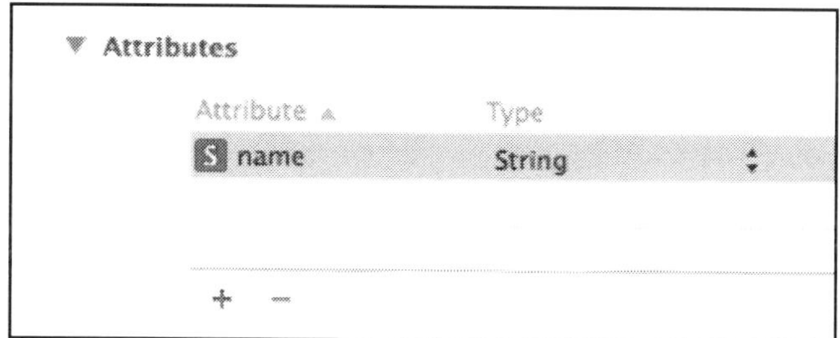

Repeat this process five more times to add the following attributes:

- A **Boolean** named **isFavorite**

- A **Date** named **lastWorn**

- A **Double** named **rating**

- A **String** named **searchKey**

- An **Integer 32** named **timesWorn**

When you're finished, your Attributes section should look like this:

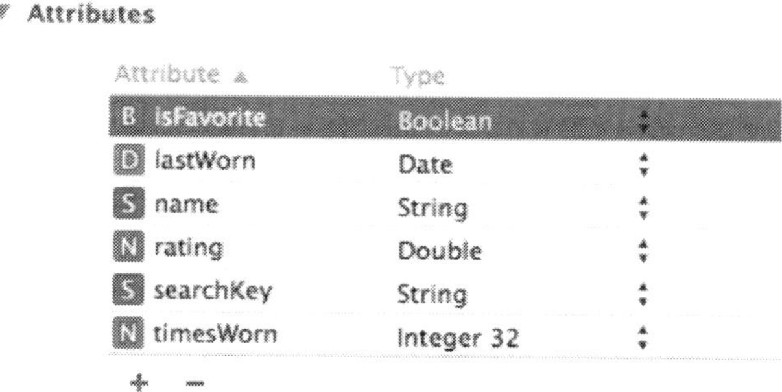

Don't worry if the order of the attributes is different — all that matters is that the attribute names and types are correct.

> **Note:** You may have noticed you have three options for the `timesWorn` integer attribute: **Integer 16**, **Integer 32** or **Integer 64**.
>
> 16, 32 and 64 refer to the number of bits that represent the integer. This is important for two reasons: the number of bits reflects how much space an integer takes up on disk as well as how many values it can represent, or its `range`. Here are the ranges for the three types of integers:
>
> Range for 16-bit integer: -32768 to 32767
>
> Range for 32-bit integer: –2147483648 to 2147483647
>
> Range for 64-bit integer: –9223372036854775808 to 9223372036854775807
>
> How do you choose? The source of your data will dictate the best type of integer. You are assuming your users *really* like bow ties, so a 32-bit integer should offer enough storage for a lifetime of bow tie wear. :]

Each bow tie has an associated image. How will you store it in Core Data? Add one more attribute to the `Bowtie` entity, name it **photoData** and change its data type to **Binary Data**:

▼ **Attributes**

Attribute ▲	Type
⏼ photoData	Binary Data
B isFavorite	Boolean
D lastWorn	Date
S name	String

Core Data provides the option of storing arbitrary blobs of binary data directly in your data model. These could be anything from images, to PDF files, to anything that can be serialized into zeroes and ones.

As you can imagine, this convenience can come at a steep cost. Storing a large amount of binary data in the same SQLite database as your other attributes will likely impact your app's performance. That means a giant binary blob would be loaded into memory each time you access an entity, even if you only need to access its name!

Luckily, Core Data anticipates this problem. With the `photoData` attribute selected, open the **Attributes Inspector** and check the **Allows External Storage** option.

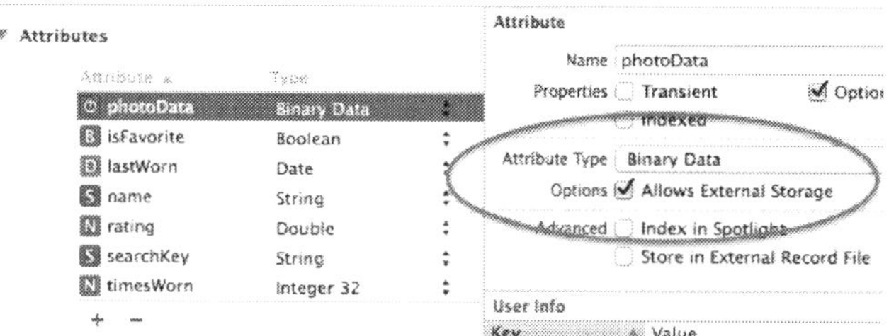

When you enable **Allows External Storage**, Core Data heuristically decides on a per-value basis if it should save the data directly in the database or store a URI that points to a separate file.

> **Note:** The **Allows External Storage** option is only available for the binary data attribute type. In addition, if you turn it on, you won't be able to query Core Data using this attribute.

In summary, besides Strings, Integers, Doubles, Booleans and Dates, Core Data can also save Binary Data, and it can do so efficiently and intelligently.

Storing non-standard data types in Core Data

Still, there are many other types of data you may want to save. For example, what would you do if you had to store an instance of `UIColor`?

With the options presented so far, you would have to deconstruct the color into its individual components and save them as integers (e.g., red: 255, green: 101, blue: 155). Then, after fetching these components, you'd have to reconstitute your color at runtime.

Alternatively, you could serialize the `UIColor` instance to NSData and save it as binary data. Then again, you'd also have to "add water" afterward to reconstitute the binary data back to the `UIColor` object you wanted in the first place.

Once again, Core Data has your back. If you took a close look at **SampleData.plist**, you probably noticed that each bow tie has an associated color. Select the `Bowtie` entity in the model editor and add a new attribute named **tintColor** of data type **Transformable**:

▼ **Attributes**

Attribute ▲	Type
T tintColor	Transformable
B isFavorite	Boolean
D lastWorn	Date
S name	String
photoData	Binary Data
N rating	Double
S searchKey	String
N timesWorn	Integer 32

You can save any data type to Core Data (even ones you define) using the `Transformable` type as long as your type conforms to the `NSCoding` protocol.

`UIColor` conforms to `NSSecureCoding`, which inherits from `NSCoding`, so it can use the transformable type out of the box. If you wanted to save your own custom object, you would first have to implement the `NSCoding` protocol.

Note: The `NSCoding` protocol is a simple way to archive and unarchive objects into data buffers so they can be saved to disk.

If you want to familiarize yourself with `NSCoding`, check out our `NSCoding` tutorial for a quick introduction:

http://www.raywenderlich.com/1914/nscoding-tutorial-for-ios-how-to-save-your-app-data

Your data model is now complete. The `Bowtie` entity has the eight attributes it needs to store all the information in **SampleData.plist**.

Managed object subclasses

In the sample project from the last chapter, you used key-value coding to access the attributes on the `Person` entity. It looked something like this:

```
// Set the name

person.setValue(aName, forKey: "name")

// Get the name

let name = person.value(forKey: "name")
```

Even though you can do everything directly on `NSManagedObject` using key-value coding, that doesn't mean you should!

The biggest problem with key-value coding is that you're accessing data using strings instead of strongly-typed classes. This is often jokingly referred to as writing `stringly typed` code. :]

As you probably know from experience, `stringly typed` code is vulnerable to silly human errors such as mistyping and misspelling. Key-value coding also doesn't take full advantage of Swift's type-checking and Xcode's auto-completion.

The best alternative to key-value coding is to create `NSManagedObject` subclasses for each entity in your data model. That means there will be a `Bowtie` class with correct types for each property.

Xcode can generate the subclass for you either manually or automatically. Why would you want Xcode to do it for you? It can be a bit of a hassle having to generate these subclass files and have them clutter up your project if you never have to look at them or change them. In Xcode 8, you can choose, on a per-entity basis, to have Xcode automatically generate and update these files, and store them in the derived data folder for your project.

This setting is in the **Codegen** field of the **Data Model** inspector when using the model editor. Because you're learning about Core Data in this book, you're not going to use automatic code generation because it helps a lot to be able to easily see the files that have been generated for you.

Make sure you still have **Bow_Ties.xcdatamodeld** open, select the `Bowties` entity and open the Data Model inspector. Set the **Codegen** dropdown to **Manual/None**, as shown below:

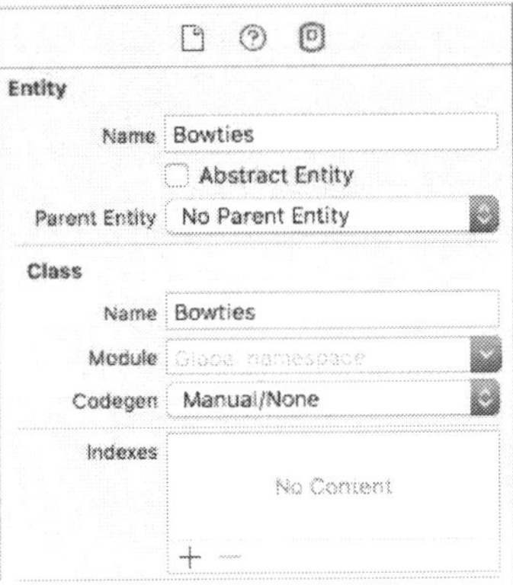

> **Note:** Make sure you change this code generation setting **before** your first compilation after you add the `Bowtie` entity to the model.
>
> If you set the code generation setting after your first compilation, you'll have two versions of the managed object subclass: one in derived data and a second one in your source code. If this happens, you'll run into problems when you try to compile again.

Now go to **Editor\Create NSManagedObject Subclass…**. Select the data model and then the `Bowtie` entity in the next two dialog boxes, then select **Swift** as the language option in the final box. Click **Create** to save the file.

Xcode generated two Swift files for you, one called **Bowtie+CoreDataClass.swift** and a second called **Bowtie+CoreDataProperties.swift**. Open **Bowtie+CoreDataClass.swift**. It should look like this:

```swift
import Foundation
import CoreData

public class Bowtie: NSManagedObject {

}
```

Next, open **Bowtie+CoreDataProperties.swift**. It should look like this:

```swift
import Foundation
import CoreData

extension Bowtie {

  @nonobjc public class func fetchRequest()
    -> NSFetchRequest<Bowtie> {
      return NSFetchRequest<Bowtie>(entityName: "Bowtie");
  }

  @NSManaged public var name: String?
  @NSManaged public var isFavorite: Bool
  @NSManaged public var lastWorn: NSDate?
  @NSManaged public var searchKey: String?
  @NSManaged public var timesWorn: Int32
  @NSManaged public var photoData: NSData?
  @NSManaged public var tintColor: NSObject?
}
```

In object-oriented parlance, an object is a set of **values** and a set of **operations** defined on those values. In this case, Xcode separates the two into two separate files. The values (i.e. the properties that correspond to the Bowtie attributes in your data model) are in **BowTie+CoreDataProperties.swift** whereas the operations are in the currently empty **Bowtie+CoreDataClass.swift**.

> **Note:** If your `Bowtie` entity changes, you can go to **Editor\Create NSManagedObject Subclass...** one more time to re-generate **BowTie+CoreDataProperties.swift**.
>
> The second time you do this, you won't re-generate **Bowtie+CoreDataClass.swift** so you don't have to worry about overwriting any methods you add in there. In fact, this is the primary reason why Core Data generates two files instead of one, as it used to do in previous versions of iOS.

Xcode has created a class with a property for each attribute in your data model.

Note there is a corresponding class in `Foundation` or in the Swift standard library for every attribute type in the model editor. Here's the full mapping of attribute types to runtime classes:

- **String** maps to `String?`

- **Integer 16** maps to `Int16`

- **Integer 32** maps to `Int32`

- **Integer 64** maps to `Int64`

- **Float** maps to `Float`

- **Double** maps to `Double`

- **Boolean** maps to `Bool`

- **Decimal** maps to `NSDecimalNumber?`

- **Date** maps to `NSDate?`

- **Binary data** maps to `NSData?`

- **Transformable** maps to `NSObject?`

> **Note:** Similar to `@dynamic` in Objective-C, the `@NSManaged` attribute informs the Swift compiler that the backing store and implementation of a property will be provided at runtime instead of compile time.
>
> The normal pattern is for a property to be backed by an instance variable in memory. A property on a managed object is different: It's backed by the managed object context, so the source of the data is not known at compile time.

Congratulations, you've just made your first managed object subclass in Swift! Compared with key-value coding, this is a much better way of working with Core Data entities. There are two main benefits:

1. Managed object subclasses unleash the syntactic power of Swift properties. By accessing attributes using properties instead of key-value coding, you again befriend Xcode and the compiler.

2. You gain the ability to override existing methods or to add your own. Note there are some `NSManagedObject` methods you must never override. Check Apple's documentation of `NSManagedObject` for a complete list.

To make sure everything is hooked up correctly between the data model and your new managed object subclass, you'll perform a small test.

Open **AppDelegate.swift** and replace `application(_:didFinishLaunchingWithOptions:)` with the following implementation:

```swift
func application(_ application: UIApplication,
                 didFinishLaunchingWithOptions
  launchOptions: [UIApplicationLaunchOptionsKey: Any]?) -> Bool
  {
```

```swift
    // Save test bow tie
    let bowtie = NSEntityDescription.insertNewObject(
      forEntityName: "Bowtie",
      into: self.persistentContainer.viewContext) as! Bowtie
    bowtie.name = "My bow tie"
    bowtie.lastWorn = NSDate()

    // Retrieve test bow tie
    do {
      let request = NSFetchRequest<Bowtie>(entityName: "Bowtie")
      let ties =
        try self.persistentContainer.viewContext.fetch(request)

      let sample = ties.first
      print("Name :\(sample?.name), Worn: \(sample?.lastWorn)")

    } catch let error as NSError {
      print("Fetching error: \(error), \(error.userInfo)")
    }
    return true
}
```

On app launch, this test creates a bow tie and sets its `name` and `lastWorn` properties before saving the managed object context.

Immediately after that, it fetches all `Bowtie` entities and prints the name and the `lastWorn` date of the first one to the console; there should only be one at this point. Build and run the application and pay close attention to the console:

```
Name: Optional("My bow tie"),  Worn: Optional(2015-07-14 11:53:08 +0000)
```

If you've been following along carefully, `name` and `lastWorn` print to the console as expected. This means you were able to save and fetch a `Bowtie` managed object subclass successfully. With this new knowledge under your belt, it's time to implement the entire sample app.

Propagating a managed context

Open **ViewController.swift** and add the following below `import UIKit`:

```swift
import CoreData
```

Next, add the following below the last `IBOutlet` property:

```
// MARK: - Properties
var managedContext: NSManagedObjectContext!
```

To reiterate, before you can do anything in Core Data, you first have to get an
`NSManagedObjectContext` to work with. Knowing how to **propagate** a managed object
context to different parts of your app is an important aspect of Core Data programming.

Open **AppDelegate.swift** and replace
`application(_:didFinishLaunchingWithOptions:)`, which currently contains the
test code, with the following implementation:

```
func application(_ application: UIApplication,
                 didFinishLaunchingWithOptions
  launchOptions: [UIApplicationLaunchOptionsKey: Any]?) -> Bool
{

  guard let vc =
    window?.rootViewController as? ViewController else {
      return true
  }

  vc.managedContext = persistentContainer.viewContext

  return true
}
```

In the previous chapter, you gained access to the app delegate's managed object context
using the delegate more or less as a global variable. In this chapter, you'll use another
approach: pass the managed object context from class to class via a property.

Since the caller is responsible for setting the managed object context, `ViewController`
can use it without needing to know where it came from. The benefit here is cleaner code
since the context moves **down** the chain rather than each object accessing some global
state.

You've got seven bowties dying to enter your Core Data store. Open
ViewController.swift and add the following two methods:

```
// Insert sample data
func insertSampleData() {

  let fetch = NSFetchRequest<Bowtie>(entityName: "Bowtie")
  fetch.predicate = NSPredicate(format: "searchKey != nil")

  let count = try! managedContext.count(for: fetch)

  if count > 0 {
```

```swift
    // SampleData.plist data already in Core Data
    return
  }

  let path = Bundle.main.path(forResource: "SampleData",
                              ofType: "plist")
  let dataArray = NSArray(contentsOfFile: path!)!

  for dict in dataArray {
    let entity = NSEntityDescription.entity(
      forEntityName: "Bowtie",
      in: managedContext)!
    let bowtie = Bowtie(entity: entity,
                        insertInto: managedContext)
    let btDict = dict as! [String: AnyObject]

    bowtie.name = btDict["name"] as? String
    bowtie.searchKey = btDict["searchKey"] as? String
    bowtie.rating = btDict["rating"] as! Double
    let colorDict = btDict["tintColor"] as! [String: AnyObject]
    bowtie.tintColor = UIColor.color(dict: colorDict)

    let imageName = btDict["imageName"] as? String
    let image = UIImage(named: imageName!)
    let photoData = UIImagePNGRepresentation(image!)!
    bowtie.photoData = NSData(data: photoData)

    bowtie.lastWorn = btDict["lastWorn"] as? NSDate
    let timesNumber = btDict["timesWorn"] as! NSNumber
    bowtie.timesWorn = timesNumber.int32Value
    bowtie.isFavorite = btDict["isFavorite"] as! Bool
  }

  try! managedContext.save()
}
```

Xcode will complain about a missing method declaration on `UIColor`. Fix this by
scrolling to the end of the file, past the last curly brace, and add a private `UIColor`
extension:

```swift
private extension UIColor {

  static func color(dict: [String : AnyObject]) -> UIColor? {

    guard let red = dict["red"] as? NSNumber,
      let green = dict["green"] as? NSNumber,
      let blue = dict["blue"] as? NSNumber else {
        return nil
    }

    return UIColor(red: CGFloat(red)/255.0,
```

```
          green: CGFloat(green)/255.0,
          blue: CGFloat(blue)/255.0,
          alpha: 1)
  }
}
```

That's quite a bit of code, but it's all fairly simple. The first method, `insertSampleData`, checks for any bow ties; you'll learn how this works later. If none are present, it grabs the bow tie information in **SampleData.plist**, iterates through each bow tie dictionary and inserts a new `Bowtie` entity into your Core Data store. At the end of this iteration, it saves the managed object context property to commit these changes to disk.

The `color(_:)` method you added to `UIColor` via private extension is also simple. **SampleData.plist** stores colors in a dictionary containing three keys: `red`, `green` and `blue`. This class method takes in this dictionary and returns a bona fide `UIColor`.

Notice two things:

1. **The way you store images in Core Data.** The property list contains a file name for each bow tie, not the file image — the actual images are in the project's asset catalog. With this file name, you instantiate the `UIImage` and immediately convert it into `NSData` by means of `UIImagePNGRepresentation()` before storing it in the `imageData` property.

2. **The way you store the color.** Even though the color is stored in a transformable attribute, it doesn't require any special treatment before you store it in `tintColor`. You simply set the property and you're good to go.

The previous methods insert all the bow tie data you had in **SampleData.plist** into Core Data. Now you need to access the data from somewhere!

Replace `viewDidLoad()` with the following implementation:

```
override func viewDidLoad() {
  super.viewDidLoad()

  //1
  insertSampleData()

  //2
  let request = NSFetchRequest<Bowtie>(entityName: "Bowtie")
  let firstTitle = segmentedControl.titleForSegment(at: 0)!
  request.predicate = NSPredicate(
    format: "searchKey == %@", firstTitle)

  do {
    //3
    let results = try managedContext.fetch(request)
```

```
    //4
    populate(bowtie: results.first!)
  } catch let error as NSError {
    print("Could not fetch \(error), \(error.userInfo)")
  }
}
```

This is where you fetch the bow ties from Core Data and populate the UI.

Step by step, here's what you're doing with this code:

1. You call `insertSampleData()`, which you implemented earlier. Since `viewDidLoad()` can be called every time the app is launched, `insertSampleData()` performs a fetch to make sure it isn't inserting the sample data into Core Data multiple times.

2. You create a fetch request for the purpose of fetching the newly inserted `Bowtie` entities. The segmented control has tabs to filter by color, so the predicate adds the condition to find the bow ties matching the selected color. Predicates are both very flexible and very powerful — you'll read more about them in Chapter 4, "Intermediate Fetching."

    For now, know that this particular predicate is looking for bow ties with their `searchKey` property set to the segmented control's first button title: in this case, **R**.

3. As always, the managed object context does the heavy lifting for you. It executes the fetch request you crafted moments earlier and returns an array of `Bowtie` objects.

4. You populate the user interface with the first bow tie in the `results` array. If there was an error, print the error to the console.

You haven't defined the **populate** method yet, so Xcode throws a warning. Add the following implementation:

```
func populate(bowtie: Bowtie) {

  guard let imageData = bowtie.photoData as? Data,
    let lastWorn = bowtie.lastWorn as? Date,
    let tintColor = bowtie.tintColor as? UIColor else {
      return
  }

  imageView.image = UIImage(data: imageData)
  nameLabel.text = bowtie.name
  ratingLabel.text = "Rating: \(bowtie.rating)/5"

  timesWornLabel.text = "# times worn: \(bowtie.timesWorn)"

  let dateFormatter = DateFormatter()
```

```
    dateFormatter.dateStyle = .short
    dateFormatter.timeStyle = .none

    lastWornLabel.text =
      "Last worn: " + dateFormatter.string(from: lastWorn)

    favoriteLabel.isHidden = !bowtie.isFavorite
    view.tintColor = tintColor
}
```

There's a UI element for every one of the attributes defined in a bow tie. Since Core Data only stores the image as a blob of binary data, it's your job to reconstitute it back into an image so the view controller's image view can use it.

Similarly, you can't use the `lastWorn` date attribute directly. You first need to create a date formatter to turn the date into a string humans can understand.

Finally, the `tintColor` transformable attribute that stores your bow tie's color changes the color of not one, but `all` the elements on the screen. Simply set the tint color on the view controller's view and voilà! Everything is now tinted the same color.

> **Note:** Xcode generates some `NSManagedObject` subclass properties as optional types. That's why inside the `populate` method, you unwrap some of the Core Data properties on `Bowtie` using a `guard` statement at the beginning of the method.

Build and run the app. The red bow tie appears on the screen, like so:

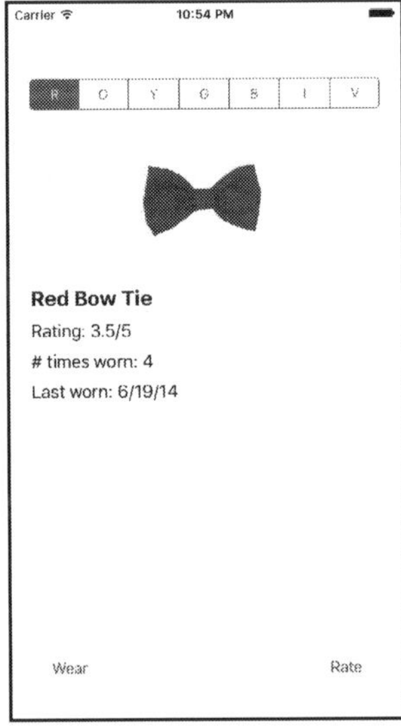

The **Wear** and **Rate** buttons do nothing at the moment. Tapping on the different parts of the segmented controls also does nothing. You've still got work to do!

First, you need to keep track of the currently selected bow tie so you can reference it from anywhere in your class. Add a new property to do this below `managedContext`:

```
var currentBowtie: Bowtie!
```

Next, replace the `do-catch` statement in `vicwDidLoad()` to use your new property:

```
do {
  let results = try managedContext.fetch(request)
  currentBowtie = results.first

  populate(bowtie: results.first!)
} catch let error as NSError {
  print("Could not fetch \(error), \(error.userInfo)")
}
```

Keeping track of the currently selected bow tie is necessary to implement the **Wear** and **Rate** buttons since these actions only affect the current bow tie.

Every time the user taps on **Wear**, the button executes the `wear` action method. But `wear` is empty at the moment. Add the following implementation:

```
@IBAction func wear(_ sender: AnyObject) {

  let times = currentBowtie.timesWorn
  currentBowtie.timesWorn = times + 1

  currentBowtie.lastWorn = NSDate()

  do {
    try managedContext.save()
    populate(bowtie: currentBowtie)
  } catch let error as NSError {
    print("Could not fetch \(error), \(error.userInfo)")
  }
}
```

This method takes the currently selected bow tie and increments its `timesWorn` attribute by one. Then, you change the `lastWorn` date to today and save the managed object context to commit these changes to disk. Finally, you populate the user interface to visualize these changes.

Run the application and tap **Wear** as many times as you'd like. It looks like you thoroughly enjoy the timeless elegance of a red bow tie!

Similarly, every time the user taps on **Rate**, it executes the `rate` action method in your code. `Rate` is currently empty. Add the following implementation:

```swift
@IBAction func rate(_ sender: AnyObject) {

  let alert = UIAlertController(title: "New Rating",
                               message: "Rate this bow tie",
                               preferredStyle: .alert)

  alert.addTextField { (textField) in
    textField.keyboardType = .decimalPad
  }

  let cancelAction = UIAlertAction(title: "Cancel",
                                   style: .default)

  let saveAction = UIAlertAction(title: "Save",
                                 style: .default) {
    [unowned self] action in

    guard let textField = alert.textFields?.first else {
      return
    }

    self.update(rating: textField.text)
  }

  alert.addAction(cancelAction)
  alert.addAction(saveAction)
```

```
      present(alert, animated: true)
  }
```

Tapping on **Rate** now brings up an alert view with a single text field, a cancel button and a save button. Tapping the save button calls `update(_:)`, which...

Whoops, you haven't defined it yet. Appease Xcode by implementing it below:

```
func update(rating: String?) {

  guard let ratingString = rating,
    let rating = Double(ratingString) else {
      return
  }

  do {
    currentBowtie.rating = rating
    try managedContext.save()
    populate(bowtie: currentBowtie)
  } catch let error as NSError {
    print("Could not save \(error), \(error.userInfo)")
  }
}
```

You convert the text from the alert view's text field into a `Double` and use it to update the current bow ties `rating` property.

Finally, you commit your changes as usual by saving the managed object context and refresh the UI to see your changes in real time.

Try it out. Build and run the app and tap **Rate**:

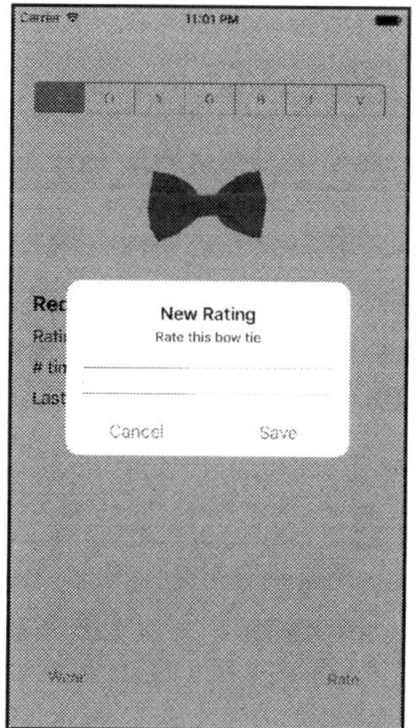

Enter any decimal number from 0 to 5 and tap **Save**. As you would expect, the rating label updates to the new value you entered.

Now tap **Rate** one more time. Remember the timeless elegance of a red bow tie? Let's say you like it so much you decide to rate it a 6 out of 5. Tap **Save** to refresh the user interface:

While you may absolutely love the color red, this is neither the time nor the place for hyperbole. Your app let you save a 6 for a value that's only supposed to go up to 5. You've got invalid data on your hands.

Data validation in Core Data

Your first instinct may be to write client-side validation—something like, "Only save the new rating if the value is greater than 0 and less than 5." Fortunately, you don't have to write this code yourself. Core Data supports validation for most attribute types out of the box.

Open your data model, select the **rating** attribute and open the data model inspector.

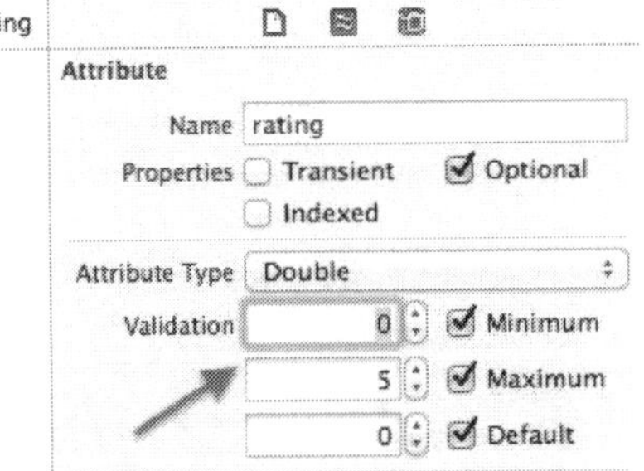

Next to **Validation**, type **0** for minimum and **5** for maximum. That's it! No need to write any Swift to reject invalid data.

> **Note:** Normally, you have to **version** your data model if you want to change it after you've shipped your app. You'll learn more about this in Chapter 6, "Versioning and Migration."
>
> Attribute validation is one of the few exceptions. If you add it to your app after shipping, you don't have to version your data model. Lucky you!

But what does this do, exactly?

Validation kicks in immediately after you call `save()` on your managed object context. The managed object context checks with the model to see if any of the new values conflict with the validation rules you've put in place.

If there's a validation error, the save fails. Remember that `NSError` in the `do-catch` block wrapping the `save` method? Up until now, you've had no reason to do anything special if there's an error other than log it to the console. Validation changes that.

Build and run the app once more. Give the red bowtie a rating of 6 out of 5 and save. A rather cryptic error message will spill out onto your console:

```
Could not save Error Domain=NSCocoaErrorDomain Code=1610 "The
operation couldn't be completed. (Cocoa error 1610.)"
UserInfo={NSValidationErrorObject=<Bow_Ties.Bowtie:
0x6180000c3100> (entity: Bowtie; id: 0xd000000000180000 <x-
coredata://D33D3FDD-1AF7-401C-9D3A-B2414A4AC197/Bowtie/p6> ;
data: {
    isFavorite = 0;
    lastWorn = "2016-08-24 12:53:34 +0000";
    name = "Red Bow Tie";
    photoData = <89504e47 0d0a1a0a 0000000d 49484452 00000124
0000012c 08020000 00e5c859 d6000000 01735247 4200aece 1ce90000
001c>;
    rating = 6;
    searchKey = R;
    timesWorn = 15;
    tintColor = "UIExtendedSRGBColorSpace 0.937255 0.188235
0.141176 1";
}), NSValidationErrorValue=6, NSValidationErrorKey=rating,
NSLocalizedDescription=The operation couldn't be completed.
(Cocoa error 1610.)}, [AnyHashable("NSLocalizedDescription"):
The operation couldn't be completed. (Cocoa error 1610.),
AnyHashable("NSValidationErrorValue"): 6,
AnyHashable("NSValidationErrorObject"): <Bow_Ties.Bowtie:
0x6180000c3100> (entity: Bowtie; id: 0xd000000000180000 <x-
coredata://D33D3FDD-1AF7-401C-9D3A-B2414A4AC197/Bowtie/p6> ;
```

```
data: {
    isFavorite = 0;
    lastWorn = "2016-08-24 12:53:34 +0000";
    name = "Red Bow Tie";
    photoData = <89504e47 0d0a1a0a 0000000d 49484452 00000124
0000012c 08020000 00e5c859 d6000000 01735247 4200aece 1ce90000
001c>;
    rating = 6;
    searchKey = R;
    timesWorn = 15;
    tintColor = "UIExtendedSRGBColorSpace 0.937255 0.188235
0.141176 1";
}), AnyHashable("NSValidationErrorKey"): rating]
```

The `userInfo` dictionary that comes with the error contains all kinds of useful
information about why Core Data aborted your save operation. It even has a localized
error message that you can show your users, under the key `NSLocalizedDescription`:
`The operation couldn't be completed.`

What you do with this error, however, is entirely up to you. Open **ViewController.swift**
and re-implement `update(_:)` to handle the error appropriately:

```swift
func update(rating: String?) {

  guard let ratingString = rating,
    let rating = Double(ratingString) else {
      return
  }

  do {

    currentBowtie.rating = rating
    try managedContext.save()
    populate(bowtie: currentBowtie)

  } catch let error as NSError {

    if error.domain == NSCocoaErrorDomain &&
      (error.code == NSValidationNumberTooLargeError ||
        error.code == NSValidationNumberTooSmallError) {
      rate(currentBowtie)
    } else {
      print("Could not save \(error), \(error.userInfo)")
    }
  }
}
```

If there's an error and it happened because the new rating was either too large or too
small, then you present the alert view again.

Otherwise, you populate the user interface with the new rating as before.

But wait… Where did `NSValidationNumberTooLargeError` and
`NSValidationNumberTooSmallError` come from? Go back to the previous console
reading and look closely at the first line:

```
Could not save Error Domain=NSCocoaErrorDomain Code=1610 "The
operation couldn't be completed. (Cocoa error 1610.)"
```

`NSValidationNumberTooLargeError` is an error code that maps to the integer 1610.

For a full list of Core Data errors and code definitions, you can consult
CoreDataErrors.h in Xcode by Cmd-clicking on
`NSValidationNumberTooLargeError`.

> **Note:** When an `NSError` is involved, it's standard practice to check the domain
> and code for the error to determine what went wrong. You can read more about
> this in Apple's `Error Handling Programming Guide`:
>
> https://developer.apple.com/library/mac/documentation/Cocoa/Conceptual/
> ErrorHandlingCocoa/CreateCustomizeNSError/CreateCustomizeNSError.html

Build and run the app. Verify that the new validation rules work properly by once again
showing the red tie some love.

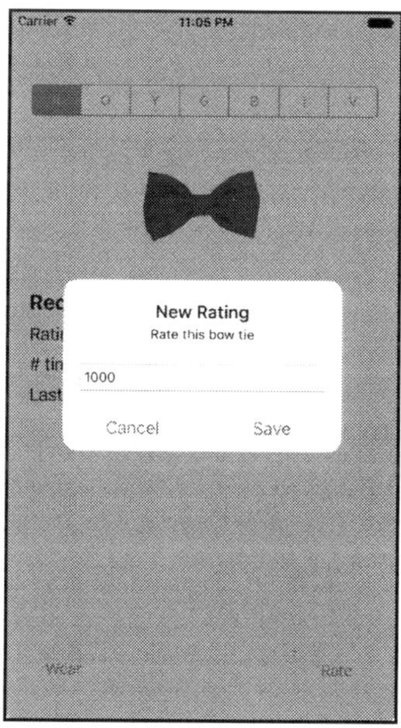

If you enter any value above 5 and try to save, the app rejects your rating and asks you to
try again with a new alert view. Success!

Tying everything up

The **Wear** and **Rate** buttons are working properly but the app can only display one tie. Tapping the different values on the segmented control is supposed to switch ties. You will finish up this sample project by implementing that feature.

Every time the user taps the segmented control, it executes the `segmentedControl` action method in your code. Add the following implementation:

```swift
@IBAction func segmentedControl(_ sender: AnyObject) {
  guard let control = sender as? UISegmentedControl else {
    return
  }

  let selectedValue = control.titleForSegment(
    at: control.selectedSegmentIndex)

  let request = NSFetchRequest<Bowtie>(entityName: "Bowtie")
  request.predicate =
    NSPredicate(format: "searchKey == %@", selectedValue!)

  do {
    let results = try managedContext.fetch(request)
    currentBowtie = results.first
    populate(bowtie: currentBowtie)

  } catch let error as NSError {
    print("Could not fetch \(error), \(error.userInfo)")
  }
}
```

The title of each segment in the segmented control conveniently corresponds to a particular tie's `searchKey` attribute. Grab the title of the currently selected segment and fetch the appropriate bow tie using a well-crafted `NSPredicate`.

Then, use the first bow tie in the array of results (there should only be one per `searchKey`) to populate the user interface.

Once again, build and run the app. Tap different letters on the segmented control for a psychedelic treat.

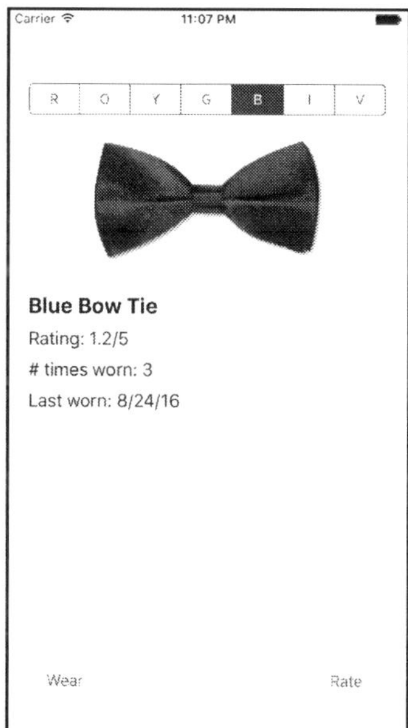

You did it! With this bow tie app under your belt, you're well on your way to becoming a Core Data master.

Where to go from here?

In this chapter, on top of practicing what you already knew about fetching and saving, you learned how to create your own managed object subclasses in Swift, explored different types of Core Data attributes and learned about validation.

Even though this is just the second chapter, you've probably already started to appreciate the flexibility and power of Core Data as a framework. But you've only scratched the surface. There's a lot more to learn — and you'll do exactly that in Chapter 3, "The Core Data Stack."

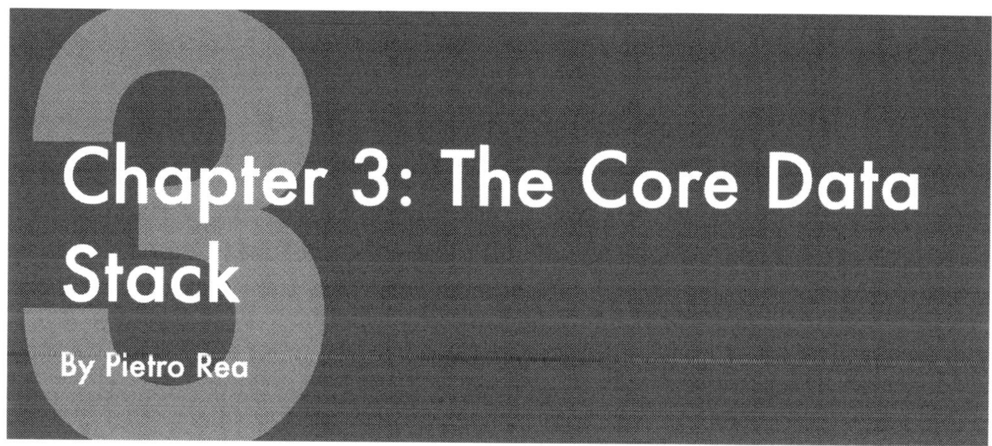

Until now, you've been relying on Xcode's Core Data template. There's nothing wrong with getting help from Xcode (that's what it's there for!), but if you really want to know how Core Data works, building your own Core Data stack is a must.

The stack is made up of four Core Data classes:

- `NSManagedObjectModel`

- `NSPersistentStore`

- `NSPersistentStoreCoordinator`

- `NSManagedObjectContext`

Of these four classes, you've only encountered `NSManagedObjectContext` so far in this book. But the other three were there behind the scenes the whole time, supporting your managed context.

In this chapter, you'll learn the details of what these four classes do. Rather than rely on the default starter template, you'll build your own Core Data stack: a customizable **wrapper** around these classes.

Getting started

The sample project for this chapter is a simple dog-walking app. This application lets you save the date and time of your dog walks in a simple table view. Use this app regularly and your pooch (and his bladder) will love you.

You'll find the sample project **Dog Walk** in the resources accompanying this book. Open **Dog Walk.xcodeproj**, then build and run the starter project.

As you can see, the sample app is already a fully-working (albeit simple) prototype. Tapping on the plus (+) button on the top-right adds a new entry to the list of walks. The image represents the dog you're currently walking, but otherwise does nothing.

The app has all the functionality it needs, except for one important feature: The list of walks doesn't persist. If you terminate **Dog Walk** and re-launch, your entire history is gone. How will you remember if you walked your pooch this morning?

Your task in this chapter is to save the list of walks in Core Data. If that sounds like something you've already done in Chapters 1 and 2, here's the twist: you'll be writing your own Core Data stack to really understand what's really going on under the hood!

Rolling your own Core Data stack

Knowing how the Core Data stack works is more than a **nice to know**. If you're working with a more advanced setup, such as migrating data from an old persistent store, digging into the stack is essential.

Before you jump into the code, let's consider what each of the four classes in the Core Data stack — `NSManagedObjectModel`, `NSPersistentStore`, `NSPersistentStoreCoordinator` and `NSManagedObjectContext` — does in detail.

> **Note:** This is one of the few parts of the book where you'll read about the theory before using the concepts in practice. It's almost impossible to separate one component from the rest of the stack and use it in isolation.

The managed object model

The `NSManagedObjectModel` represents each object type in your app's data model, the properties they can have, and the relationships between them. Other parts of the Core Data stack use the model to create objects, store properties and save data.

As mentioned earlier in the book, it can be helpful to think about `NSManagedObjectModel` as a database schema. If your Core Data stack uses SQLite under the hood, `NSManagedObjectModel` represents the schema for the database.

However, SQLite is only one of many persistent store types you can use in Core Data (more on this later), so it's better to think of the managed object model in more general terms.

> **Note:** You may be wondering how `NSManagedObjectModel` relates to the data model editor you've been using all along. Good question!
>
> The visual editor creates and edits an **xcdatamodel** file. There's a special compiler, `momc`, that compiles the model file into a set of files in a **momd** folder.
>
> Just as your Swift code is compiled and optimized so it can run on a device, the compiled model can be accessed efficiently at runtime. Core Data uses the compiled contents of the **momd** folder to initialize an `NSManagedObjectModel` at runtime.

The persistent store

`NSPersistentStore` reads and writes data to whichever storage method you've decided to use. Core Data provides four types of `NSPersistentStore` out of the box: three atomic and one non-atomic.

An **atomic** persistent store needs to be completely deserialized and loaded into memory before you can make any read or write operations. In contrast, a **non-atomic** persistent store can load chunks of itself onto memory as needed.

Here's a brief overview of the four built-in Core Data store types:

1. **NSQLiteStoreType** is backed by an SQLite database. It's the only non-atomic store type Core Data supports out of the box, giving it a lightweight and efficient memory footprint. This makes it the best choice for most iOS projects. Xcode's Core Data template uses this store type by default.

2. **NSXMLStoreType** is backed by an XML file, making it the most human-readable of all the store types. This store type is atomic, so it can have a large memory footprint. `NSXMLStoreType` is only available on OS X.

3. **NSBinaryStoreType** is backed by a binary data file. Like `NSXMLStoreType`, it's also an atomic store, so the entire binary file must be loaded onto memory before you can do anything with it. You'll rarely find this type of persistent store in real-world applications.

4. **NSInMemoryStoreType** is the in-memory persistent store type. In a way, this store type is not really `persistent`. Terminate the app or turn off your phone, and the data stored in an in-memory store type disappears into thin air. Although this may seem to defeat the purpose of Core Data, in-memory persistent stores can be helpful for unit testing and some types of caching.

> **Note:** Were you holding your breath for a persistent store type backed by a JSON file or a CSV file? Bummer. The good news is you can create your own type of persistent store by subclassing `NSIncrementalStore`.
>
> Refer to Apple's Incremental Store Programming Guide if you're curious about this option:
>
> https://developer.apple.com/library/ios/documentation/DataManagement/Conceptual/IncrementalStorePG/Introduction/Introduction.html

The persistent store coordinator

`NSPersistentStoreCoordinator` is the bridge between the managed object model and the persistent store. It's responsible for using the model and the persistent stores to do most of the hard work in Core Data. It understands the `NSManagedObjectModel` and knows how to send information to, and fetch information from, the `NSPersistentStore`.

`NSPersistentStoreCoordinator` also hides the implementation details of how your persistent store or stores are configured. This is useful for two reasons:

1. `NSManagedObjectContext` (coming next!) doesn't have to know if it's saving to an SQLite database, XML file or even a custom incremental store.

2. If you have multiple persistent stores, the persistent store coordinator presents a unified interface to the managed context. As far as the managed context is concerned, it always interacts with a single, aggregate persistent store.

The managed object context

On a day-to-day basis, you'll work with `NSManagedObjectContext` the most out of the four stack components. You'll probably only see the other three components when you need to do something more advanced with Core Data.

Since working with `NSManagedObjectContext` is so common, understanding how contexts work is very important! Here are some things you may have already picked up from the book so far:

- A context is an in-memory scratchpad for working with your managed objects.

- You do all of the work with your Core Data objects within a managed object context.

- Any changes you make won't affect the underlying data on disk until you call `save()` on the context.

Now here are five things about contexts not mentioned before. A few of them are very important for later chapters, so pay close attention:

1. The context `manages` the lifecycle of the objects it creates or fetches. This lifecycle management includes powerful features such as faulting, inverse relationship handling and validation.

2. A managed object cannot exist without an associated context. In fact, a managed object and its context are so tightly coupled that every managed object keeps a reference to its context, which can be accessed like so:

```
let managedContext = employee.managedObjectContext
```

3. Contexts are very territorial; once a managed object has associated with a particular context, it will remain associated with the same context for the duration of its lifecycle.

4. An application can use more than one context — most non-trivial Core Data applications fall into this category. Since a context is an in-memory scratch pad for

what's on disk, you can actually load the same Core Data object onto two different contexts simultaneously.

5. A context is not thread-safe. The same goes for a managed object — you can only interact with contexts and managed objects on the same thread in which they were created.

Apple has provided many ways to work with contexts in multithreaded applications. You'll read all about different concurrency models in Chapter 9, "Multiple Managed Object Contexts."

The persistent store container

If you thought there were only 4 pieces to the Core Data stack, you're in for a suprise! As of iOS 10, there is a new class to orchestrate all four Core Data stack classes — the managed model, the store coordinator, the persistent store and the managed context.

The name of this class is `NSPersistentContainer` and as its name implies, it's a container that holds everything together. Instead of wasting your time writing boilerplate code to wire up all four stack components together, you can simply initialize an `NSPersistentContainer`, load its persistent stores, and you're good to go.

Creating your stack object

Now you know what each component does, it's time to return to **Dog Walk** and implement your own Core Data stack.

As you know from previous chapters, Xcode creates its Core Data stack in the app delegate. You're going to do it differently. Instead of mixing app delegate code with Core Data code, you'll create a separate class to encapsulate the stack.

Go to **File\New\File…**, select the **iOS\Source\Swift File** template and click **Next**. Name the file **CoreDataStack** and click **Create** to save the file.

Go to the newly created **CoreDataStack.swift**. You'll be creating this file piece by piece. Start by replacing the contents of the file with the following:

```swift
import Foundation
import CoreData

class CoreDataStack {

  private let modelName: String
```

```swift
  init(modelName: String) {
    self.modelName = modelName
  }

  private lazy var storeContainer: NSPersistentContainer = {

    let container = NSPersistentContainer(name: self.modelName)
    container.loadPersistentStores {
      (storeDescription, error) in
      if let error = error as NSError? {
        print("Unresolved error \(error), \(error.userInfo)")
      }
    }
    return container
  }()
}
```

You start by importing the `Foundation` and `CoreData` modules. Next, create an initializer to pass `modelName` into the store container.

Next, set up a lazily instantiated `NSPersistentContainer`, passing the `modelName` you received during initialization. The only other thing you need to do is call `loadPersistentStores(completionHandler:)` on the persitent container, which typically runs asynchronously.

Finally, add the following lazily instantiated property as shown below:

```swift
lazy var managedContext: NSManagedObjectContext = {
  return self.storeContainer.viewContext
}()
```

Even though `NSPersistentContainer` has public accessors for its managed context, the managed model, the store coordinator and the persistent stores (via its `[NSPersistentStoreDescription]` property), `CoreDataStack` works a bit differently.

For instance, the only publicly accessible part of `CoreDataStack` is the `NSManagedObjectContext` because of the lazy property you just added. Everything else is marked `private`. Why is this?

The managed context is the only entry point required to access the rest of the stack. The persistent store coordinator is a public property on the `NSManagedObjectContext`. Similarly, both the managed object model and the array of persistent stores are public properties on the `NSPersistentStoreCoordinator`.

Finally, add the following method:

```swift
func saveContext () {
  guard managedContext.hasChanges else { return }

  do {
    try managedContext.save()
  } catch let error as NSError {
    print("Unresolved error \(error), \(error.userInfo)")
  }
}
```

This is a convenience method to save the stack's managed object context and handle any resulting errors.

Switch to **ViewController.swift** and make the following changes. First, import the Core Data module below `import UIKit`:

```swift
import CoreData
```

Next, add a property below `dateFormatter` to hold the managed object context:

```swift
var managedContext: NSManagedObjectContext!
```

As in the previous chapter, you'll follow the pattern of each view controller having a reference to the managed object context.

Next, open **AppDelegate.swift** and make the following changes. Again, you need to import the Core Data framework below `import UIKit`:

```swift
import CoreData
```

Next, below `window`, add a property to hold the Core Data stack:

```swift
lazy var coreDataStack = CoreDataStack(modelName: "Dog Walk")
```

You initialize the Core Data stack object as a lazy variable on the application delegate. This means the stack won't be set up until the first time you access the property.

Still in **AppDelegate.swift**, replace `application(_:didFinishLaunchingWithOptions:)` with the following:

```swift
func application(_ application: UIApplication,
                 didFinishLaunchingWithOptions
  launchOptions: [UIApplicationLaunchOptionsKey: Any]?)
  -> Bool {

  guard let navController =
```

```
      window?.rootViewController as? UINavigationController,
    let viewController =
      navController.topViewController as? ViewController else {
        return true
  }

  viewController.managedContext = coreDataStack.managedContext
  return true
}
```

This code propagates the managed context from your `CoreDataStack` object (initializing the whole stack in the process) to `ViewController`.

Finally, add the following two `UIApplicationDelegate` methods:

```
func applicationDidEnterBackground(
  _ application: UIApplication) {
    coreDataStack.saveContext()
}

func applicationWillTerminate(_ application: UIApplication) {
  coreDataStack.saveContext()
}
```

These methods ensure Core Data saves any pending changes before the app is either sent to the background or terminated for whatever reason.

Modeling your data

Now your shiny new Core Data stack is securely fastened to your application delegate, it's time to create your data model.

Head over to your Project Navigator and... Wait a second. There's no data model file! That's right. Since you generated this sample application without enabling the option to use Core Data, there's no **.xcdatamodeld** file.

No worries. Go to **File\New\File...**, select the **iOS\Core Data\Data Model** template and click **Next**. Name the file **Dog Walk.xcdatamodeld** and click **Create** to save the file.

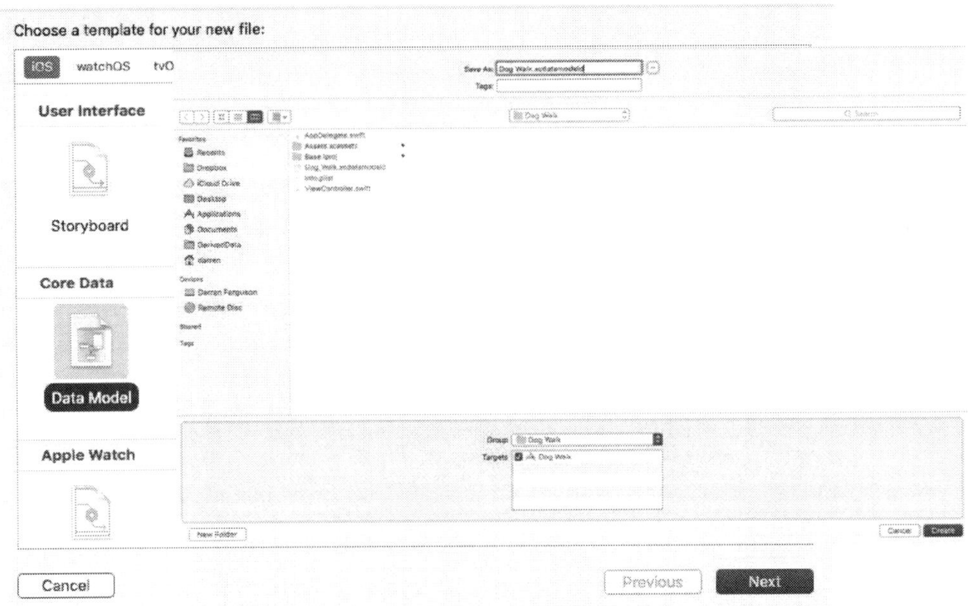

Note: You'll have problems later on if you don't name your data model file precisely **Dog Walk.xcdatamodeld**. This is because **CoreDataStack.swift** expects to find the compiled version at **Dog Walk.momd**.

Open the data model file and create a new entity named **Dog**. You should be able to do this on your own by now, but in case you forgot how, click the **Add Entity** button on the bottom left.

Add an attribute named **name** of type **String**. Your data model should look like this:

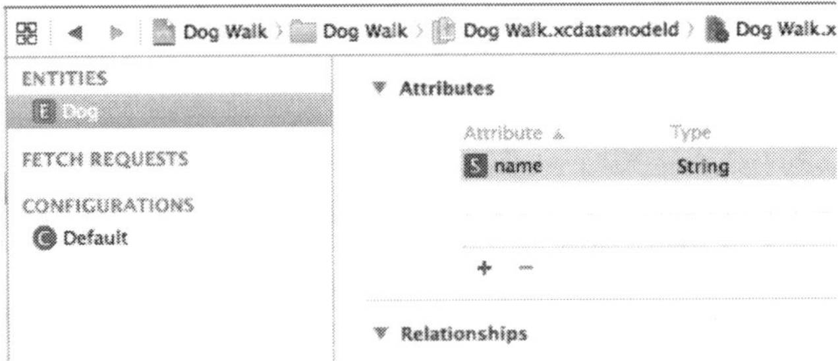

You also want to keep track of the walks for a particular dog. After all, that's the whole point of the app!

Define another entity and name it **Walk**. Then add an attribute named **date** and set its type to **Date**.

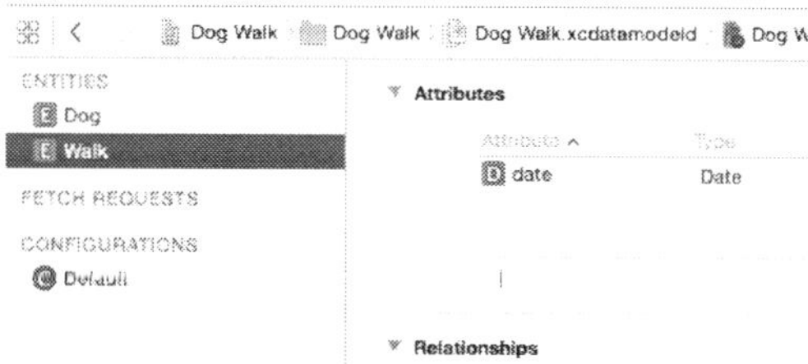

Go back to the `Dog` entity. You might think you need to add a new attribute of type **Array** to hold the walks, but there is no array type in Core Data. Instead, the way to do this is to model it as a relationship. Add a new relationship and name it **walks**:

Set the destination to **Walk**. You can think of the destination as the receiving end of a relationship.

Every relationship begins as a to-one relationship by default, which means you can only track one walk per dog at the moment. Unless you don't plan on keeping your dog for very long, you probably want to track more than one walk.

To fix this, with the **walks** relationship selected, open the **Data Model** Inspector:

Click on the **Type** dropdown, select **To Many** and check **Ordered**. This means one dog can have many walks and the order of the walks matters, since you'll be displaying the walks sorted by date.

Select the **Walk** entity and create an inverse relationship back to **Dog**. Set the destination as **dog** and the inverse as **walks**.

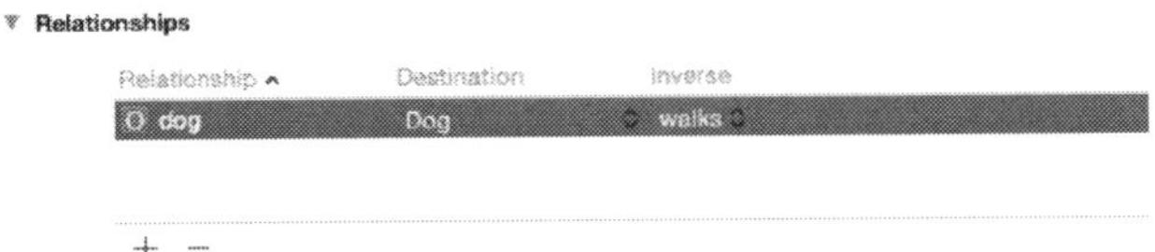

It's OK to leave this relationship as a to-one relationship. A dog can have many walks, but a walk can only belong to one dog — for the purposes of this app, at least. :]

The inverse lets the model know how to find its way back, so to speak. Given a walk record, you can follow the relationship to the dog. Thanks to the inverse, the model knows to follow the **walks** relationship to get back to the walk record.

This is a good time to let you know the data model editor has another view style. This entire time you've been looking at the table editor style. Toggle the segmented control on the bottom-right to switch to the graph editor style:

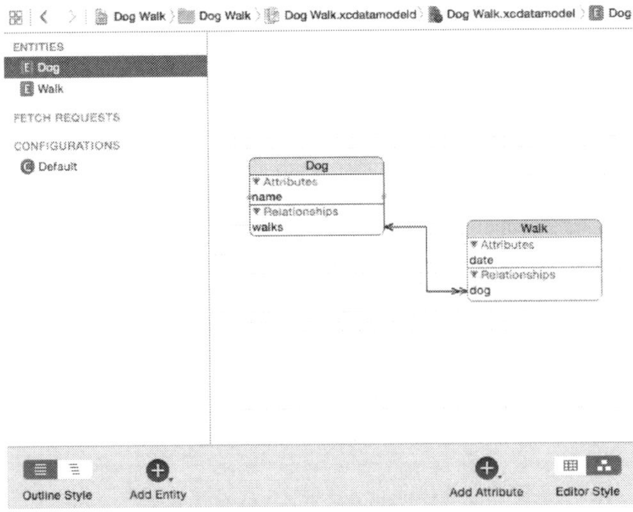

The graph editor style is a great tool to visualize the relationships between your Core Data entities. Here the to-many relationship from `Dog` to `Walk` is represented with a double arrow. `Walk` points back to `Dog` with a single arrow, indicating a to-one relationship.

Feel free to switch back and forth between the two editor styles. You might find it easier to use the table style to add and remove entities and attributes, and the graph style to see the big picture of your data model.

Adding managed object subclasses

In the previous chapter you learned how to create custom managed object subclasses for your Core Data entities. It's more convenient to work this way, so this is what you'll do for `Dog` and `Walk` as well.

Like in the previous chapter, you're going to generate custom managed object subclasses manually instead of letting Xcode do it for you so you can see what's going on behind the scenes. Open **Dog Walk.xcdatamodeld**, slect the `Dog` entity and set the **Codegen** dropdown in the Data Model inspector to **Manual/None**. Repeat the same process for the `Walk` entity.

Then, go to **Editor\Create NSManagedObject Subclass…** and choose the **Dog Walk** model, and then both the **Dog** and **Walk** entities. Click **Create** on the next screen to create the files.

As you saw in Chapter 2, doing this creates two files per entity: one for the Core Data properties you defined in the model editor and one for any future functionality you may add to your managed object subclass.

Dog+CoreDataProperties.swift should look like this:

```swift
import Foundation
import CoreData

extension Dog {

  @nonobjc public class func fetchRequest()
    -> NSFetchRequest<Dog> {
      return NSFetchRequest<Dog>(entityName: "Dog");
  }

  @NSManaged public var name: String?
  @NSManaged public var walks: NSOrderedSet?
}

// MARK: Generated accessors for walks
extension Dog {

  @objc(insertObject:inWalksAtIndex:)
  @NSManaged public func insertIntoWalks(_ value: Walk,
                          at idx: Int)
```

```
    @objc(removeObjectFromWalksAtIndex:)
    @NSManaged public func removeFromWalks(at idx: Int)

    @objc(insertWalks:atIndexes:)
    @NSManaged public func insertIntoWalks(_ values: [Walk],
                                    at indexes: NSIndexSet)

    @objc(removeWalksAtIndexes:)
    @NSManaged public func removeFromWalks(at indexes: NSIndexSet)

    @objc(replaceObjectInWalksAtIndex:withObject:)
    @NSManaged public func replaceWalks(at idx: Int,
                                  with value: Walk)

    @objc(replaceWalksAtIndexes:withWalks:)
    @NSManaged public func replaceWalks(at indexes: NSIndexSet,
                                  with values: [Walk])

    @objc(addWalksObject:)
    @NSManaged public func addToWalks(_ value: Walk)

    @objc(removeWalksObject:)
    @NSManaged public func removeFromWalks(_ value: Walk)

    @objc(addWalks:)
    @NSManaged public func addToWalks(_ values: NSOrderedSet)

    @objc(removeWalks:)
    @NSManaged public func removeFromWalks(_ values: NSOrderedSet)
}
```

Like before, the name attribute is a String optional. But what about the walks
relationship? Core Data represents to-many relationships using sets, not arrays. Because
you made the walks relationship ordered, you've got an NSOrderedSet.

> **Note:** NSSet seems like an odd choice, doesn't it? Unlike arrays, sets don't allow
> accessing their members by index. In fact, there's no ordering at all! Core Data
> uses NSSet because a set forces uniqueness in its members. The same object can't
> feature more than once in a to-many relationship.
>
> If you need to access individual objects by index, you can check the **Ordered**
> checkbox in the visual editor, as you've done here. Core Data will then represent
> the relationship as an NSOrderedSet.

Similarly, **Walk+CoreDataProperties.swift** should look like this:

```swift
import Foundation
import CoreData

extension Walk {

  @nonobjc public class func fetchRequest()
    -> NSFetchRequest<Walk> {
      return NSFetchRequest<Walk>(entityName: "Walk");
  }

  @NSManaged public var date: NSDate?
  @NSManaged public var dog: Dog?
}
```

The inverse relationship back to `Dog` is simply a property of type `Dog`. Easy as pie.

Note: Sometimes Xcode will create relationship properties with the generic `NSManagedObject` type instead of the specific class, especially if you're making lots of subclasses at the same time. If this happens, just correct the type yourself or generate the specific file again.

A walk down persistence lane

Now your setup is complete: your Core Data stack, your data model and your managed object subclasses. It's time to convert **Dog Walk** to use Core Data. You've done this several times before, so this should be an easy section for you.

Pretend for a moment this application will at some point support tracking multiple dogs. The first step is to track the currently selected dog. Open **ViewController.swift** and replace the `walks` array with the following property:

```swift
var currentDog: Dog?
```

Next, add the following code to the end of `viewDidLoad()`:

```swift
let dogName = "Fido"
let dogFetch: NSFetchRequest<Dog> = Dog.fetchRequest()
dogFetch.predicate = NSPredicate(format: "%K == %@",
#keyPath(Dog.name), dogName)

do {
  let results = try managedContext.fetch(dogFetch)
```

```swift
  if results.count > 0 {
    // Fido found, use Fido
    currentDog = results.first
  } else {
    // Fido not found, create Fido
    currentDog = Dog(context: managedContext)
    currentDog?.name = dogName
    try managedContext.save()
  }
} catch let error as NSError {
  print("Fetch error: \(error) description: \(error.userInfo)")
}
```

First, you fetch all **Dog** entities with names of **"Fido"** from Core Data. You'll learn more about fancy fetch requests like this in the next chapter. If the fetch request came back with results, you set the first entity (there should only be one) as the currently selected dog. If the fetch request comes back with zero results, this probably means it's the user's first time opening the app. If this is the case, you insert a new dog, name it "Fido", and set it as the currently selected dog.

> **Note:** You've just implemented what's often referred to as the **Find or Create** pattern. The purpose of this pattern is to manipulate an object stored in Core Data without running the risk of adding a duplicate in the process.
>
> In iOS 9, Apple introduced the ability to specify **unique constraints** on your Core Data entities. With unique constraints, you can specify in your data model which attributes must always be unique on an entity to avoid adding duplicates.

Next, replace the implementation of `tableView(_:numberOfRowsInSection:)` with the following:

```swift
func tableView(_ tableView: UITableView,
              numberOfRowsInSection section: Int) -> Int {

  guard let walks = currentDog?.walks else {
    return 1
  }

  return walks.count
}
```

As you can probably guess, this ties the number of rows in the table view to the number of walks set in the currently selected dog. If there is no currently selected dog, return 1.

Next, replace `tableView(_:cellForRowAt:)` as follows:

```swift
func tableView(_ tableView: UITableView,
               cellForRowAt indexPath: IndexPath)
               -> UITableViewCell {

  let cell =
    tableView.dequeueReusableCell(withIdentifier: "Cell",
                                  for: indexPath)

  guard let walk = currentDog?.walks?[indexPath.row] as? Walk,
    let walkDate = walk.date as? Date else {
      return cell
  }

  cell.textLabel?.text = dateFormatter.string(from: walkDate)
  return cell
}
```

Only two lines of code have changed. Now, you take the date of each walk and display it in the corresponding table view cell.

The `add(_:)` method still has a reference to the old `walks` array. Comment it out for now — you'll re-implement this method in the next step:

```swift
@IBAction func add(_ sender: UIBarButtonItem) {
  // walks.append(NSDate())
  tableView.reloadData()
}
```

Build and run to make sure you have everything hooked up correctly.

Hooray! If you've gotten this far, you've just inserted a dog into Core Data and are currently populating the table view with his list of walks. This list doesn't have any walks at the moment, so the table doesn't look very exciting.

Tap the plus (+) button, and it understandably does nothing. You haven't implemented it yet! Before transitioning to Core Data, add(_:) simply added an NSDate object to an array and reloaded the table view. Re-implement it as shown below:

```swift
@IBAction func add(_ sender: UIBarButtonItem) {

  // Insert a new Walk entity into Core Data

  let walk = Walk(context: managedContext)
  walk.date = NSDate()

  // Insert the new Walk into the Dog's walks set

  if let dog = currentDog,
    let walks = dog.walks?.mutableCopy()
                  as? NSMutableOrderedSet {
    walks.add(walk)
    dog.walks = walks
  }

  // Save the managed object context

  do {
    try managedContext.save()
  } catch let error as NSError {
    print("Save error: \(error),
          description: \(error.userInfo)")
  }

  // Reload table view

  tableView.reloadData()
}
```

As you can see, the Core Data version of this method is much more complicated. First, you have to create a new Walk entity and set its date attribute to now. Next, you have to insert this walk into the currently selected dog's list of walks.

However, the walks attribute is of type NSOrderedSet. NSOrderedSet is immutable, so you first have to create a mutable copy (NSMutableOrderedSet), insert the new walk and then reset an immutable copy of this mutable ordered set back on the dog.

> **Note:** Is adding a new object into a to-many relationship making your head spin? Many people can sympathize, which is why **Dog+CoreDataProperties** contains generated accessors to the `walks` ordered set that will handle all of this for you.

For example, you can replace the entire `if-let` statement in the last code snippet with the following:

```
currentDog?.addToWalks(walk)
```

Give it a try!

Core Data can make things easier for you, though. If the relationship weren't ordered, you'd just be able to set the one side of the relationship (e.g., walk.dog = currentDog) rather than the many side and Core Data would use the inverse relationship defined in the model editor to add the walk to the dog's set of walks.

Finally, you commit your changes to the persistent store by calling `save()` on the managed object context, and you reload the table view.

Build and run the app, and tap the plus (+) button a few times:

Great! The list of walks should now be saved in Core Data. Verify this by terminating the app in the fast app switcher and re-launching from scratch.

Deleting objects from Core Data

Let's say you were too trigger-friendly and tapped the plus (+) button when you didn't mean to. You didn't actually walk your dog, so you want to delete the walk you just added.

You've added objects to Core Data, you've fetched them, modified them and saved them again. What you haven't yet done is delete them — but you're about to do that next.

First, add the following method to the `UITableViewDataSource` extension in **ViewController.swift**:

```swift
func tableView(_ tableView: UITableView,
               canEditRowAt indexPath: IndexPath) -> Bool {
  return true
}
```

You're going to use `UITableView`'s default behavior for deleting items: swipe left to reveal the red **Delete** button, then tap on it to delete. The table view calls this `UITableViewDataSource` method to ask if a particular cell is editable, and returning true means all the cells should be editable.

Next, add the following method:

```swift
func tableView(_ tableView: UITableView,
               commit editingStyle: UITableViewCellEditingStyle,
               forRowAt indexPath: IndexPath) {

  //1
  guard let walkToRemove =
    currentDog?.walks?[indexPath.row] as? Walk,
    editingStyle == .delete else {
      return
  }

  //2
  managedContext.delete(walkToRemove)

  do {
    //3
    try managedContext.save()

    //4
    tableView.deleteRows(at: [indexPath], with: .automatic)
  } catch let error as NSError {
    print("Saving error: \(error),
          description: \(error.userInfo)")
  }
}
```

This table view data source method is called when you tap the red Delete button. Let's go step by step through the code:

1. First, you get a reference to the `walk` you want to delete.

2. Remove the walk from Core Data by calling `NSManagedObjectContext`'s `delete()` method. Core Data also takes care of removing the deleted walk from the current dog's walks relationship.

3. No changes are final until you save your managed object context, not even deletions!

4. Finally, if the save operation succeeds you animate the table view to tell the user about the deletion.

Build and run the app one more time. You should have several walks from previous runs. Pick any and swipe to the left:

Tap on the Delete button to remove the walk. Verify that the walk is actually gone by terminating the app and re-launching from scratch. The walk you just removed is gone for good. Core Data giveth and Core Data taketh away.

> **Note:** Deletion used to be one of the most "dangerous" Core Data operations. Why is this? When you remove something from Core Data you have to delete both the record on disk as well as any outstanding references in code.
>
> Trying to access an `NSManagedObject` that had no Core Data backing store resulted in the the much-feared `inaccessible fault` Core Data crash.

> Starting with iOS 9, deletion is safer than ever. Apple introduced the property `shouldDeleteInaccessibleFaults` on `NSManagedObjectContext`, which is turned on by default. This marks bad faults as deleted and treats missing data as `NULL/nil/0`.

Where to go from here?

If you followed this chapter all the way through, then you've spent a lot of time on setup and the underlying pieces that make up Core Data. This was intentional! Core Data has a reputation for its steep learning curve. This is partly because of all the setup it requires just to get started: the stack, the data model, the managed object subclasses, et cetera. In addition, you got some firsthand experience with relationships and deletion.

These last three chapters were not only a tour of Core Data but also a thorough introduction to the entire framework. Even though you didn't spend long on any one particular topic, you're now familiar with the basics of fetching, saving, editing and deleting objects from a Core Data store backed by an SQLite database.

In the next chapter, you'll spend less time on setup and dig much deeper into fetching data. You got a small taste of the basic operations in this chapter, but there's a lot more to learn. Head into the next chapter to continue your journey!

Chapter 4: Intermediate Fetching

By Pietro Rea

In the first three chapters of this book, you began to explore the foundations of Core Data, including very basic methods of saving and fetching data with Core Data persistent store.

To this point, you've mostly performed simple, unrefined fetches such as "fetch all `Bowtie` entities." Sometimes this is all you need to do. Often, you'll want to exert more control over how you retrieve information from Core Data.

Building on what you've learned so far, this chapter dives deep into the topic of **fetching**. Fetching is a large topic in Core Data, and you have many tools at your disposal. By the end of this chapter, you'll know how to:

- Fetch only what you need to

- Refine your fetched results using predicates

- Fetch in the background to avoid blocking the UI

- Avoid unnecessary fetching by updating objects directly in the persistent store

This chapter is a toolbox sampler; its aim is to expose you to many fetching techniques, so that when the time comes you can use the right tool.

NSFetchRequest: the star of the show

As you've learned in previous chapters, you fetch records from Core Data by creating an instance of `NSFetchRequest`, configuring it as you like and handing it over to `NSManagedObjectContext` to do the heavy lifting.

Seems simple enough, but there are actually **five** different ways to get hold of a fetch request. Some are more popular than others, but you'll likely encounter all of them at some point as a Core Data developer.

Before jumping to the starter project for this chapter, here are the five different ways to set up a fetch request so you're not caught by surprise:

```swift
// 1
let fetchRequest1 = NSFetchRequest<Venue>()
let entity =
  NSEntityDescription.entity(forEntityName: "Venue",
                             in: managedContext)!
fetchRequest1.entity = entity

// 2
let fetchRequest2 = NSFetchRequest<Venue>(entityName: "Venue")

// 3
let fetchRequest3: NSFetchRequest<Venue> = Venue.fetchRequest()

// 4
let fetchRequest4 =
  managedObjectModel.fetchRequestTemplate(forName: "venueFR")

// 5
let fetchRequest5 =
  managedObjectModel.fetchRequestFromTemplate(
    withName: "venueFR",
    substitutionVariables: ["NAME" : "Vivi Bubble Tea"])
```

Going through each in turn:

1. You initialize an instance of `NSFetchRequest` as generic type:
    `NSFetchRequest<Venue>`. At a minimum, you must specify an
    `NSEntityDescription` for the fetch request. In this case, the entity is `Venue`. You
    initialize an instance of `NSEntityDescription` and use it to set the fetch request's
    `entity` property.

2. Here you use `NSFetchRequest`'s convenience initializer. It initializes a new fetch
    request and sets its `entity` property in one step. You simply need to provide a string
    for the entity name rather than a full-fledged `NSEntityDescription`.

3. Just as the second example was a contraction of the first, the third is a contraction of
    the second. When you generate an `NSManagedObject` subclass, this step also
    generates a class method that returns an `NSFetchRequest` already set up to fetch
    corresponding entity types. This is where `Venue.fetchRequest()` comes from. This
    code lives in **Venue+CoreDataProperties.swift**.

4. In the fourth example, you retrieve your fetch request from your `NSManagedObjectModel`. You can configure and store commonly used fetch requests in Xcode's data model editor. You'll learn how to do this later in the chapter.

5. The last case is similar to the fourth. Retrieve a fetch request from your managed object model, but this time, you pass in some extra variables. These "substitution" variables are used in a predicate to refine your fetched results.

The first three examples are the simple cases you've already seen. You'll see even more of these simple cases in the rest of this chapter, in addition to stored fetch requests and other tricks of `NSFetchRequest`!

> **Note:** In case you didn't know, `NSFetchRequest` is a generic type. If you inspect `NSFetchRequest`'s initializer, you'll notice it takes in type as a parameter `<ResultType : NSFetchRequestResult>`.
>
> `ResultType` specifies the type of objects you **expect** as a result of the fetch request. For example, if you're expecting an array of `Venue` objects, the result of the fetch request is now going to be `[Venue]` instead of `[AnyObject]`. This is helpful because you don't have to cast down to `[Venue]` anymore.

Introducing the Bubble Tea app

This chapter's sample project is a bubble tea app. For those of you who don't know about bubble tea (also known as "boba tea"), it's a Taiwanese tea-based drink containing large tapioca pearls. It's very yummy!

You can think of this bubble tea app as an ultra-niche Yelp. Using the app, you can find locations near you selling your favorite Taiwanese drink.

For this chapter, you'll only be working with static venue data from Foursquare: that's about 30 locations in New York City that sell bubble tea. You'll use this data to build the filter/sort screen to arrange the list of static venues as you see fit.

Go to this chapter's files and open **Bubble Tea Finder.xcodeproj**. Build and run the starter project.

You'll see the following:

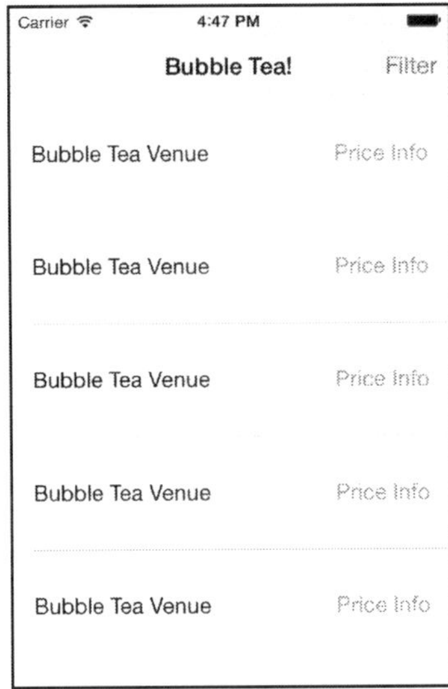

The sample app consists of a number of table view cells with static information. Although the sample project isn't very exciting at the moment, there's a lot of setup already done for you.

Open the project navigator and take a look at the full list of files in the starter project:

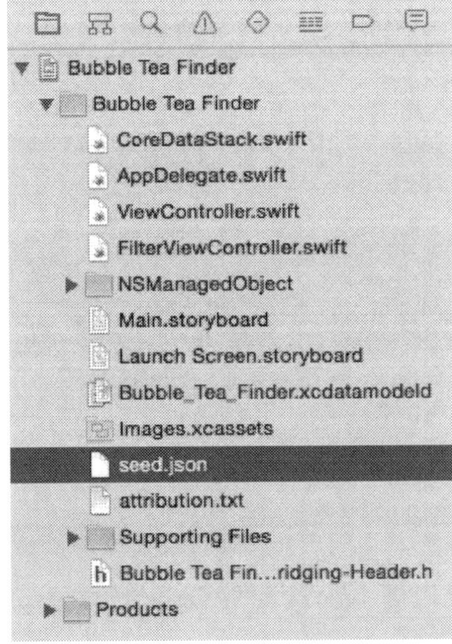

It turns out most of the Core Data setup you had to do in the first section of the book comes ready for you to use. Below is a quick overview of the components you get in the starter project, grouped into categories:

- **Seed data: seed.json** is a JSON file containing real-world venue data for venues in New York City serving bubble tea. Since this is real data coming from Foursquare, the structure is more complex than previous seed data used in this book.

- **Data model:** Click on **Bubble_Tea_Finder.xcdatamodeld** to open Xcode's model editor. The most important entity is `Venue`. It contains attributes for a venue's name, phone number and the number of specials it's offering at the moment.

  Since the JSON data is rather complex, the data model breaks down a venue's information into other entities. These are `Category`, `Location`, `PriceInfo` and `Stats`. For example, `Location` has attributes for city, state, country, and others.

- **Managed object subclasses:** All the entities in your data model also have corresponding `NSManagedObject` subclasses. These are **Venue+CoreDataClass.swift**, **Location+CoreDataClass.swift**, **PriceInfo+CoreDataClass.swift**, **Category+CoreDataClass.swift** and **Stats+CoreDataClass.swift**. You can find these in the **NSManagedObject** group along with their accompanying **EntityName+CoreDataProperties.swift** file.

- **App Delegate:** On first launch, the app delegate reads from **seed.json**, creates corresponding Core Data objects and saves them to the persistent store.

- **CoreDataStack:** As in previous chapters, this object wraps an `NSPersistentStoreContainer` object, which itself contains the cadre of Core Data objects known as the "stack": the context, the model, the persistent store and the persistent store coordinator. No need to set this up — it comes ready-to-use.

- **View Controllers:** The initial view controller that shows you the list of venues is **ViewController.swift**. Tapping the **Filter** button on the top-right brings up **FilterViewController.swift**. There's not much going on here at the moment. You'll add code to these two files throughout the chapter.

When you first launched the sample app, you saw only static information. However, your app delegate had already read the seed data from **seed.json**, parsed it into Core Data objects and saved them into the persistent store.

Your first task will be to fetch this data and display it in the table view. This time, you'll do it with a twist.

Stored fetch requests

As previously mentioned, you can store frequently used fetch requests right in the data model. Not only does this make them easier to access, but you also get the benefit of using a GUI-based tool to set up the fetch request parameters.

Open **Bubble_Tea_Finder.xcdatamodeld** and long-click the **Add Entity** button:

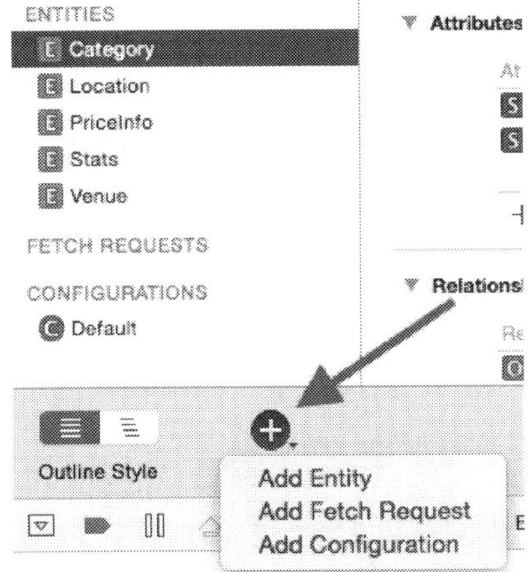

Select **Add Fetch Request** from the menu. This will create a new fetch request on the left-side bar and take you to a special fetch request editor:

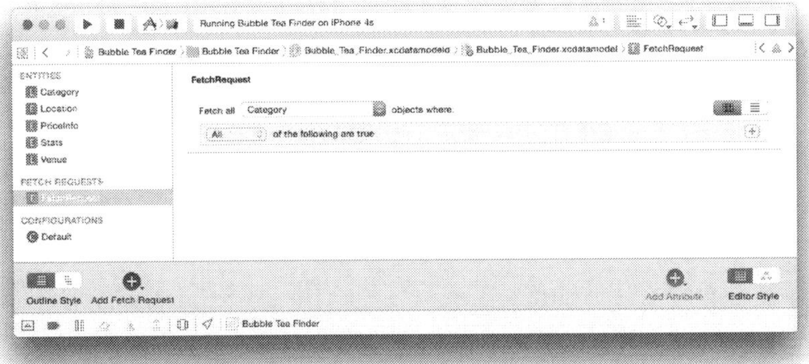

Note: You can click on the newly created fetch request on the left-hand sidebar to change its name.

You can make your fetch request as general or as specific as you want using the visual tool in Xcode's data model editor. To start, create a fetch request that retrieves all Venue objects from the persistent store.

You only need to make one change here: click the dropdown menu next to **Fetch all** and select **Venue**.

FetchRequest

Fetch all   Venue   ⬍   objects where:

[All   ⬍]   of the following are true

That's all you need to do. If you wanted to refine your fetch request with an additional predicate, you could also add conditions from the fetch request editor.

Time to take your newly created fetch request out for a spin. Open **ViewController.swift** and add the following below `import UIKit`:

```swift
import CoreData
```

Next, add the following two properties below `coreDataStack`:

```swift
var fetchRequest: NSFetchRequest<Venue>!
var venues: [Venue]!
```

The first property will hold your fetch request. The second property is the array of Venue objects you'll use to populate the table view.

Next, make the following additions to the currently empty `viewDidLoad()`:

```swift
guard let model =
  coreDataStack.managedContext
    .persistentStoreCoordinator?.managedObjectModel,
  let fetchRequest = model
    .fetchRequestTemplate(forName: "FetchRequest")
    as? NSFetchRequest<Venue> else {
      return
}

self.fetchRequest = fetchRequest
fetchAndReload()
```

Doing this connects the `fetchRequest` property you just set up to the one you created using Xcode's data model editor. There are three things to remember here:

1. Unlike other ways of getting a fetch request, this one involves the managed object model. This is why you must go through the `coreDataStack` property to retrieve your fetch request.

2. As you saw in the previous chapter, you constructed `CoreDataStack` so only the managed context is public. To retrieve the managed object model, you have to go through the managed context's persistent store coordinator.

3. `NSManagedObjectModel`'s `fetchRequestTemplate(forName:)` takes a string identifier. This identifier must exactly match the name you chose for your fetch request in the model editor. Otherwise, your app will throw an exception and crash.

The last line calls a method you haven't defined yet, so Xcode will complain about it. To fix that, add the following extension above the `UITableViewDataSource` extension:

```swift
// MARK: - Helper methods
extension ViewController {

  func fetchAndReload() {

    do {
      venues =
        try coreDataStack.managedContext.fetch(fetchRequest)
      tableView.reloadData()
    } catch let error as NSError {
      print("Could not fetch \(error), \(error.userInfo)")
    }
  }
}
```

As its name suggests, `fetchAndReload()` executes the fetch request and reloads the table view. Other methods in this class will need to see the fetched objects, so you store the fetched results in the `venues` property you defined earlier.

There's one more thing you have to do before you can run the sample project: hook up the table view's data source with the fetched `Venue` objects.

In the `UITableViewDataSource` extension, replace the placeholder implementations of `tableView(_:numberOfRowsInSection:)` and `tableView(_:cellForRowAt:)` with the following:

```swift
func tableView(_ tableView: UITableView,
               numberOfRowsInSection section: Int) -> Int {
  return venues.count
}
```

```swift
func tableView(_ tableView: UITableView,
               cellForRowAt indexPath: IndexPath)
               -> UITableViewCell {

  let cell =
    tableView.dequeueReusableCell(
      withIdentifier: venueCellIdentifier, for: indexPath)

  let venue = venues[indexPath.row]
  cell.textLabel?.text = venue.name
  cell.detailTextLabel?.text = venue.priceInfo?.priceCategory
  return cell
}
```

You've implemented these methods many times in this book, so you're probably familiar with what they do. The first method, `tableView(_:numberOfRowsInSection:)`, matches the number of cells in the table view with the number of fetched objects in the `venues` array.

The second method, `tableView(_:cellForRowAt:)`, dequeues a cell for a given index path and populates it with the information of the corresponding `Venue` in the `venues` array. In this case, the main label gets the venue's name and the detail label gets a price category that is one of three possible values: $, $$ or $$$.

Build and run the project, and you'll see the following:

Carrier 🔋	8:18 PM	🔋
	Bubble Tea!	Filter
CoCo Fresh Tea & Juice		$$
Vivi Bubble Tea		$
Tbaar		$
Boba Life NYC		$
Kung Fu Tea		$

Scroll down the list of bubble tea venues. These are all real places in New York City that sell the delicious drink.

> **Note:** When should you store fetch requests in your data model?
>
> If you know you'll be making the same fetch over and over in different parts of your app, you can use this feature to save you from writing the same code multiple times. A drawback of stored fetch requests is that there is no way to specify a sort order for the results.

Fetching different result types

All this time, you've probably been thinking of `NSFetchRequest` as a fairly simple tool. You give it some instructions and you get some objects in return. What else is there to it?

If this is the case, you've been underestimating this class. `NSFetchRequest` is the multi-function Swiss army knife of the Core Data framework!

You can use it to fetch individual values, compute statistics on your data such as the average, minimum, maximum, and more.

How is this possible, you ask? `NSFetchRequest` has a property named `resultType`. So far, you've only used the default value, `NSManagedObjectResultType`. Here are all the possible values for a fetch request's `resultType`:

- **.managedObjectResultType:** Returns managed objects (default value).

- **.countResultType:** Returns the count of the objects matching the fetch request.

- **.dictionaryResultType:** This is a catch-all return type for returning the results of different calculations.

- **.managedObjectIDResultType:** Returns unique identifiers instead of full-fledged managed objects.

Let's go back to the sample project and apply these concepts in practice.

With the sample project running, tap **Filter** in the top-right corner to bring up the UI for the filter screen.

You won't implement the actual filters or sorts right now. Instead, you'll focus on the following four labels:

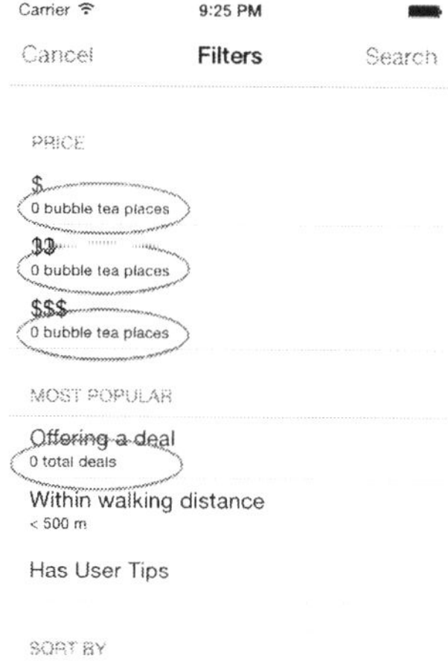

The filter screen is divided into three sections: **Price**, **Most Popular** and **Sort By**. That last section is not technically made up of "filters", but sorting usually goes hand-in-hand with filters, so you'll leave it like that. :]

Below each price filter is space for the total number of venues that fall into that price category. Similarly, there's a spot for the total number of deals across all venues. You'll implement these next.

Returning a count

Open **FilterViewController.swift** and add the following below `import UIKit`:

```
import CoreData
```

Next, add the following property below the last `@IBOutlet` property:

```
// MARK: - Properties
var coreDataStack: CoreDataStack!
```

This will hold the `CoreDataStack` object you've been using in the app delegate and **ViewController.swift**.

Open **ViewController.swift** and replace the `prepare(for:sender:)` implementation with the following:

```
override func prepare(for segue: UIStoryboardSegue,
                      sender: Any?) {
```

```swift
    guard segue.identifier == filterViewControllerSegueIdentifier,
      let navController = segue.destination
        as? UINavigationController,
      let filterVC = navController.topViewController
        as? FilterViewController else {
        return
    }

    filterVC.coreDataStack = coreDataStack
}
```

The new line of code propagates the `CoreDataStack` object from `ViewController` to `FilterViewController`. The filter screen is now ready to use Core Data.

Open **FilterViewController.swift** and add the following lazy property below `coreDataStack`:

```swift
lazy var cheapVenuePredicate: NSPredicate = {
  return NSPredicate(format: "%K == %@",
    #keyPath(Venue.priceInfo.priceCategory), "$")
}()
```

You'll use this lazily-instantiated `NSPredicate` to calculate the number of venues in the lowest price category.

> **Note:** `NSPredicate` supports key paths. This is why you can drill down from the Venue entity into the `PriceInfo` entity using `priceInfo.priceCategory`, and use the `#keyPath` keyword to get safe, compile-time checked values for the key path.

Next, add the following extension below the `UITableViewDelegate` extension:

```swift
// MARK: - Helper methods
extension FilterViewController {

  func populateCheapVenueCountLabel() {

    let fetchRequest =
      NSFetchRequest<NSNumber>(entityName: "Venue")
    fetchRequest.resultType = .countResultType
    fetchRequest.predicate = cheapVenuePredicate

    do {
      let countResult =
        try coreDataStack.managedContext.fetch(fetchRequest)

      let count = countResult.first!.intValue
```

```
      firstPriceCategoryLabel.text =
        "\(count) bubble tea places"
    } catch let error as NSError {
      print("Count not fetch \(error), \(error.userInfo)")
    }
  }
}
```

This extension provides the `populateCheapVenueCountLabel()` method which creates a fetch request to fetch `Venue` entities. You then set the result type to `.countResultType` and set the fetch request's `predicate` to `cheapVenuePredicate`. Notice that for this to work correctly, the fetch request's type parameter has to be `NSNumber`, not `Venue`.

When you set a fetch result's result type to `.countResultType`, the return value becomes a Swift array containing a single `NSNumber`. The integer inside the `NSNumber` is the total count you're looking for.

Once again, you execute the fetch request against `CoreDataStack`'s `NSManagedObjectContext` property. Then you extract the integer from the resulting `NSNumber` and use it to populate `firstPriceCategoryLabel`.

Before you run the sample app, add the following to `viewDidLoad()`:

```
populateCheapVenueCountLabel()
```

Now build and run to test if these changes took effect. Tap **Filter** to bring up the filter/sort menu:

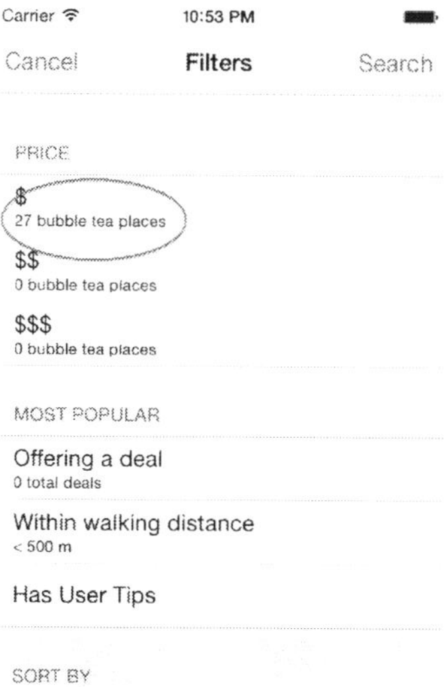

The label under the first price filter now says "27 bubble tea places." Hooray! You've successfully used `NSFetchRequest` to calculate a count.

> **Note:** You may be thinking that you could have just as easily fetched the actual Venue objects and gotten the count from the array's `count` property. That's true. Fetching counts instead of objects is mainly a performance optimization. For example, if you had census data for New York City and wanted to know how many people lived in its metropolitan area, would you prefer Core Data gave you the number 8,300,000 (an integer) or an array of 8,300,000 records?
>
> Obviously, getting the count directly is more memory-efficient. There's a whole chapter devoted to Core Data performance. If you want to learn more about performance optimization in Core Data, check out Chapter 8, "Measuring and Boosting Performance."

Now that you're acquainted with the count result type, you can quickly implement the count for the second price category filter. Add the following lazy property below `cheapVenuePredicate`:

```
lazy var moderateVenuePredicate: NSPredicate = {
  return NSPredicate(format: "%K == %@",
    #keyPath(Venue.priceInfo.priceCategory), "$$")
}()
```

This `NSPredicate` is almost identical to the cheap venue predicate, except this one matches against $$ instead of $. Similarly, add the following method below `populateCheapVenueCountLabel()`:

```
func populateModerateVenueCountLabel() {

  let fetchRequest =
    NSFetchRequest<NSNumber>(entityName: "Venue")
  fetchRequest.resultType = .countResultType
  fetchRequest.predicate = moderateVenuePredicate

  do {

    let countResult =
      try coreDataStack.managedContext.fetch(fetchRequest)

    let count = countResult.first!.intValue
    secondPriceCategoryLabel.text = "\(count) bubble tea places"
  } catch let error as NSError {
    print("Count not fetch \(error), \(error.userInfo)")
  }
}
```

Finally, add the following line to the bottom of `viewDidLoad()` to invoke your newly defined method:

```
populateModerateVenueCountLabel()
```

Build and run the sample project. As before, tap **Filter** on the top right to reach the filter/sort screen:

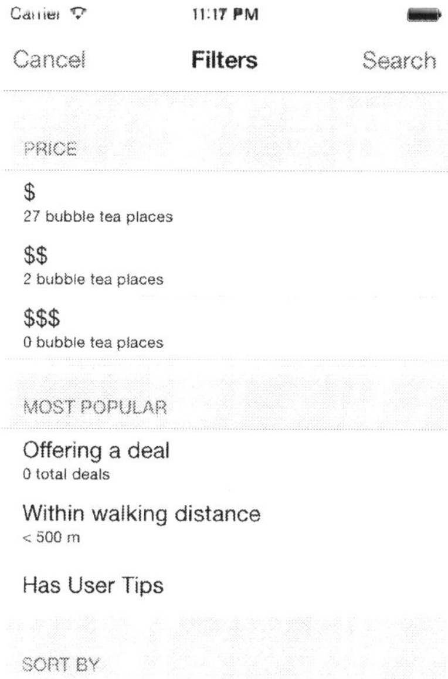

Great news for bubble tea lovers! Only two places are moderately expensive. Bubble tea as a whole seems to be quite accessible. :]

An alternate way to fetch a count

Now that you're familiar with `.countResultType`, it's a good time to mention that there's an alternate API for fetching a count directly from Core Data.

Since there's one more price category count to implement, you'll use this alternate API now. Add the follow lazy property below `moderateVenuePredicate`:

```
lazy var expensiveVenuePredicate: NSPredicate = {
  return NSPredicate(format: "%K == %@",
    #keyPath(Venue.priceInfo.priceCategory), "$$$")
}()
```

Next, implement the following method below
`populateModerateVenueCountLabel()`:

```swift
func populateExpensiveVenueCountLabel() {

  let fetchRequest: NSFetchRequest<Venue> = Venue.fetchRequest()
  fetchRequest.predicate = expensiveVenuePredicate

  do {
    let count =
      try coreDataStack.managedContext.count(for: fetchRequest)

    thirdPriceCategoryLabel.text = "\(count) bubble tea places"
  } catch let error as NSError {
    print("Count not fetch \(error), \(error.userInfo)")
  }
}
```

Like the previous two scenarios, you create a fetch request for retrieving Venue objects.
Next, you set the predicate that you defined as a lazy property moments earlier,
`expensiveVenuePredicate`. The difference between this scenario and the last two is
here, you don't set the result type to `.countResultType`. Rather than the usual
`fetch(_:)`, you use `NSManagedObjectContext`'s method `count(for:)` instead.

The return value for `count(for:)` is an integer that you can use directly to populate the
third price category label.

Finally, add the following line to the bottom of `viewDidLoad()` to invoke your newly
defined method:

```swift
populateExpensiveVenueCountLabel()
```

Build and run to see if your latest changes took effect. The filter/sort screen should look
like this:

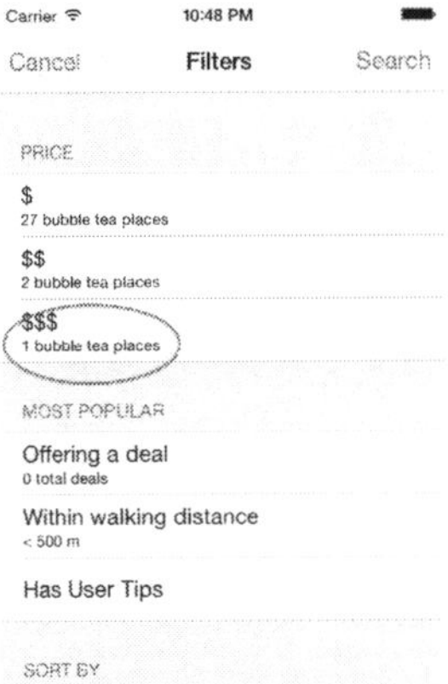

There's only one bubble tea venue that falls into the $$$ category. Maybe they use real pearls instead of tapioca?

Performing calculations with fetch requests

All three price category labels are populated with the number of venues that fall into each category. The next step is to populate the label under "Offering a deal." It currently says "0 total deals." That can't be right!

Where exactly does this information come from? Venue has a `specialCount` attribute that captures the number of deals the venue is currently offering. Unlike the labels under the price category, you now need to know the total sum of deals across **all** venues since a particularly savvy venue could have many deals at once.

The naïve approach would be to load all venues into memory and sum their deals using a for-loop. If you're hoping for a better way, you're in luck: Core Data has built-in support for a number of different functions such as average, sum, min and max.

Open **FilterViewController.swift**, and add the following method below `populateExpensiveVenueCountLabel()`:

```swift
func populateDealsCountLabel() {

  // 1
  let fetchRequest =
    NSFetchRequest<NSDictionary>(entityName: "Venue")
  fetchRequest.resultType = .dictionaryResultType

  // 2
  let sumExpressionDesc = NSExpressionDescription()
  sumExpressionDesc.name = "sumDeals"

  // 3
  let specialCountExp =
    NSExpression(forKeyPath: #keyPath(Venue.specialCount))
  sumExpressionDesc.expression =
    NSExpression(forFunction: "sum:",
              arguments: [specialCountExp])
  sumExpressionDesc.expressionResultType =
    .integer32AttributeType

  // 4
  fetchRequest.propertiesToFetch = [sumExpressionDesc]

  // 5
  do {

    let results =
      try coreDataStack.managedContext.fetch(fetchRequest)
```

```
    let resultDict = results.first!
    let numDeals = resultDict["sumDeals"]!
    numDealsLabel.text = "\(numDeals) total deals"

  } catch let error as NSError {
    print("Count not fetch \(error), \(error.userInfo)")
  }
}
```

This method contains a few classes you've not encountered in the book before, so here is each explained in turn:

1. You begin by creating your typical fetch request for retrieving `Venue` objects. Next, you specify the result type to be `.dictionaryResultType`.

2. You create an `NSExpressionDescription` to request the sum, and give it the name `sumDeals` so you can read its result out of the result dictionary you'll get back from the fetch request.

3. You give the expression description an `NSExpression` to specify you want the sum function. Next, give **that** expression another `NSExpression` to specify what property you want to sum over — in this case, `specialCount`. Finally, you have to set the return data type of your expression description, so you set it to `integer32AttributeType`.

4. You tell your original fetch request to fetch the `sum` by setting its `propertiesToFetch` property to the expression description you just created.

5. Finally, execute the fetch request in the usual `do-catch` statement. The result type is an `NSDictionary` array, so you retrieve the result of your expression using your expression description's name (`sumDeals`) and you're done!

> **Note:** What other functions does Core Data support? To name a few: count, min, max, average, median, mode, absolute value and many more. For a comprehensive list, check out Apple's documentation for `NSExpression`.

Fetching a calculated value from Core Data requires you to follow many, often unintuitive steps, so make sure you have a good reason for using this technique, such as performance considerations.

Finally, add the following line to the bottom of `viewDidLoad()`:

```
populateDealsCountLabel()
```

Build the sample project and open the filter/sort screen to verify your changes.

Great! There are 12 total deals across all `venues` stored in Core Data.

You've now used three of the four supported `NSFetchRequest` result types: `.managedObjectResultType`, `.countResultType` and `.dictionaryResultType`.

The remaining result type is `.managedObjectIDResultType`. When you fetch with this type, the result is an array of `NSManagedObjectID` objects rather the actual managed objects they represent. An `NSManagedObjectID` is a compact universal identifier for a managed object. It works like the primary key in the database!

Prior to iOS 5, fetching by ID was popular because `NSManagedObjectID` is thread-safe and using it helped developers implement the thread confinement concurrency model.

Now that thread confinement has been deprecated in favor of more modern concurrency models, there's little reason to fetch by object ID anymore.

> **Note:** You can set up multiple managed object contexts to run concurrent operations and keep long-running operations off the main thread. For more information, check out Chapter 9, "Multiple Managed Object Contexts."

You've gotten a taste of all the things a fetch request can do for you. But just as important as the information a fetch request returns, is the information it **doesn't** return.

For practical reasons, you have to cap the incoming data at some point.

Why? Imagine a perfectly connected object graph, one where each Core Data object is connected to every other object through a series of relationships. If Core Data didn't put limits on the information a fetch request returned, you'd be fetching the entire object graph every single time! That's not memory efficient.

There are ways you can manually limit the information you get back from a fetch request. For example, `NSFetchRequest` supports fetching batches. You can use the properties `fetchBatchSize`, `fetchLimit` and `fetchOffset` to control the batching behavior.

Core Data also tries to minimize its memory consumption for you by using a technique called **faulting**. A fault is a placeholder object representing a managed object that hasn't yet been fully brought into memory.

Finally, another way to limit your object graph is to use predicates, as you've done to populate the venue count labels above. Let's add the filters to the sample app using predicates.

Open **FilterViewController.swift**, and add the following protocol declaration above your class definition:

```swift
protocol FilterViewControllerDelegate: class {
  func filterViewController(
    filter: FilterViewController,
    didSelectPredicate predicate: NSPredicate?,
    sortDescriptor: NSSortDescriptor?)
}
```

This protocol defines a delegate method that will notify the delegate when the user selects a new sort/filter combination.

Next, add the following three properties below `coreDataStack`:

```swift
weak var delegate: FilterViewControllerDelegate?
var selectedSortDescriptor: NSSortDescriptor?
var selectedPredicate: NSPredicate?
```

This first property will hold a reference to `FilterViewController`'s delegate. It's a `weak` property instead of a strongly-retained property in order to avoid retain cycles. The second and third properties will hold references to the currently selected `NSSortDescriptor` and `NSPredicate`, respectively.

Next, re-implement `saveButtonTapped(_:)` as shown below:

```swift
@IBAction func saveButtonTapped(_ sender: UIBarButtonItem) {
  delegate?.filterViewController(
```

```swift
      filter: self,
    didSelectPredicate: selectedPredicate,
    sortDescriptor: selectedSortDescriptor)

  dismiss(animated: true)
}
```

This means every time you tap **Search** in the top-right corner of the filter/sort screen, you'll notify the delegate of your selection and dismiss the filter/sort screen to reveal the list of venues behind it.

You need to make one more change in this file. Find `tableView(_:didSelectRowAt:)` and implement it as shown below:

```swift
override func tableView(_ tableView: UITableView, didSelectRowAt
indexPath: IndexPath) {

  guard let cell = tableView.cellForRow(at: indexPath) else {
    return
  }

  // Price section
  switch cell {
  case cheapVenueCell:
    selectedPredicate = cheapVenuePredicate
  case moderateVenueCell:
    selectedPredicate = moderateVenuePredicate
  case expensiveVenueCell:
    selectedPredicate = expensiveVenuePredicate
  default: break
  }

  cell.accessoryType = .checkmark
}
```

When the user taps on any of the first three price category cells, this method will map the selected cell to the appropriate predicate. You store a reference to this predicate in `selectedPredicate` so it's ready when you notify the delegate of the user's selection.

Next, open **ViewController.swift** and add the following extension to conform to the `FilterViewControllerDelegate` protocol:

```swift
// MARK: - FilterViewControllerDelegate
extension ViewController: FilterViewControllerDelegate {

  func filterViewController(
    filter: FilterViewController,
    didSelectPredicate predicate: NSPredicate?,
    sortDescriptor: NSSortDescriptor?) {
```

```
      fetchRequest.predicate = nil
      fetchRequest.sortDescriptors = nil

      fetchRequest.predicate = predicate

      if let sr = sortDescriptor {
        fetchRequest.sortDescriptors = [sr]
      }

      fetchAndReload()
    }
  }
```

Adding the `FilterViewControllerDelegate` Swift extension tells the compiler that this class will conform to this protocol. This delegate method fires every time the user selects a new filter/sort combination. Here, you reset your fetch request's `predicate` and `sortDescriptors`, then set the predicate and sort descriptor passed into the method and reload the data.

There's one more thing you need to do before you can test your price category filters. Find `prepare(for:sender:)` and add the following line to the end of the method:

```
filterVC.delegate = self
```

This formally sets `ViewController` as `FilterViewController`'s delegate.

Build and run the sample project. Go to the **Filter** screen, tap the first price category cell ($) and then tap **Search** in the top-right corner.

Your app crashes with the following error message in the console:

```
2016-09-05 14:42:57.960 Bubble Tea Finder[5697:1288181] ***
Terminating app due to uncaught exception
'NSInternalInconsistencyException', reason: 'Can't modify a
named fetch request in an immutable model.'
```

What happened? Earlier in the chapter, you defined your fetch request in the data model. It turns out if you use that technique, the fetch request becomes immutable. You can't change its predicate at runtime, or else you'll crash spectacularly. If you want to set a fetch request in advance, you have to do it in the data model editor.

Open **ViewController.swift**, and replace `viewDidLoad()` with the following:

```
override func viewDidLoad() {
  super.viewDidLoad()

  fetchRequest = Venue.fetchRequest()
  fetchAndReload()
}
```

You removed the lines that retrieves the fetch request from the template in the managed object model. Instead, you get an instance of `NSFetchRequest` directly from the `Venue` entity.

Build and run the sample app one more time. Go to the **Filter** screen, tap the second price category cell (\$\$) and then tap **Search** in the top-right corner. This is the result:

As expected, there are only two venues in this category. Test the first (\$) and third (\$\$\$) price category filters as well, making sure the filtered list contains the correct number of venues for each.

You'll practice writing a few more predicates for the remaining filters. The process is similar to what you've done already, so this time you'll do it with less explanation.

Open **FilterViewController.swift** and add these three lazy properties below `expensiveVenuePredicate`:

```swift
lazy var offeringDealPredicate: NSPredicate = {
  return NSPredicate(format: "%K > 0",
    #keyPath(Venue.specialCount))
}()

lazy var walkingDistancePredicate: NSPredicate = {
  return NSPredicate(format: "%K < 500",
    #keyPath(Venue.location.distance))
}()

lazy var hasUserTipsPredicate: NSPredicate = {
```

```
    return NSPredicate(format: "%K > 0",
      #keyPath(Venue.stats.tipCount))
}()
```

The first predicate specifies venues that are currently offering one or more deals, the second predicate specifies venues that are less than 500 meters away from your current location and the third predicate specifies venues that have at least one user tip.

> **Note:** So far in the book, you've written predicates with a single condition. You should also know that you can write predicates that check two conditions instead of one by using compound predicate operators such as **AND, OR** and **NOT**.
>
> Alternatively, you can string two simple predicates into one compound predicate by using the class `NSCompoundPredicate`.
>
> `NSPredicate` isn't technically part of Core Data (it's part of `Foundation`) so this book won't cover it in depth, but you can seriously improve your Core Data chops by learning the ins and outs of this nifty class. For more information, make sure to check out Apple's Predicate Programming Guide:
>
> https://developer.apple.com/library/ios/documentation/Cocoa/Conceptual/
> Predicates/AdditionalChapters/Introduction.html

Next, scroll down to `tableView(_:didSelectRowAt:)`. You're going to add three more cases to the switch statement you added earlier:

```
override func tableView(_ tableView: UITableView, didSelectRowAt
indexPath: IndexPath) {

  guard let cell = tableView.cellForRow(at: indexPath)else {
    return
  }

  switch cell {
  // Price section
  case cheapVenueCell:
    selectedPredicate = cheapVenuePredicate
  case moderateVenueCell:
    selectedPredicate = moderateVenuePredicate
  case expensiveVenueCell:
    selectedPredicate = expensiveVenuePredicate

  // Most Popular section
  case offeringDealCell:
    selectedPredicate = offeringDealPredicate
  case walkingDistanceCell:
    selectedPredicate = walkingDistancePredicate
```

```
case userTipsCell:
  selectedPredicate = hasUserTipsPredicate
default: break
}

cell.accessoryType = .checkmark
}
```

Above, you added cases for `offeringDealCell`, `walkingDistanceCell` and `userTipsCell`. These are the three new filters for which you're now adding support.

That's all you need to do. Build and run the sample app. Go to the **Filters** page, select the **Offering Deals** filter and tap **Search**:

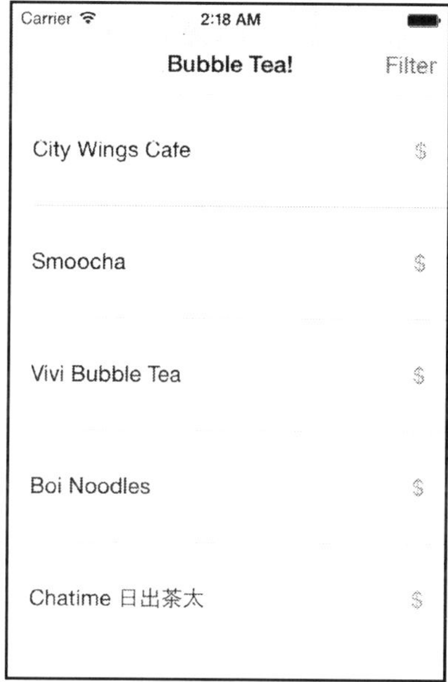

You'll see a total of six venues. Note since you didn't specify a sort descriptor, your list of venues may be in a different order than the venues in the screenshot. You can verify these venues have specials by looking them up in **seed.json**. For example, City Wing Cafe is currently offering four specials. Woo-hoo!

Sorting fetched results

Another powerful feature of `NSFetchRequest` is its ability to sort fetched results for you. It does this by using yet another handy `Foundation` class, `NSSortDescriptor`. These sorts happen at the SQLite level, not in memory. This makes sorting in Core Data fast and efficient.

In this section, you'll implement four different sorts to complete the filter/sort screen.

Open **FilterViewController.swift** and add the following three lazy properties below `hasUserTipsPredicate`:

```swift
lazy var nameSortDescriptor: NSSortDescriptor = {
  let compareSelector =
    #selector(NSString.localizedStandardCompare(_:))
  return NSSortDescriptor(key: #keyPath(Venue.name),
                          ascending: true,
                          selector: compareSelector)
}()

lazy var distanceSortDescriptor: NSSortDescriptor = {
  return NSSortDescriptor(
    key: #keyPath(Venue.location.distance),
    ascending: true)
}()

lazy var priceSortDescriptor: NSSortDescriptor = {
  return NSSortDescriptor(
    key: #keyPath(Venue.priceInfo.priceCategory),
    ascending: true)
}()
```

The way to add sort descriptors is very similar to the way you added filters. Each sort descriptor maps to one of these three lazy `NSSortDescriptor` properties.

To initialize an instance of `NSSortDescriptor` you need three things: a key path to specify the attribute which you want to sort, a specification of whether the sort is ascending or descending and an optional selector to perform the comparison operation.

> **Note:** If you've worked with `NSSortDescriptor` before, then you probably know there's a block-based API that takes a comparator instead of a selector. Unfortunately, Core Data doesn't support this method of defining a sort descriptor.
>
> The same thing goes for the block-based method of defining an `NSPredicate`. Core Data doesn't support this either. The reason is filtering and sorting happens in the SQLite database, so the predicate/sort descriptor has to match nicely to something that can be written as an SQLite statement.

The three sort descriptors are going to sort by name, distance and price category, respectively, in ascending order. Before moving on, take a closer look at the first sort descriptor, `nameSortDescriptor`. The initializer takes in an optional selector, `NSString.localizedStandardCompare(_:)`. What is that?

Any time you're sorting user-facing strings, Apple recommends that you pass in
`NSString.localizedStandardCompare(_:)` to sort according to the language rules of
the current locale. This means sort will "just work" and do the right thing for languages
with special characters. It's the little things that matter, *bien sûr*! :]

Next, find `tableView(_:didSelectRowAt:)` and add the following cases to the end of
the `switch` statement above the `default` case:

```
//Sort By section

case nameAZSortCell:
  selectedSortDescriptor = nameSortDescriptor
case nameZASortCell:
  selectedSortDescriptor =
    nameSortDescriptor.reversedSortDescriptor
    as? NSSortDescriptor
case distanceSortCell:
  selectedSortDescriptor = distanceSortDescriptor
case priceSortCell:
  selectedSortDescriptor = priceSortDescriptor
```

Like before, this `switch` statement matches the user tapped cell with the appropriate
sort descriptor, so it's ready to pass to the delegate when the user taps **Search**.

The only wrinkle is the `nameZA` sort descriptor. Rather than creating a separate sort
descriptor, you can reuse the one for A-Z and simply call the method
`reversedSortDescriptor`. How handy!

Everything else is hooked up for you to test the sorts you just implemented. Build and
run the sample app and go to the **Filter** screen. Tap the **Name (Z-A)** sort and then tap
Search. You'll see search results ordered like so:

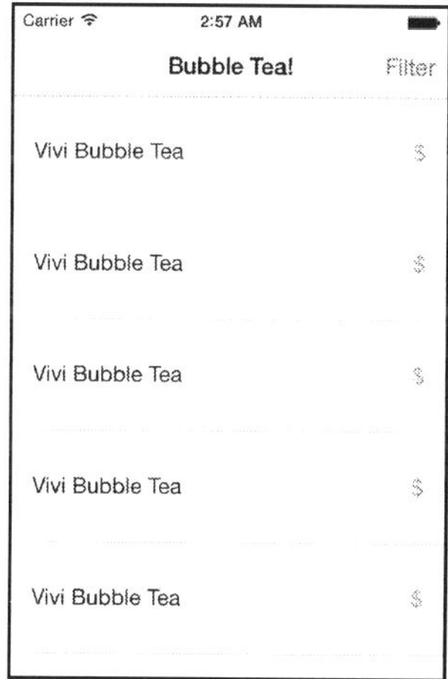

No, you're not seeing double. There really are seven Vivi Bubble Tea venues in the data set — it's a popular bubble tea chain in New York City.

As you scroll down the table view, you'll see the app has indeed sorted the venues alphabetically from Z to A.

You've now completed your **Filter** screen, setting it up so the user can combine any one filter with any one sort. Try different combinations to see what you get. The venue cell doesn't show much information, so if you need to verify a sort, you can go straight to the source and consult **seed.json**.

Asynchronous fetching

If you've reached this point, there's both good news and bad news (and then more good news). The good news is you've learned a lot about what you can do with a plain `NSFetchRequest`. The bad news is that every fetch request you've executed so far has blocked the main thread while you waited for the results to come back.

When you block the main thread, it makes the screen unresponsive to incoming touches and creates a slew of other problems. You haven't felt this blocking of the main thread because you've made simple fetch requests fetching a few objects at a time.

Since the beginning of Core Data, the framework has given developers several techniques to perform fetches in the background. As of iOS 8, Core Data has an API for performing long-running fetch requests in the background and getting a completion callback when the fetch completes.

Let's see this new API in action. Open **ViewController.swift** and add the following property below `venues`:

```
var asyncFetchRequest: NSAsynchronousFetchRequest<Venue>!
```

There you have it. The new class responsible for this asynchronous magic is aptly called `NSAsynchronousFetchRequest`. Don't be fooled by its name, though. It's not directly related to `NSFetchRequest`; it's actually a subclass of `NSPersistentStoreRequest`.

Next, replace the contents of `viewDidLoad()` with the following:

```
override func viewDidLoad() {
  super.viewDidLoad()

  // 1
  fetchRequest = Venue.fetchRequest()

  // 2
```

```swift
asyncFetchRequest =
  NSAsynchronousFetchRequest<Venue>(
    fetchRequest: fetchRequest) {
      [unowned self] (result: NSAsynchronousFetchResult) in

      guard let venues = result.finalResult else {
        return
      }

      self.venues = venues
      self.tableView.reloadData()
  }

  // 3
  do {
    try coreDataStack.managedContext.execute(asyncFetchRequest)
    // Returns immediately, cancel here if you want
  } catch let error as NSError {
    print("Could not fetch \(error), \(error.userInfo)")
  }
}
```

There's a lot that you haven't seen before, so let's cover it step by step:

1. Notice here that an asynchronous fetch request doesn't replace the regular fetch request. Rather, you can think of an asynchronous fetch request as a `wrapper` around the fetch request you already had.

2. To create an `NSAsynchronousFetchRequest` you need two things: a regular `NSFetchRequest` and a completion handler. Your fetched venues are contained in `NSAsynchronousFetchResult`'s `finalResult` property. Within the completion handler, you update the `venues` property and reload the table view.

3. Specifying the completion handler is not enough! You still have to execute the asynchronous fetch request. Once again, `CoreDataStack`'s `managedContext` property handles the heavy lifting for you. However, notice the method you use is different — this time, it's `execute(_:)` instead of the usual `fetch(_:)`.

    `execute(_:)` returns immediately. You don't need to do anything with the return value since you're going to update the table view from within the completion block. The return type is `NSAsynchronousFetchResult`.

> **Note:** As an added bonus to this API, you can cancel the fetch request with `NSAsynchronousFetchResult`'s `cancel()` method.

If you were to build and run the sample app at this point, it would crash on launch. There is one more change you need to make. Replace the `venues` property in **ViewController.swift** with the following:

```
var venues: [Venue] = []
```

Since the original fetch request is asynchronous, it will finish after the table view does its initial load. The table view will try to unwrap the `venues` property but since there are no results yet, your app will crash.

You fix this issue by initializing venues to an empty array. This way, on first load, your table view will simply be empty if there are no results.

Time to see if your asynchronous fetch delivers as promised. If everything goes well, you shouldn't notice any difference in the user interface.

Build and run the sample app, and you should see the list of venues as before:

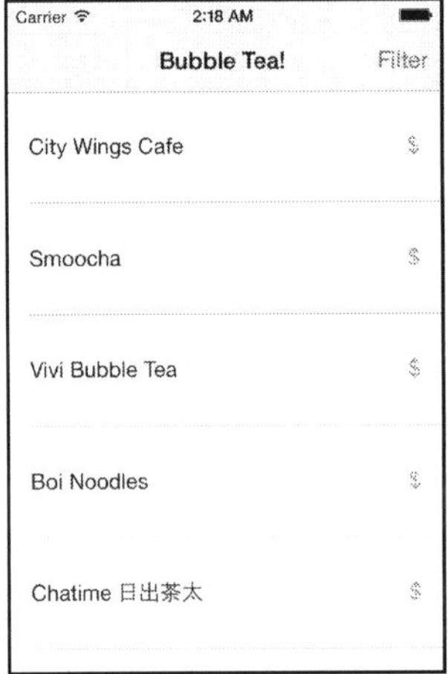

Hooray! You've mastered asynchronous fetching. The filters and sorts will also work, except they still use a plain `NSFetchRequest` to reload the table view.

Batch updates: no fetching required

Sometimes the only reason you fetch objects from Core Data is to change a single attribute. Then, after you make your changes, you have to commit the Core Data objects back to the persistent store and call it a day. This is the normal process you've been following all along.

But what if you want to update a hundred thousand records all at once? It would take a lot of time and a lot of memory to fetch all of those objects just to update one attribute. No amount of tweaking your fetch request would save your user from having to stare at a spinner for a long, long time.

Luckily, as of iOS 8 there has been new way to update Core Data objects without having to fetch anything into memory: `batch updates`. This new technique greatly reduces the amount of time and memory required to make those huge kinds of updates.

The new technique bypasses the `NSManagedObjectContext` and goes straight to the persistent store. The classic use case for batch updates is the "Mark all as read" feature in a messaging application or e-mail client. For this sample app, you're going to do something more fun. Since you love bubble tea so much, you're going to mark every `Venue` in Core Data as your favorite. :]

Let's see this in practice. Open **ViewController.swift** and add the following to `viewDidLoad()` below the `super.viewDidLoad()` call:

```swift
let batchUpdate = NSBatchUpdateRequest(entityName: "Venue")
batchUpdate.propertiesToUpdate =
  [#keyPath(Venue.favorite) : true]

batchUpdate.affectedStores =
  coreDataStack.managedContext
    .persistentStoreCoordinator?.persistentStores

batchUpdate.resultType = .updatedObjectsCountResultType

do {
  let batchResult =
    try coreDataStack.managedContext.execute(batchUpdate)
      as! NSBatchUpdateResult
  print("Records updated \(batchResult.result!)")
} catch let error as NSError {
  print("Could not update \(error), \(error.userInfo)")
}
```

You create an instance of `NSBatchUpdateRequest` with the entity you want to update, `Venue` in this case. Next, set up your batch update request by setting `propertiesToUpdate` to a dictionary that contains the key path of the attribute you want to update, `favorite`, and its new value, `true`. Next, set `affectedStores` to your persistent store coordinator's `persistentStores` array. Finally, set the result type to return a count and execute your batch update request.

Build and run your sample app. If everything works properly, you'll see the following printed to your console log:

```
Records updated 30
```

Great! You've surreptitiously marked every bubble tea venue in New York City as your favorite. :]

Now you know how to update your Core Data objects without loading them into memory. Is there another use case where you may want to bypass the managed context and change your Core Data objects directly in the persistent store?

Of course there is — batch deletion!

You shouldn't have to to load objects into memory just to delete them, particularly if you're handling a large number of them. As of iOS 9, you've had `NSBatchDeleteRequest` for this purpose.

As the name suggests, a batch delete request can efficiently delete a large number Core Data objects in one go.

Like `NSBatchUpdateRequest`, `NSBatchDeleteRequest` is also a subclass of `NSPersistentStoreRequest`. Both types of batch request behave similarly since they both operate directly on the persistent store.

> **Note:** Since you're sidestepping your `NSManagedObjectContext`, you won't get any validation if you use a batch update request or a batch delete request. Your changes also won't be reflected in your managed context. Make sure you're sanitizing and validating your data properly before using a persistent store request!

Where to go from here?

Whew! If you followed the chapter all the way through, then you've spent a lot of time fetching from your Core Data persistent store. I hope these examples gave you insight into how powerful and flexible fetching is in Core Data.

Among other things, you've learned how to store fetch requests in your data model and how to refine your fetched results using predicates and sort descriptors. There is much more to learn about fetching! In the next chapter, you'll work with `NSFetchedResultsController`, a helpful class that makes using table views a breeze.

If you're thirsty and need a break before continuing — perhaps you now feel like a nice refreshing bubble tea?

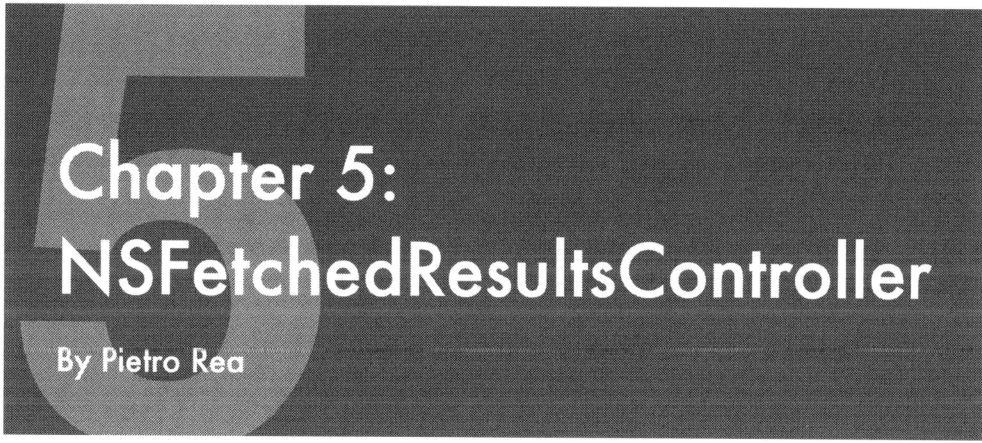

If you followed the previous chapters closely, you probably noticed that most of the sample projects use table views. That's because Core Data fits nicely with table views. Set up your fetch request, fetch an array of managed objects and plug the result into the table view's data source. This is a common, everyday scenario.

If you see a tight relationship between Core Data and `UITableView`, you're in good company. The authors of the Core Data framework at Apple thought the same way! In fact, they saw *so* much potential for a close connection between `UITableView` and Core Data they penned a class to formalize this bond: `NSFetchedResultsController`.

As the name suggests, `NSFetchedResultsController` is a controller, but it's not a *view* controller. It has no user interface. Its purpose is to make developers' lives easier by abstracting away much of the code needed to synchronize a table view with a data source backed by Core Data.

Set up an `NSFetchedResultsController` correctly, and your table will "magically" mimic its data source without you have to write more than a few lines of code. In this chapter, you'll learn the ins and outs of this class. You'll also learn when to use it and when not to use it. Are you ready?

Introducing the World Cup app

This chapter's sample project is a World Cup scoreboard app for iOS. On startup, the one-page application will list all the teams contesting for the World Cup. Tapping on a country's cell will increase the country's wins by one. In this simplified version of the World Cup, the country with the most taps wins the tournament. This ranking simplifies the real elimination rules quite a bit, but it's good enough for demonstration purposes.

Go to this chapter's files and find the **starter** folder. Open **WorldCup.xcodeproj**. Build and run the starter project:

The sample application consists of 20 static cells in a table view. Those bright blue boxes are where the teams' flags should be. Instead of real names, you see "Team Name." Although the sample project isn't too exciting, it actually does a lot of the setup for you.

Open the project navigator and take a look at the full list of files in the starter project:

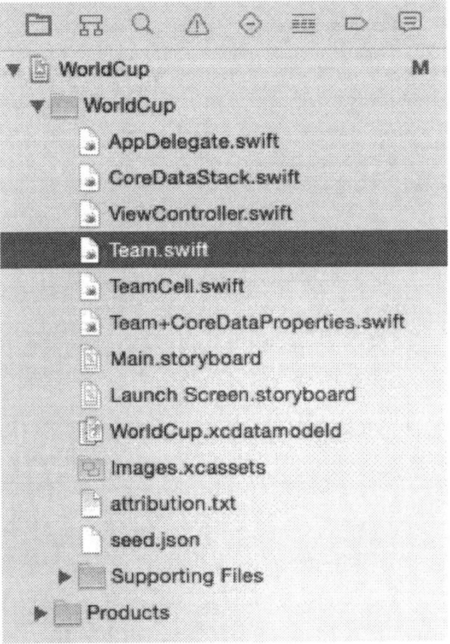

Before jumping into the code, let's briefly go over what each class does for you out of the box. You'll find a lot of the setup you did manually in previous chapters comes already implemented for you. Hooray!

- **AppDelegate**: On first launch, the app delegate reads from **seed.json**, creates corresponding Core Data objects and saves them to the persistent store.

- **CoreDataStack**: As in previous chapters, this object wraps an instance of `NSPersistentContainer`, which in turn contains the cadre of Core Data objects known as the "stack": the context, the model, the persistent store and the persistent store coordinator. No need to set this up. It comes ready to be used.

- **ViewController**: The sample project is a one-page application, and this file represents that one page. If you're curious about its UI elements, head over to **Main.storyboard**. There's a table, a navigation bar and a single prototype cell.

- **Team+CoreDataClass & Team+CoreDataProperties**: These files represent a country's team. It's an `NSManagedObject` subclass with properties for each of its four attributes: `teamName`, `qualifyingZone`, `imageName` and `wins`. If you're curious about its entity definition, head over to **WorldCup.xcdatamodel**.

- **Images.xcassets**: The sample project's asset catalog contains a flag image for every country in **seed.json**.

The first three chapters of this book covered the Core Data concepts mentioned above. If "managed object subclass" doesn't ring a bell or if you're unsure what a Core Data stack is supposed to do, you may want to go back and reread the relevant chapters. `NSFetchedResultsController` will be here when you return. :]

Otherwise, if you're ready to proceed, you'll begin implementing the World Cup application. You probably already know who won the World Cup last time, but this is your chance to rewrite history for the country of your choice, with just a few taps!

It all begins with a fetch request...

At its core, `NSFetchedResultsController` is a wrapper around the results of an `NSFetchRequest`. Right now, the sample project contains static information. You're going to create a fetched results controller to display the list of teams from Core Data in the table view.

Open **ViewController.swift** and add the following below `import UIKit`:

```
import CoreData
```

Next, add a property to hold your fetched results controller below `coreDataStack`:

```
var fetchedResultsController: NSFetchedResultsController<Team>!
```

Like NSFetchRequest, NSFetchedResultsController requires a generic type paremeter, Team in this case, to specify the type of entity you *expect* to be working with. Next, add the following code to the end of viewDidLoad() to set up your fetched results controller property:

```
// 1
let fetchRequest: NSFetchRequest<Team> = Team.fetchRequest()

// 2
fetchedResultsController = NSFetchedResultsController(
  fetchRequest: fetchRequest,
  managedObjectContext: coreDataStack.managedContext,
  sectionNameKeyPath: nil,
  cacheName: nil)

// 3
do {
  try fetchedResultsController.performFetch()
} catch let error as NSError {
  print("Fetching error: \(error), \(error.userInfo)")
}
```

Setting up a fetched results controller is a little more complicated than setting up a simple fetch request. Let's go step by step through the process:

1. The fetched results controller handles the coordination between Core Data and your table view, but it still needs you to provide an NSFetchRequest. Remember the NSFetchRequest class is highly customizable. It can take sort descriptors, predicates, etc.

   In this example, you get your NSFetchRequest directly from the Team class because you want to fetch all Team objects.

2. The initializer method for a fetched results controller takes four parameters: first is the fetch request you just created.

   The second parameter is an instance of NSManagedObjectContext. Like NSFetchRequest, the fetched results controller class needs a managed object context to execute the fetch. It can't actually fetch anything by itself.

   The other two parameters are optional: sectionNameKeyPath and cacheName. Leave them blank for now; you'll read more about them later in the chapter.

3. You execute the fetch request. If there's an error, you log the error to the console.

Wait a minute... where are your fetched results? While fetching with NSFetchRequest returns an array of results, fetching with NSFetchedResultsController doesn't return anything.

`NSFetchedResultsController` is both a wrapper around a fetch request and a container for its fetched results. You can get them either with the `fetchedObjects` property or the `object(at:)` method.

Next, you'll connect the fetched results controller to the usual table view data source methods. The fetched results determine both the number of sections and the number of rows per section.

With this in mind, re-implement `numberOfSections(in:)` and `tableView(_:numberOfRowsInSection:)`, as shown below:

```swift
func numberOfSections(in tableView: UITableView) -> Int {

  guard let sections = fetchedResultsController.sections else {
    return 0
  }

  return sections.count
}

func tableView(_ tableView: UITableView,
               numberOfRowsInSection section: Int)
               -> Int {

  guard let sectionInfo =
    fetchedResultsController.sections?[section] else {
      return 0
  }

  return sectionInfo.numberOfObjects
}
```

The number of sections in the table view corresponds to the number of sections in the fetched results controller. You may be wondering how this table view can have more than one section. Aren't you simply fetching and displaying all teams?

That's correct. You will only have one section this time around, but keep in mind `NSFetchedResultsController` can split up your data into sections. You'll see an example of this later in the chapter.

Furthermore, the number of rows in each table view section corresponds to the number of objects in each fetched results controller section. You can query information about a fetched results controller section through its `sections` property.

> **Note:** The `sections` array contains opaque objects that implement the `NSFetchedResultsSectionInfo` protocol. This lightweight protocol provides information about a section, such as its title and number of objects.

Implementing `tableView(_:cellForRowAt:)` would typically be the next step. A quick look at the method, however, reveals it's already vending `TeamCell` cells as needed. What you need to change is the helper method that populates the cell.

Find `configure(_:for:)` and replace it with the following:

```swift
func configure(cell: UITableViewCell,
               for indexPath: IndexPath) {

  guard let cell = cell as? TeamCell else {
    return
  }

  let team = fetchedResultsController.object(at: indexPath)
  cell.flagImageView.image = UIImage(named: team.imageName!)
  cell.teamLabel.text = team.teamName
  cell.scoreLabel.text = "Wins: \(team.wins)"
}
```

This method takes in a table view cell and an index path. You use this index path to grab the corresponding `Team` object from the fetched results controller. Next, you use the `Team` object to populate the cell's flag image, team name and score label.

Notice again there's no array variable holding your teams. They're all stored inside the fetched results controller and you access them via `object(at:)`.

It's time to test your creation. Build and run the app. Ready, set and... crash?

```
*** Terminating app due to uncaught exception
'NSInvalidArgumentException', reason: 'An instance of
NSFetchedResultsController requires a fetch request with sort
descriptors'
*** First throw call stack:
(
    0   CoreFoundation                      0x00000001057c534b
__exceptionPreprocess + 171
    1   libobjc.A.dylib                     0x0000000104e0921e
objc_exception_throw + 48
    2   CoreData                            0x0000000105430682 -
[NSFetchedResultsController
initWithFetchRequest:managedObjectContext:sectionNameKeyPath:cac
heName:] + 2130
    3   WorldCup                            0x00000001048112e7
_TTOFCSo26NSFetchedResultsControllercfT12fetchRequestGCSo14NSFet
chRequestx_20managedObjectContextCSo22NSManagedObjectContext18se
ctionNameKeyPathGSqSS_9cacheNameGSqSS__GS_x_ + 311
    4   WorldCup                            0x000000010480f375
_TFCSo26NSFetchedResultsControllerCfT12fetchRequestGCSo14NSFetch
Requestx_20managedObjectContextCSo22NSManagedObjectContext18sect
ionNameKeyPathGSqSS_9cacheNameGSqSS__GS_x_ + 309
    5   WorldCup                            0x000000010480ed08
```

```
_TFC8WorldCup14ViewController11viewDidLoadfT_T_ + 552
    6   WorldCup                        0x000000010480f582
_TToFC8WorldCup14ViewController11viewDidLoadfT_T_ + 34
    7   UIKit                           0x0000000105d87e55 -
[UIViewController loadViewIfRequired] + 1258
    8   UIKit                           0x0000000105dc8237 -
[UINavigationController _layoutViewController:] + 55
    9   UIKit                           0x0000000105dc8b1f -
[UINavigationController
_updateScrollViewFromViewController:toViewController:] + 471
    10  UIKit                           0x0000000105dc8c96 -
[UINavigationController
_startTransition:fromViewController:toViewController:] + 133
    11  UIKit                           0x0000000105dc9ea1 -
[UINavigationController _startDeferredTransitionIfNeeded:] + 874
    12  UIKit                           0x0000000105dcaf83 -
[UINavigationController __viewWillLayoutSubviews] + 58
    13  UIKit                           0x0000000105fb773f -
[UILayoutContainerVicw layoutSubviews] + 223
    14  UIKit                           0x0000000105cacae4 -
[UIView(CALayerDelegate) layoutSublayersOfLayer:] + 1237
    15  QuartzCore                      0x000000010ac45cdc -
[CALayer layoutSublayers] + 146
    16  QuartzCore                      0x000000010ac397a0
_ZN2CA5Layer16layout_if_neededEPNS_11TransactionE + 366
    17  QuartzCore                      0x000000010ac3961e
_ZN2CA5Layer28layout_and_display_if_neededEPNS_11TransactionE +
24
    18  QuartzCore                      0x000000010abc762c
_ZN2CA7Context18commit_transactionEPNS_11TransactionE + 280
    19  QuartzCore                      0x000000010abf4713
_ZN2CA11Transaction6commitEv + 475
    20  QuartzCore                      0x000000010abf5083
_ZN2CA11Transaction17observer_callbackEP19__CFRunLoopObservermPv
+ 113
    21  CoreFoundation                  0x0000000105769e17
__CFRUNLOOP_IS_CALLING_OUT_TO_AN_OBSERVER_CALLBACK_FUNCTION__ +
23
    22  CoreFoundation                  0x0000000105769d87
__CFRunLoopDoObservers + 391
    23  CoreFoundation                  0x000000010574e4b6
CFRunLoopRunSpecific + 454
    24  UIKit                           0x0000000105be28f6 -
[UIApplication _run] + 434
    25  UIKit                           0x0000000105be8a74
UIApplicationMain + 159
    26  WorldCup                        0x0000000104817cff
main + 111
    27  libdyld.dylib                   0x0000000108dab68d
start + 1
)
libc++abi.dylib: terminating with uncaught exception of type
NSException
```

What happened? `NSFetchedResultsController` is helping you out here, though it may not feel like it! If you want to use it to populate a table view and have it know which managed object should appear at which index path, you can't just throw it a basic fetch request. The key part of the crash log is this:

```
'An instance of NSFetchedResultsController requires a fetch
 request with sort descriptors'
```

A regular fetch request doesn't require a sort descriptor. Its minimum requirement is you set an entity description, and it will fetch all objects of that entity type. `NSFetchedResultsController`, however, requires at least one sort descriptor. Otherwise, how would it know the right order for your table view?

Go back to `viewDidLoad()` and add the following lines after `let fetchRequest: NSFetchRequest<Team> = Team.fetchRequest()`:

```swift
let sort = NSSortDescriptor(key: #keyPath(Team.teamName),
  ascending: true)
fetchRequest.sortDescriptors = [sort]
```

Adding this sort descriptor will show the teams in alphabetical order from A to Z and fix the earlier crash.

Build and run the application. Your screen will look like this:

Success! The full list of World Cup participants is on your device or iOS Simulator. Notice, however, that every country has zero wins and there's no way to increment the score. Some people say that soccer is a low-scoring sport, but this is absurd!

Modifying data

Let's fix everyone's zero score and add some code to increment the number of wins. Replace the currently empty implementation of the table view delegate method `tableView(_:didSelectRowAt:)` with the following:

```swift
func tableView(_ tableView: UITableView,
              didSelectRowAt indexPath: IndexPath) {

  let team = fetchedResultsController.object(at: indexPath)
  team.wins = team.wins + 1
  coreDataStack.saveContext()
}
```

When the user taps on a row, you grab the `Team` corresponding to the selected index path, increment its number of wins and commit the change to Core Data's persistent store.

You might think a *fetched results controller* is only good for getting results, but the `Team` objects you get back are the same old managed object subclasses. You can update their values and save just as you've always done.

Build and run once again, and tap on the first country on the list (Algeria) five times:

What's going on here? You're tapping away but the number of wins is not going up. You're updating Algeria's number of wins in Core Data's underlying persistent store, but you aren't triggering a UI refresh.

Go back to Xcode, stop the app, and build and run again:

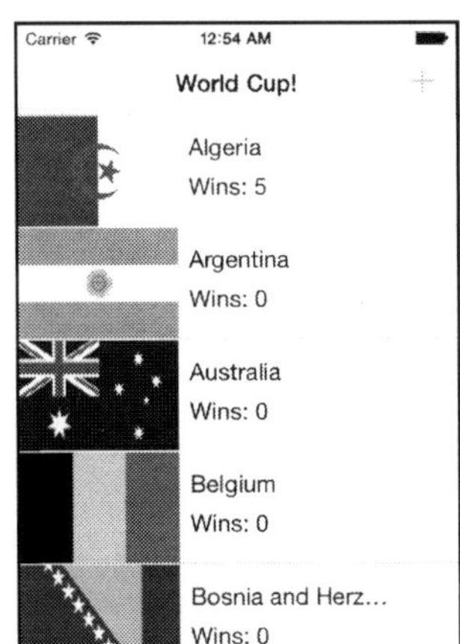

Just as you suspected, re-launching the app from scratch forced a UI refresh, showing Algeria's real score of 5. `NSFetchedResultsController` has a nice solution to this problem, but for now, let's use the brute force solution.

Add the follow line to the end of `tableView(_:didSelectRowAt:)`:

```
tableView.reloadData()
```

In addition to incrementing a team's number of wins, tapping a cell now reloads the entire table view. This approach is heavy-handed, but it does the job for now.

Build and run the app one more time. Tap as many countries as you want as many times as you want. Verify that the UI is always up to date.

There you go. You've got a fetched results controller up and running. Excited?

If this were all `NSFetchedResultsController` could do, you would probably feel a little disappointed. After all, you can accomplish the same thing using an `NSFetchRequest` and a simple array.

The real magic comes in the remaining sections of this chapter. `NSFetchedResultsController` earned its keep in the Cocoa Touch frameworks with features such as section handling and change monitoring, covered next.

Grouping results into sections

There are six qualifying zones in the World Cup: Africa, Asia, Oceania, Europe, South America and North/Central America. The `Team` entity has a string attribute named `qualifyingZone` storing this information.

In this section, you'll split up the list of countries into their respective qualifying zones. `NSFetchedResultsController` makes this very simple.

Let's see it in action. Go back to `viewDidLoad()` and make the following change to the fetched results controller's initializer:

```
fetchedResultsController = NSFetchedResultsController(
  fetchRequest: fetchRequest,
  managedObjectContext: coreDataStack.managedContext,
  sectionNameKeyPath: #keyPath(Team.qualifyingZone),
  cacheName: nil)
```

The difference here is you're passing in a value for the optional `sectionNameKeyPath` parameter. You can use this parameter to specify an attribute the fetched results controller should use to group the results and generate sections.

How exactly are these sections generated? Each unique attribute value becomes a section. `NSFetchedResultsController` then groups its fetched results into these sections. In this case, it will generate sections for each unique value of `qualifyingZone` such as "Africa", "Asia", "Oceania" and so on. This is exactly what you want!

> **Note:** `sectionNameKeyPath` takes a keyPath string. It can take the form of an attribute name such as `qualifyingZone` or `teamName`, or it can drill deep into a Core Data relationship, such as `employee.address.street`. Use the `#keyPath` syntax to defend against typos and stringly typed code.

The fetched results controller will now report the sections and rows to the table view, but the current UI won't look any different. To fix this problem, add the following method to the `UITableViewDataSource` extension:

```
func tableView(_ tableView: UITableView,
               titleForHeaderInSection section: Int)
    -> String? {
  let sectionInfo = fetchedResultsController.sections?[section]
  return sectionInfo?.name
}
```

Implementing this data source method adds section headers to the table view, making it easy to see where one section ends and another one begins. In this case, the section gets its title from the qualifying zone. Like before, this information comes directly from the `NSFetchedResultsSectionInfo` protocol.

Build and run the application. Your app will look something like the following:

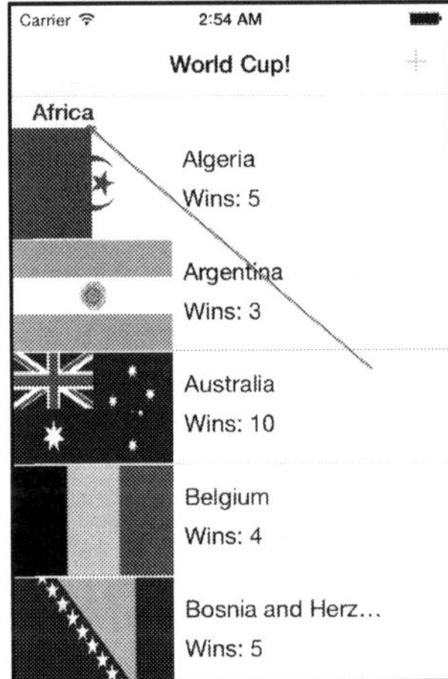

Scroll down the page. There's good news and bad news. The good news is the app accounts for all six sections. Hooray! The bad news is the world is upside down.

Take a closer look at the sections. You'll see Argentina in Africa, Cameroon in Asia and Russia in South America. How did this happen? It's not a problem with the data; you can open **seed.json** and verify each team lists the correct qualifying zone.

Have you figured it out? The list of countries is still shown alphabetically and the fetched results controller is simply splitting up the table into sections as if all teams of the same qualifying zone were grouped together.

Go back to `viewDidLoad()` and make the following change to fix the problem. Replace the existing code that creates and sets the sort descriptor on the fetch request with the following:

```
let zoneSort = NSSortDescriptor(
  key: #keyPath(Team.qualifyingZone), ascending: true)
let scoreSort = NSSortDescriptor(
  key: #keyPath(Team.wins), ascending: false)
let nameSort = NSSortDescriptor(
  key: #keyPath(Team.teamName), ascending: true)

fetchRequest.sortDescriptors = [zoneSort, scoreSort, nameSort]
```

The problem was the sort descriptor. This is another `NSFetchedResultsController` "gotcha" to keep in mind. If you want to separate fetched results using a section keyPath, `the first sort descriptor's attribute must match the key path's attribute`.

The documentation for `NSFetchedResultsController` makes this point emphatically, and with good reason! You saw what happened when the sort descriptor doesn't match the key path — your data ends up making no sense.

Build and run one more time to verify this change fixed the problem:

Indeed it did. Changing the sort descriptor restored the geopolitical balance in your sample application. African teams are in Africa, European teams are in Europe and so on.

> **Note:** The only team that may still raise eyebrows is Australia, which appears
> under Asia's qualifying zone. This is how FIFA categorizes Australia. If you don't
> like it, you can file a bug report with them! ;]

Notice within each qualifying zone, teams are sorted by number of wins from highest to
lowest, then by name. This is because in the previous code snippet, you added three sort
descriptors: first sort by qualifying zone, then by number of wins, then finally by name.

Before moving on, take a moment to think of what you'd have needed to do to separate
the teams by qualifying zone without the fetched results controller. First, you would've
had to create a dictionary and iterated over the teams to find unique qualifying zones. As
you traversed the array of teams, you would've had to associate each team with the
correct qualifying zone. Once you have the list of teams by zone, you'd then need to sort
the data.

Of course it's not impossible to do this yourself, but it's tedious. This is what
`NSFetchedResultsController` saved you from doing. You can take the rest of the day
off and go to the beach or watch some old World Cup matches. Thank you,
`NSFetchedResultsController`!

"Cache" the ball

As you can probably imagine, grouping teams into sections is not a cheap operation.
There's no way to avoid iterating over every team.

It's not a performance problem in this case because there are only 32 teams to consider
but imagine what would happen if your data set were much larger. What if your task
were to iterate over 3 million census records and separate them by state/province?

"I'd just throw that on a background thread!" might be your first thought. The table
view, however, can't populate itself until all sections are available. You might save yourself
from blocking the main thread, but you'd still be left looking at a spinner.

There's no denying that this operation is expensive. At a bare minimum, you should only
pay the cost once: figure out the section grouping a single time, and reuse your result
every time after that.

The authors of `NSFetchedResultsController` thought about this problem and came
up with a solution: caching. You don't have to do much to turn it on.

Head back to `viewDidLoad()` and make the following modification to the fetched results controller initialization, adding a value to the `cacheName` parameter:

```
fetchedResultsController = NSFetchedResultsController(
  fetchRequest: fetchRequest,
  managedObjectContext: coreDataStack.managedContext,
  sectionNameKeyPath: #keyPath(Team.qualifyingZone),
  cacheName: "worldCup")
```

You specify a cache name to turn on `NSFetchedResultsController`'s on-disk section cache. That's all you need to do! Keep in mind that this section cache is completely separate from Core Data's persistent store, where you persist the teams.

Note: `NSFetchedResultsController`'s section cache is very sensitive to changes in its fetch request. As you can imagine, any changes — such as a different entity description or different sort descriptors — would give you a completely different set of fetched objects, invalidating the cache completely. If you make changes like this, you must delete the existing cache using `deleteCache(withName:)` or use a different cache name.

Build and run the application a few times. The second launch should be a *little* bit faster than the first. This is not the author's power of suggestion (psst, say "fast" five times in a row); it's `NSFetchedResultsController`'s cache system at work!

On the second launch, `NSFetchedResultsController` reads directly from your cache. This saves a round trip to Core Data's persistent store, as well as the time needed to compute those sections. Hooray!

You'll learn about measuring performance and seeing if your code changes really did make things faster in Chapter 8, "Measuring and Boosting Performance".

In your own apps, consider using `NSFetchedResultsController`'s cache if you're grouping results into sections and either have a very large data set or are targeting older devices.

Monitoring changes

This chapter has already covered two of the three main benefits of using `NSFetchedResultsController`: sections and caching. The third and last benefit is somewhat of a double-edged sword: it's powerful but also easy to misuse.

Earlier in the chapter, when you implemented the tap to increment the number of wins, you added a line of code to reload the table view to show the updated score. This was a brute force solution, but it worked.

Sure, you could have reloaded only the selected cell by being smart about the `UITableView` API, but that wouldn't have solved the root problem.

Not to get too philosophical, but the root problem is *change*. Something changed in the underlying data and you had to be explicit about reloading the user interface.

Imagine for a moment what a second version of the World Cup app would look like. Maybe there's a detail screen for every team where you can change the score. Maybe the app calls an API endpoint and gets new score information from the web service. It would be your job to refresh the table view `for every code path` that updates the underlying data.

Doing it explicitly is error-prone, not to mention a little boring. Isn't there a better way? Yes, there is. Once again, fetched results controller comes to the rescue.

`NSFetchedResultsController` can listen for changes in its result set and notify its delegate, `NSFetchedResultsControllerDelegate`. You can use this delegate to refresh the table view as needed any time the underlying data changes.

What does it mean a fetched results controller can monitor changes in its "result set"? It means it can monitor changes in all objects, old and new, it *would* have fetched, in addition to objects it has already fetched. This distinction will become clearer later in this section.

Let's see this in practice. Add the following extension to the bottom of the file:

```swift
// MARK: - NSFetchedResultsControllerDelegate
extension ViewController: NSFetchedResultsControllerDelegate {

}
```

This simply tells the compiler the `ViewController` class will implement some of the fetched results controller's delegate method.

Next, go back to `viewDidLoad()` and set the view controller as the fetched results controller's delegate. Add the following line of code after you initialize the fetched results controller:

```swift
fetchedResultsController.delegate = self
```

That's all you need to start monitoring changes! Of course, the next step is to do something when those change reports come in. You'll do that next.

> **Note:** A fetched results controller can only monitor changes made via the managed object context specified in its initializer. If you create a separate `NSManagedObjectContext` somewhere else in your app and start making changes there, your delegate method won't run until those changes have been saved and merged with the fetched results controller's context.

Responding to changes

First, remove the `reloadData()` call from `tableView(_:didSelectRowAt:)`. As mentioned before, this was the brute force approach that you're now going to replace.

`NSFetchedResultsControllerDelegate` has four methods that come in varying degrees of granularity. To start out, implement the broadest delegate method, the one that says: "Hey, something just changed!"

Add the following method inside the `NSFetchedResultsControllerDelegate` extension:

```swift
func controllerDidChangeContent(_ controller:
  NSFetchedResultsController<NSFetchRequestResult>) {
    tableView.reloadData()
}
```

The change may seem small, but implementing this method means that any change whatsoever, no matter the source, will refresh the table view.

Build and run the application. Verify that the table view's cells still update correctly by tapping on a few cells:

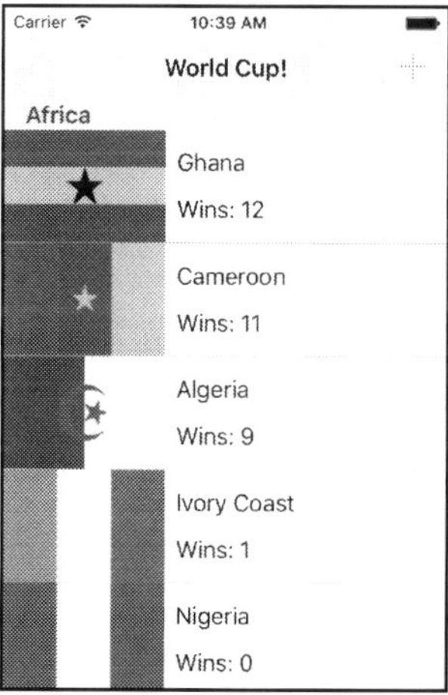

The score labels update as before, but there's something else happening. When one country has more points than another country in the same qualifying zone, it will "jump" on top of it. This is the fetched results controller noticing a change in the sort order of its fetched results and readjusting the table view's data source accordingly.

When the cells do move around, it's pretty jumpy, almost as if you were completely reloading the table every time something changed. :]

Next, you'll go from reloading the entire table to refreshing only what needs to change. The fetched results controller delegate can tell you if a specific index path needs to be moved, inserted or deleted due to a change in the fetched results controller's result set.

Replace the contents of the `NSFetchedResultsControllerDelegate` extension, with the following three delegate methods to see this in action:

```swift
func controllerWillChangeContent(_ controller:
  NSFetchedResultsController<NSFetchRequestResult>) {
    tableView.beginUpdates()
}

func controller(_ controller:
  NSFetchedResultsController<NSFetchRequestResult>,
  didChange anObject: Any,
  at indexPath: IndexPath?,
  for type: NSFetchedResultsChangeType,
  newIndexPath: IndexPath?) {

  switch type {
  case .insert:
    tableView.insertRows(at: [newIndexPath!], with: .automatic)
  case .delete:
    tableView.deleteRows(at: [indexPath!], with: .automatic)
  case .update:
    let cell = tableView.cellForRow(at: indexPath!) as! TeamCell
    configure(cell: cell, for: indexPath!)
  case .move:
    tableView.deleteRows(at: [indexPath!], with: .automatic)
    tableView.insertRows(at: [newIndexPath!], with: .automatic)
  }
}

func controllerDidChangeContent(_ controller:
  NSFetchedResultsController<NSFetchRequestResult>) {
    tableView.endUpdates()
}
```

Whew! That's a wall of code. Fortunately, it's mostly boilerplate and easy to understand. Let's briefly go over all three methods you just added or modified:

- **controllerWillChangeContent(_:)**: This delegate method notifies you that changes are about to occur. You ready your table view using `beginUpdates()`.

- **controller(_:didChange...)**: This method is quite a mouthful. And with good reason — it tells you exactly which objects changed, what type of change occurred (insertion, deletion, update or reordering) and what the affected index paths are.

  This middle method is the proverbial glue that synchronizes your table view with Core Data. No matter how much the underlying data changes, your table view will stay true to what's going on in the persistent store.

- **controllerDidChangeContent(_:)**: The delegate method you had originally implemented to refresh the UI turned out to be the third of three delegate methods that notify you of changes. Rather than refreshing the entire table view, you just need to call `endUpdates()` to apply the changes.

> **Note:** What you end up doing with the change notifications depends on your individual app. The implementation you see above is an example Apple provided in the `NSFetchedResultsControllerDelegate` documentation.

Note the order and nature of the methods ties in very neatly to the "begin updates, make changes, end updates" pattern used to update table views. This is not a coincidence!

Build and run to see your work in action. Right off the bat, each qualifying zone lists teams by the number of wins. Tap on different countries a few times. You'll see the cells animate smoothly to maintain this order.

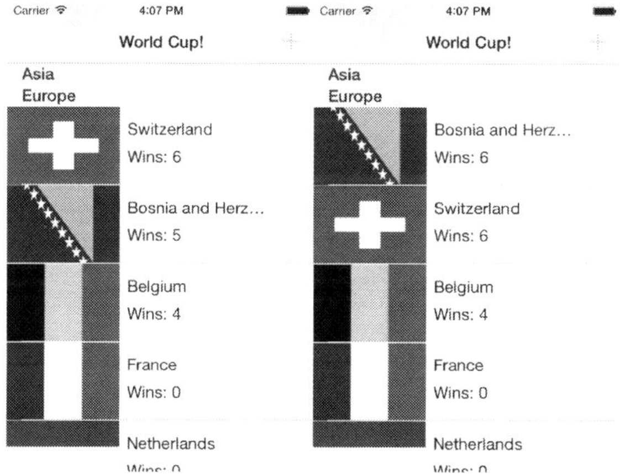

For example, in the first screenshot, Switzerland leads Europe with 6 wins. Tapping on Bosnia & Herzegovina brings their score to 6 and moves the cell on top of Switzerland with a nice animation. This is the fetched results controller delegate in action!

There is one more delegate method in **NSFetchedResultsControllerDelegate**. Add it to the extension:

```swift
func controller(_ controller:
  NSFetchedResultsController<NSFetchRequestResult>,
  didChange sectionInfo: NSFetchedResultsSectionInfo,
  atSectionIndex sectionIndex: Int,
  for type: NSFetchedResultsChangeType) {

  let indexSet = IndexSet(integer: sectionIndex)

  switch type {
  case .insert:
    tableView.insertSections(indexSet, with: .automatic)
  case .delete:
    tableView.deleteSections(indexSet, with: .automatic)
  default: break
  }
}
```

This delegate method is similar to `controllerDidChangeContent(_:)` but notifies you of changes to sections rather than to individual objects. Here, you handle the cases where changes in the underlying data trigger the creation or deletion of an entire section.

Take a moment and think about what kind of change would trigger these notifications. Maybe if a new team entered the World Cup from a completely new qualifying zone, the fetched results controller would pick up on the uniqueness of this value and notify its delegate about the new section.

This would never happen in a standard-issue World Cup. Once the 32 qualifying teams are in the system, there's no way to add a new team. Or is there?

Inserting an underdog

For the sake of demonstrating what happens to the table view when there's an insertion in the result set, let's assume there **is** a way to add a new team.

If you were paying close attention, you may have noticed the + bar button item on the top-right. It's been disabled all this time. Perhaps the World Cup has a secret backdoor entrance!

Let's implement this now. In **ViewController.swift** add the following method below
`viewDidLoad()`:

```swift
override func motionEnded(_ motion: UIEventSubtype,
                         with event: UIEvent?) {
  if motion == .motionShake {
    addButton.isEnabled = true
  }
}
```

You override `motionEnded(_:with:)` so shaking the device enables the + bar button
item. This will be your secret way in. The `addButton` property held a reference to this
bar button item all along!

Next, add the following extension with method above the `Internal` extension:

```swift
extension ViewController {

  @IBAction func addTeam(_ sender: AnyObject) {

    let alert = UIAlertController(title: "Secret Team",
      message: "Add a new team",
      preferredStyle: .alert)

    alert.addTextField { textField in
      textField.placeholder = "Team Name"
    }

    alert.addTextField { textField in
      textField.placeholder = "Qualifying Zone"
    }

    let saveAction = UIAlertAction(title: "Save",
                                   style: .default) {
      [unowned self] action in

      guard let nameTextField = alert.textFields?.first,
        let zoneTextField = alert.textFields?.last else {
          return
      }

      let team = Team(
        context: self.coreDataStack.managedContext)

      team.teamName = nameTextField.text
      team.qualifyingZone = zoneTextField.text
      team.imageName = "wenderland-flag"
      self.coreDataStack.saveContext()
    }

    alert.addAction(saveAction)
```

```
    alert.addAction(UIAlertAction(title: "Cancel",
                                  style: .default))

    present(alert, animated: true)
  }
}
```

This is a fairly long but easy-to-understand method. When the user taps the **Add** button, it presents an alert controller prompting the user to enter a new team. The alert view has two text fields: one for entering a team name and another for entering the qualifying zone. Tapping **Save** commits the change and inserts the new team into Core Data's persistent store.

The action is already connected in the storyboard, so there's nothing more for you to do. Build and run the app one more time. If you're running on a device, shake it. If you're running on the Simulator, press **Command+Control+Z** to simulate a shake event.

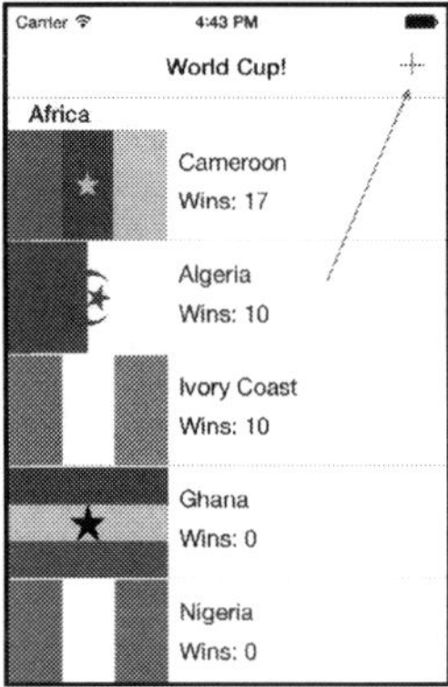

Open sesame! After much negotiation, both parties decided to "shake on it" and the **Add** button is now active!

The World Cup is officially accepting one new team. Scroll down the table to the end of the European qualifying zone and the beginning of the North, Central America & Caribbean qualifying zone. You'll see why in a moment.

Before moving on, take a few seconds to take this in. You're going to change history by adding another team to the World Cup. Are you ready?

Tap the + button on the top right. You'll be greeted by an alert view asking for the new team's details.

Enter the fictitious (yet thriving) nation of **Wenderland** as the new team. Type **Internets** for qualifying zone and tap **Save**. After a quick animation, your user interface should look like the following:

Since "Internets" is a new value for the fetched results controller's `sectionNameKeyPath`, this operation created both a new section and added a new team to the fetched results controller result set. That handles the data side of things.

Additionally, since you implemented the fetched results controller delegate methods appropriately, the table view responded by inserting a new section with one new row.

That's the beauty of `NSFetchedResultsControllerDelegate`. You can set it once and forget it. The underlying data source and your table view will always be synchronized.

As for how the Wenderland flag made it into the app: Hey, we're developers! We need to plan for all kinds of possibilities. ;]

Where to go from here?

You've seen how powerful and useful `NSFetchedResultsController` can be, and you've learned how well it works together with a table view. Table views are so common in iOS apps and you've seen first hand how the fetched results controller can save you a lot of time and code!

With some adaptation to the delegate methods, you can also use a fetched results controller to drive a collection view — the main difference being that collection views don't bracket their updates with begin and end calls, so it's necessary to store up the changes and apply them all in a batch at the end.

There are a few things you should bear in mind before using fetched results controllers in other contexts. They're not designed as general Core Data monitoring tools. There are other notifications or techniques that probably do the job better. Be mindful of how you implement the fetched results controller delegate methods. Even the slightest change in the underlying data will fire those change notifications, so avoid performing any expensive operations that you're not comfortable performing over and over.

It's not every day that a single class gets an entire chapter in a book; that honor is reserved for the select few. `NSFetchedResultsController` is one of them. As you've seen in this chapter, the reason this class exists is to save you time.

`NSFetchedResultsController` is important for another reason: it fills a gap that iOS developers have faced compared to their OS X developer counterparts. Unlike iOS, macOS has Cocoa bindings, which provide a way to tightly couple a view with its underlying data model. Sound familiar?

If you ever find yourself writing complex logic to compute sections or breaking a sweat trying to get your table view to play nicely with Core Data says, think back to this chapter!

You've seen how to design your data model and `NSManagedObject` subclasses in your Core Data apps. During app development, thorough testing can help iron out the data model well before shipping. However, changes in app usage, design or features after an app's release will inevitably lead to changes in the data model. What do you do then?

You can't predict the future, but with Core Data, you can migrate toward the future with every new release of your app. The migration process will update data created with a previous version of the data model to match the current data model. This chapter discusses the many aspects of Core Data migrations by walking you through the evolution of a note-taking app's data model.

You'll start with a simple app with only a single entity in its data model. As you add more features and data to the app, the migrations you do in this chapter will become progressively more complex.

Let the great migration begin!

When to migrate

When is a migration necessary? The easiest answer to this common question is "when you need to make changes to the data model."

However, there are some cases in which you can avoid a migration. If an app is using Core Data merely as an offline cache, when you update the app, you can simply delete and rebuild the data store. This is only possible if the source of truth for your user's data isn't in the data store. In all other cases, you'll need to safeguard your user's data.

That said, any time it's impossible to implement a design change or feature request without changing the data model, you'll need to create a new version of the data model and provide a migration path.

The migration process

When you initialize a Core Data stack, one of the steps involved is adding a store to the persistent store coordinator. When you encounter this step, Core Data does a few things prior to adding the store to the coordinator. First, Core Data analyzes the store's model version. Next, it compares this version to the coordinator's configured data model. If the store's model version and the coordinator's model version don't match, Core Data will perform a migration, when enabled.

> **Note:** If migrations aren't enabled, and the store is incompatible with the model, Core Data will simply not attach the store to the coordinator and specify an error with an appropriate reason code.

To start the migration process, Core Data needs the original data model and the destination model. It uses these two versions to load or create a mapping model for the migration, which it uses to convert data in the original store to data that it can store in the new store. Once Core Data determines the mapping model, the migration process can start in earnest.

Migrations happen in three steps:

1. First, Core Data copies over all the objects from one data store to the next.

2. Next, Core Data connects and relates all the objects according to the relationship mapping.

3. Finally, enforce any data validations in the destination model. Core Data disables destination model validations during the data copy.

You might ask, "If something goes wrong, what happens to the original source data store?" With nearly all types of Core Data migrations, nothing happens to the original store unless the migration completes without error. Only when a migration is successful, will Core Data remove the original data store.

Types of migrations

In my own experience, I've found there are a few more migration variants than the simple distinction between lightweight and heavyweight. Below, I've provided the more subtle variants of migration names, but these names are not official categories by any means. You'll start with the least complex form of migration and end with the most complex form.

Lightweight migrations

Lightweight migration is Apple's term for the migration with the least amount of work involved on your part. This happens automatically when you use `NSPersistentContainer`, or you have to set some flags when building your own Core Data stack. There are some limitations on how much you can change the data model, but because of the small amount of work required to enable this option, it's the ideal setting.

Manual migrations

Manual migrations involve a little more work on your part. You'll need to specify how to map the old set of data onto the new set, but you get the benefit of a more explicit mapping model file to configure. Setting up a mapping model in Xcode is much like setting up a data model, with similar GUI tools and some automation.

Custom manual migrations

This is level 3 on the migration complexity index. You'll still use a mapping model, but complement that with custom code to specify custom transformation logic on data. Custom entity transformation logic involves creating an `NSEntityMigrationPolicy` subclass and performing custom transformations there.

Fully manual migrations

Fully manual migrations are for those times when even specifying custom transformation logic isn't enough to fully migrate data from one model version to another. Custom version detection logic and custom handling of the migration process are necessary. In this chapter, you'll set up a fully manual migration to update data across non-sequential versions, such as jumping from version 1 to 4.

Throughout this chapter, you'll learn about each of these migration types and when to use them. Let's get started!

Getting started

Included with the resources for this book is a starter project called `UnCloudNotes`. Find the starter project and open it in Xcode.

Build and run the app in the iPhone simulator. You'll see an empty list of notes:

Tap the plus (+) button in the top-right corner to add a new note. Add a title (there is default text in the note body to make the process faster) and tap Create to save the new note to the data store. Repeat this a few times so you have some sample data to migrate.

Back in Xcode, open the **UnCloudNotesDatamodel.xcdatamodeld** file to show the entity modeling tool in Xcode. The data model is simple — just one entity, a `Note`, with a few attributes.

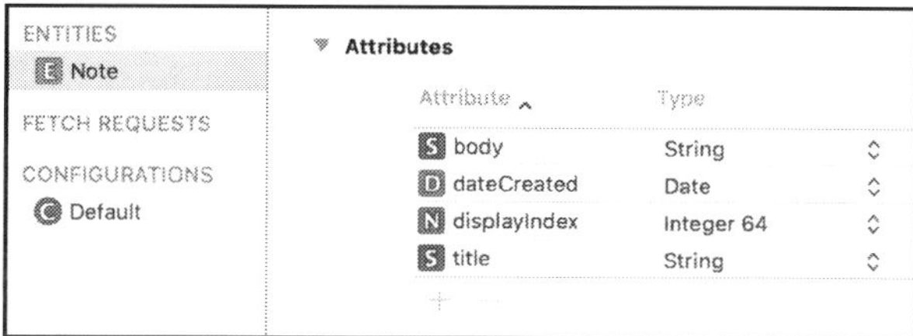

You're going to add a new feature to the app: the ability to attach a photo to a note. The data model doesn't have any place to persist this kind of information, so you'll need to add a place in the data model to hold onto the photo. But you already added a few test notes in the app. How can you change the model without breaking the existing notes?

It's time for your first migration!

> **Note:** The Xcode 8 console logs contain far more information than in previous releases. The workaround to this issue is to add **OS_ACTIVITY_MODE=disable** to the current scheme environment variables.

A lightweight migration

In Xcode, select the `UnCloudNotes` data model file if you haven't already selected it. This will show you the Entity Modeler in the main work area. Next, open the Editor menu and select **Add Model Version....** Name the new version `UnCloudNotesDataModel v2` and ensure `UnCloudNotesDataModel` is selected in the `Based on model` field. Xcode will now create a copy of the data model.

> **Note:** You can give this file any name you want. The sequential v2, v3, v4, et cetera naming helps you easily tell the versions apart.

This step will create a second version of the data model, but you still need to tell Xcode to use the new version as the current model. If you forget this step, selecting the top level **UnCloudNotesDataModel.xcdatamodeld** file will perform any changes you make to the original model file. You can override this behavior by selecting an individual model version, but it's still a good idea to make sure you don't accidentally modify the original file.

In order to perform any migration, you want to keep the original model file as it is, and make changes to an entirely new model file.

In the `File Inspector` pane on the right, there is a selection menu toward the bottom called Model Version. Change that selection to match the name of the new data model, `UnCloudNotesDataModel v2`:

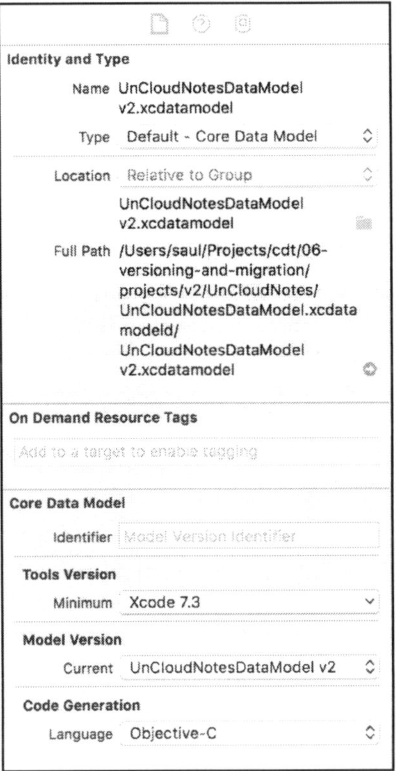

Once you've made that change, notice in the project navigator the little green check mark icon has moved from the previous data model to the v2 data model:

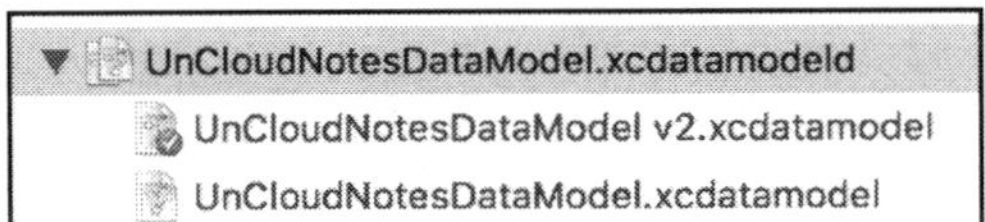

Core Data will try to first connect the persistent store with the ticked model version when setting up the stack. If a store file was found, and it isn't compatible with this model file, a migration will be triggered. The older version is there to support migration. The current model is the one Core Data will ensure is loaded prior to attaching the rest of the stack for your use.

Make sure you have the v2 data model selected and add an **image** attribute to the `Note` entity. Set the attribute's name to image and the attribute's type to **Transformable**.

Since this attribute is going to contain the actual binary bits of the image, you'll use a custom `NSValueTransformer` to convert from binary bits to a `UIImage` and back again. Just such a transformer has been provided for you in `ImageTransformer`. In the Value Transformer Name field in the Data Model Inspector on the right of the screen, enter **ImageTransformer** and enter **UnCloudNotes** in the Module field.

> **Attribute**
>
> Name `image`
>
> Properties ☐ Transient   ☑ Optional
>   ☐ Indexed
>
> Attribute Type `Transformable` ⌄
>
> Value Transfo... `ImageTransformer`
>
> Custom Class `NSObject`
>
> Module `UnCloudNotes` ⌄
>
> Advanced ☐ Index in Spotlight
>   ☐ Store in External Record File

> **Note:** When referencing code from your model files, just like in Xib and Storyboard files, you'll need to specify a **module** (`UnCloudNotes` in this case) to allow the class loader to find the exact code you want to attach.

The new model is now ready for some code! Open **Note.swift** and add the following property below `displayIndex`:

```
@NSManaged var image: UIImage?
```

Build and run the app. You'll see your notes are still magically displayed! It turns out lightweight migrations are enabled by default. This means every time you create a new data model version, and it *can* be auto migrated, it will be. What a time saver!

Inferred mapping models

It just so happens Core Data can infer a mapping model in many cases when you enable the `shouldInferMappingModelAutomatically` flag on the `NSPersistentStoreDescription`. Core Data can automatically look at the differences in two data models and create a mapping model between them.

For entities and attributes that are identical between model versions, this is a straightforward data pass through mapping. For other changes, just follow a few simple rules for Core Data to create a mapping model.

In the new model, changes must fit an obvious migration pattern, such as:

- Deleting entities, attributes or relationships

- Renaming entities, attributes or relationships using the renamingIdentifier

- Adding a new, optional attribute

- Adding a new, required attribute with a default value

- Changing an optional attribute to non-optional and specifying a default value

- Changing a non-optional attribute to optional

- Changing the entity hierarchy

- Adding a new parent entity and moving attributes up or down the hierarchy

- Changing a relationship from to-one to to-many

- Changing a relationship from non-ordered to-many to ordered to-many (and vice versa)

> **Note:** Check out Apple's documentation for more information on how Core Data infers a lightweight migration mapping:https://developer.apple.com/library/Mac/ DOCUMENTATION/Cocoa/Conceptual/CoreDataVersioning/Articles/ vmLightweightMigration.html

As you see from this list, Core Data can detect, and more importantly, automatically react to, a wide variety of common changes between data models. As a rule of thumb, all migrations, if necessary, should start as lightweight migrations and only move to more complex mappings when the need arises.

As for the migration from `UnCloudNotes` to `UnCloudNotes v2`, the image property has a default value of nil since it's an optional property. This means Core Data can easily migrate the old data store to a new one, since this change follows item 3 in the list of lightweight migration patterns.

Image attachments

Now the data is migrated, you need to update the UI to allow image attachments to new notes. Luckily, most of this work has been done for you. :]

Open **Main.storyboard** and find the `Create Note` scene. Underneath, you'll see the `Create Note With Images` scene that includes the interface to attach an image.

The `Create Note` scene is attached to a navigation controller with a root view controller relationship. `Control-drag` from the navigation controller to the `Create Note With Images` scene and select the root view controller relationship segue.

This will disconnect the old `Create Note` scene and connect the new, image-powered one instead:

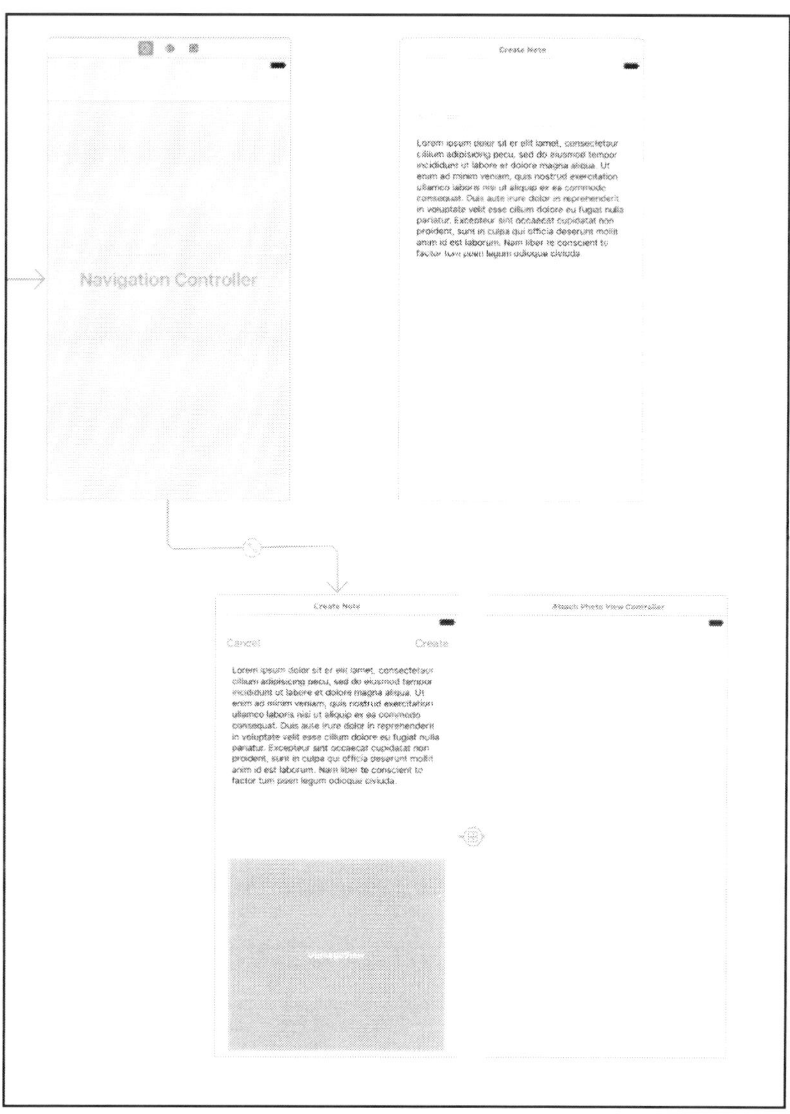

Next, open **AttachPhotoViewController.swift** and add the following method to the
`UIImagePickerControllerDelegate` extension:

```swift
func imagePickerController(_ picker: UIImagePickerController,
    didFinishPickingMediaWithInfo info: [String: Any]) {

  guard let note = note else { return }

  note.image =
    info[UIImagePickerControllerOriginalImage] as? UIImage

  _ = navigationController?.popViewController(animated: true)
}
```

This will populate the new image property of the note once the user selects an image
from the standard image picker.

Next, open **CreateNoteViewController.swift** and replace `viewDidAppear` with the
following:

```swift
override func viewDidAppear(_ animated: Bool) {
  super.viewDidAppear(animated)

  guard let image = note?.image else {
    titleField.becomeFirstResponder()
    return
  }

  attachedPhoto.image = image
  view.endEditing(true)
}
```

This will display the new image if the user has added one to the note.

Next, open **NotesListViewController.swift** and update `tableView(_:cellForRowAt)`
with the following:

```swift
override func tableView(_ tableView: UITableView,
                        cellForRowAt indexPath: IndexPath)
                        -> UITableViewCell {

  let note = notes.object(at: indexPath)
  let cell: NoteTableViewCell
  if note.image == nil {
    cell = tableView.dequeueReusableCell(
      withIdentifier: "NoteCell",
      for: indexPath) as! NoteTableViewCell
  } else {
    cell = tableView.dequeueReusableCell(
      withIdentifier: "NoteCellWithImage",
      for: indexPath) as! NoteImageTableViewCell
```

```
    }

    cell.note = note
    return cell
}
```

This will dequeue the correct `UITableViewCell` subclass based on the note having an image present or not. Finally, open **NoteImageTableViewCell.swift** and add the following to `updateNoteInfo(note:)`:

```
    noteImage.image = note.image
```

This will update the `UIImageView` inside the `NoteImageTableViewCell` with the image from the note.

Build and run, and choose to add a new note:

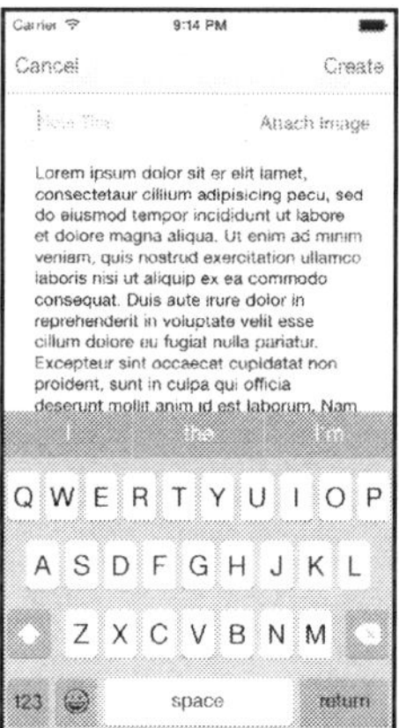

Tap the `Attach Image` button to add an image to the note. Choose an image from your simulated photo library and you'll see it in your new note:

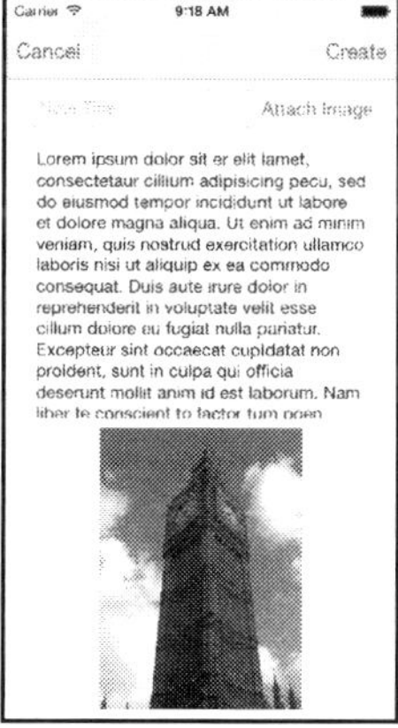

The app uses the standard `UIImagePickerController` to add photos as attachments to notes.

> **Note:** To add your own images to the Simulator's photo album, drag an image file onto the open Simulator window. Thankfully, the iOS 10 Simulator comes with a library of photos ready for your use. :]

If you're using a device, open **AttachPhotoViewController.swift** and set the `sourceType` attribute on the image picker controller to `.camera` to take photos with the device camera. The existing code uses the photo album, since there is no camera in the Simulator.

Add a couple of sample notes with photos, since in the next section you'll be using the sample data to move forward with a slightly more complex migration.

> **Note:** At this point, you might want to make a copy of the v2 source code into a different folder to come back to later. Or if you're using source control, set a tag here so you can come back to this point. You may also want to save a copy of the data store file and append the name with "v2" for this version of the application as you'll use this later on for more complex migrations.

Congratulations; you've successfully migrated your data and added a new feature based on the migrated data.

A manual migration

The next step in the evolution of this data model is to move from attaching a single image to a note to attaching multiple images. The note entity will stay, and you'll need a new entity for an image. Since a note can have many images, there will be a to-many relationship.

Splitting one entity into two isn't exactly on the list of things lightweight migrations can support. It's time to level up to a custom manual migration!

The first step in every migration is to create a new model version. As before, select the **UnCloudNotesDataModel.xcdatamodeld** file and from the `Editor` menu item, select `Add Model Version...` Name this model `UnCloudNotesDataModel v3` and base it on the `v2` data model. Set the new model version as the default model using the option in the `File Inspector Pane`.

Next, you'll add a new entity to the new data model. In the lower-left corner, click the Add Entity button. Rename this entity `Attachment`. Select the entity and in the Data Model Inspector pane, set the Class Name to Attachment, and the Module to `UnCloudNotes`.

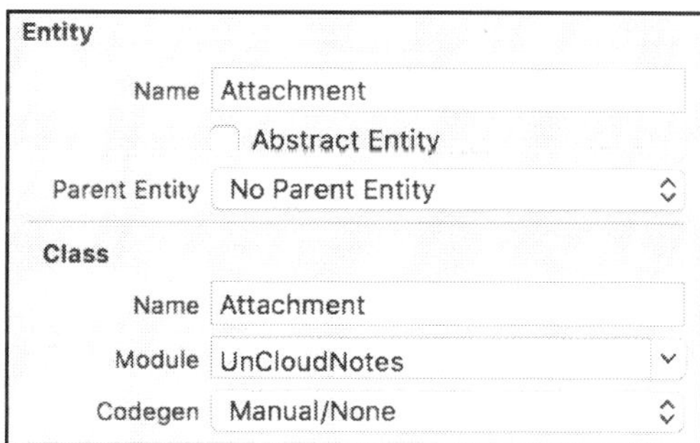

Create two attributes in the `Attachment` entity. Add a non-optional attribute named `image` of type `Transformable`, with the Value Transformer field set to `ImageTransformer` and Module field set to `UnCloudNotes`. This is the same as the image attribute you added to the `Note` entity earlier. Add a second required attribute called `dateCreated` and make it a `Date` type.

Next, add a relationship to the `Note` entity from the `Attachment` entity. Set the relationship name to `note` and its destination to `Note`.

Select the `Note` entity and delete the `image` attribute. Finally, create a to-many relationship from the `Note` entity to the `Attachment` entity. Leave it marked as *Optional*. Name the relationship `attachments`, set the destination to `Attachment` and select the `note` relationship you just created as the inverse.

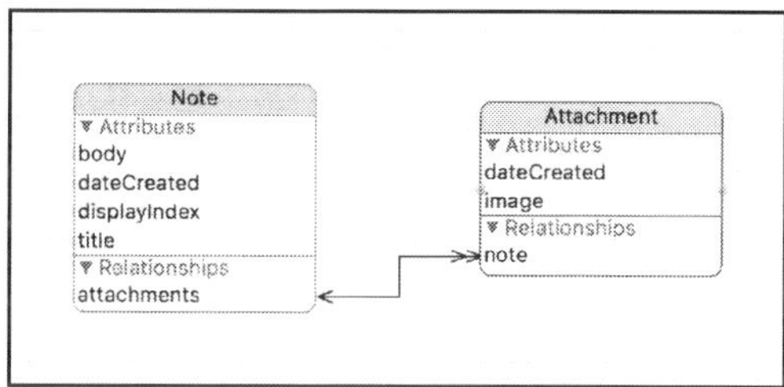

The data model is now ready for migration! While the Core Data model is ready, the code in your app will need some updates to use the changes to the data entities. Remember, you're not working with the `image` property on a `Note` any more, but with multiple `attachments`.

Create a new file called **Attachment.swift** and replace its contents with the following:

```swift
import Foundation
import UIKit
```

```swift
import CoreData

class Attachment: NSManagedObject {
  @NSManaged var dateCreated: Date
  @NSManaged var image: UIImage?
  @NSManaged var note: Note?
}
```

Next, open **Note.swift** and replace the `image` property with the following:

```swift
@NSManaged var attachments: Set<Attachment>?
```

The rest of your app still depends on an `image` property, so you'll get a compile error if
you try to build the app. Add the following to the `Note` class:

```swift
var image: UIImage? {
  return latestAttachment?.image
}

var latestAttachment: Attachment? {
  guard let attachments = attachments,
    let startingAttachment = attachments.first else {
      return nil
  }

  return Array(attachments).reduce(startingAttachment) {
    $0.dateCreated.compare($1.dateCreated)
      == .orderedAscending ? $0 : $1
  }
}
```

This implementation uses a computed property, which gets the image from the latest
attachment. If there are several attachments, `latestAttachment` will, as its name
suggests, grab the latest one and return it.

Next, open **AttachPhotoViewController.swift**. Update it to create a new `Attachment`
object when the user chooses an image. Add the Core Data import to the top of the file:

```swift
import CoreData
```

Next, replace `imagePickerController(_:didFinishPickingMediaWithInfo:)`
with the following:

```swift
func imagePickerController(_ picker: UIImagePickerController,
  didFinishPickingMediaWithInfo info: [String: Any]) {

  guard let note = note,
    let context = note.managedObjectContext else {
      return
```

```
}

let attachment = Attachment(context: context)
attachment.dateCreated = Date()
attachment.image =
  info[UIImagePickerControllerOriginalImage] as? UIImage
attachment.note = note

_ = navigationController?.popViewController(animated: true)
}
```

This implementation creates a new `Attachment` entity adding the image from the `UIImagePickerController` as the `image` property then sets the `note` property of the `Attachment` as the current note.

Mapping models

With lightweight migrations, Core Data can automatically create a mapping model to migrate data from one model version to another when the changes are simple. When the changes aren't as simple, you can manually set up the steps to migrate from one model version to another with a mapping model.

It's important to know that before creating a mapping model, you must complete and finalize your target model. During the process for creating a new Mapping Model, you'll essentially lock in the source and destination model versions into the Mapping Model file. This means any changes you make to the actual data model after creating the mapping model will not be seen by the Mapping Model.

Now that you've finished making changes to the v3 data model, you know lightweight migration isn't going to do the job. To create a mapping model, open the File menu in Xcode and select **New\File**. Navigate to the iOS\Core Data section and select Mapping Model:

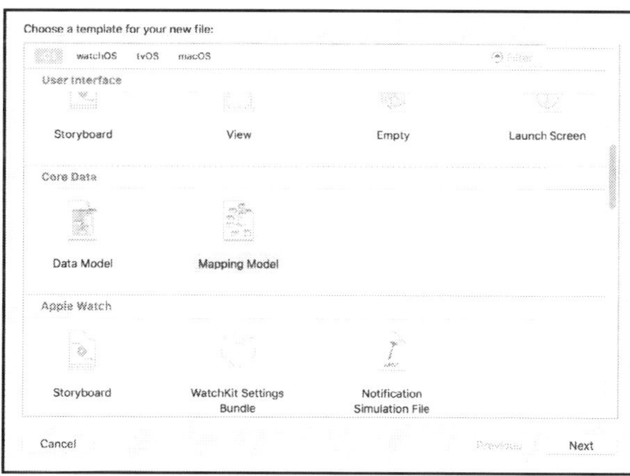

Click Next, select the v2 data model as the source model and select the v3 data model as the target model.

Name the new file **UnCloudNotesMappingModel_v2_to_v3**. The file naming convention I typically use is the data model name along with the source version and destination version. As an application collects more and more mapping models over time, this file naming convention makes it easier to distinguish between files and the order in which they have changed over time.

Open **UnCloudNotesMappingModel_v2_to_v3.xcmappingmodel**. Luckily, the mapping model doesn't start completely from scratch — Xcode examines the source and target models and infers as much as it can, so you're starting out with a mapping model that consists of the basics.

Attribute mapping

There are two mappings, one named `NoteToNote` and another simply named `Attachment`. `NoteToNote` describes how to migrate the v2 Note entity to the v3 Note entity.

Select `NoteToNote` and you'll see two sections: **Attribute Mappings** and **Relationship Mappings**.

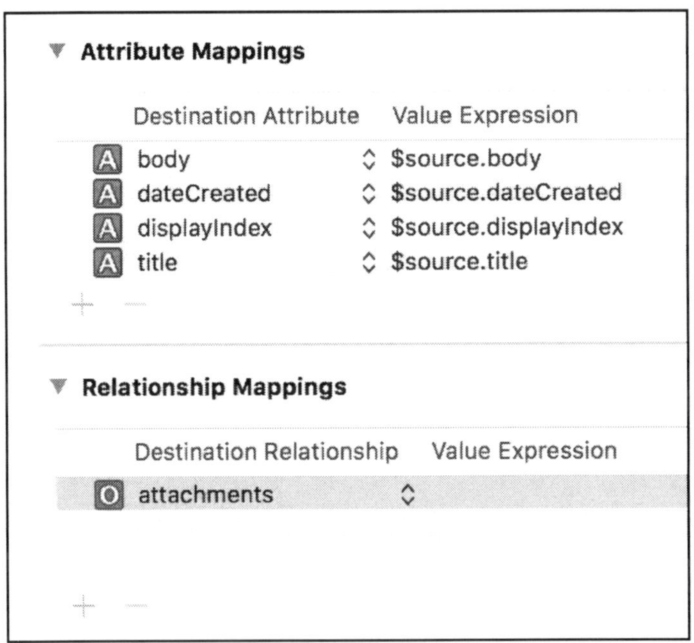

The attributes mappings here are fairly straightforward. Notice the value expressions with the pattern `$source`. `$source` is a special token for the mapping model editor, representing a reference to the source instance. Remember, with Core Data, you're not dealing with rows and columns in a database. Instead, you're dealing with objects, their attributes and classes.

In this case, the values for `body`, `dateCreated`, `displayIndex` and `title` will be transferred directly from the source. Those are the easy cases!

The `attachments` relationship is new, so Xcode couldn't fill in anything from the source. But, it turns out you'll not be using this particular relationship mapping, so delete this mapping. You'll get to the proper relationship mapping shortly.

Select the `Attachment` mapping and make sure the Utilities panel on the right is open. Select the last tab in the Utilities panel to open the `Entity Mapping` inspector:

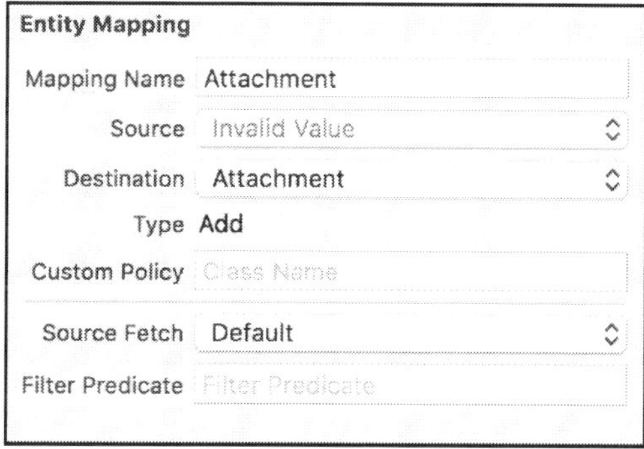

Select `Note` as the source entity in the drop-down list. Once you select the source entity, Xcode will try to resolve the mappings automatically based on the names of the attributes of the source and destination entities. In this case, Xcode will fill in the `dateCreated` and `image` mappings for you:

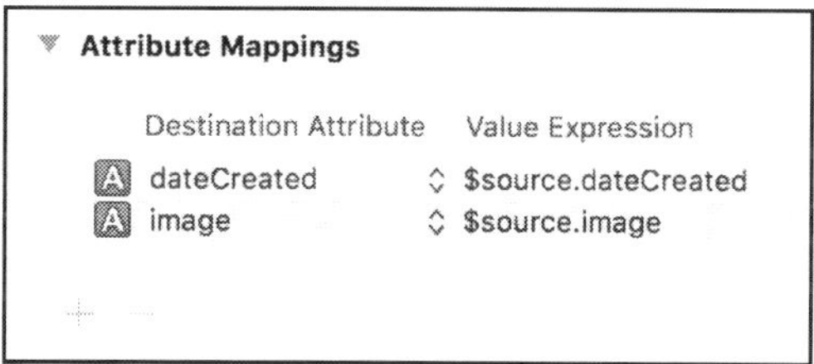

Xcode will also rename the entity mapping from `Attachment` to `NoteToAttachment`. Xcode is being helpful again; it just needs a small nudge from you specifying the source entity. Since the attribute names match, Xcode will fill in the value expressions for you. What does it mean to map data from `Note` entities to `Attachment` entities? Think of this as saying, "For each Note, make an Attachment and copy the image and dateCreated attributes across."

This mapping will create an `Attachment` for every `Note`, but you really only want an `Attachment` if there was an image attached to the note. Make sure the `NoteToAttachment` entity mapping is selected and in the inspector, set the Filter Predicate field to **image != nil**. This will ensure the `Attachment` mapping only occurs when an image is present in the source.

Relationship mapping

The migration is able to copy the images from `Notes` to `Attachments`, but as of yet, there's no relationship linking the `Note` to the `Attachment`. The next step to get that behavior is to add a relationship mapping.

In the `NoteToAttachment` mapping, you'll see a relationship mapping called `note`. Like the relationship mapping you saw in `NoteToNote`, the value expression is empty since Xcode doesn't know how to automatically migrate the relationship.

Select the **NoteToNote** mapping. Select the `attachments` relationship row in the list of relationships so that the Inspector changes to reflect the properties of the relationship mapping. In the Source Fetch field, select **Auto Generate Value Expression**. Enter `$source` in the `Key Path` field and select **NoteToNote** from the `Mapping Name` field.

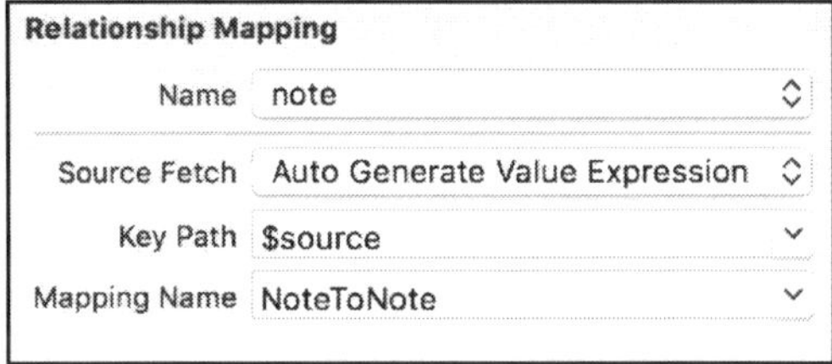

This should generate a value expression that looks like this:

```
FUNCTION($manager,
  "destinationInstancesForEntityMappingNamed:sourceInstances:",
  "NoteToNote", $source)
```

The **FUNCTION** statement resembles the objc_msgSend syntax; that is, the first argument is the object instance, the second argument is the selector and any further arguments are passed into that method as parameters.

So, the mapping model is calling a method on the $manager object. The $manager token is a special reference to the `NSMigrationManager` object handling the migration process.

> **Note:** Using FUNCTION expressions still relies on some knowledge of
> Objective-C syntax. It might be some time until Apple gets around to revamping
> Core Data 100% to Swift! :]

Core Data creates the migration manager during the migration. The migration manager
keeps track of which source objects are associated with which destination objects. The
method `destinationInstancesForEntityMappingNamed:sourceInstances:` will
look up the destination instances for a source object.

The expression on the previous page says "set the note relationship to whatever the
`$source` object for this mapping gets migrated to by the `NoteToNote` mapping," which
in this case will be the `Note` entity in the new data store.

You've completed your custom mapping! You now have a mapping that is configured to
split a single entity into two and relate the proper data objects together.

One last thing

Before running this migration, you need to update the Core Data setup code to use this
mapping model and not try to infer one on its own.

Open **CoreDataStack.swift** and look for the `storeDescription` property on to which
you set the flags for enabling migrations in the first place. Change the flags to the
following:

```
description.shouldMigrateStoreAutomatically = true
description.shouldInferMappingModelAutomatically = false
```

By setting `shouldInferMappingModelAutomatically` to false, you've ensured that the
persistent store coordinator will now use the new mapping model to migrate the store.
Yes, that's all the code you need to change; there is no new code!

When Core Data is told not to infer or generate a mapping model, it will look for the
mapping model files in the default or main bundle. The mapping model contains the
source and destination versions of the model. Core Data will use that information to
determine which mapping model, if any, to use to perform a migration. It really is as
simple as changing a single option to use the custom mapping model.

Strictly speaking, setting `shouldMigrateStoreAutomatically` to true isn't necessary
here as true is the value by default. But, let's just say, we're going to need this again later.

Build and run the app. You'll notice not a whole lot has changed on the surface! However, if you still see your notes and images as before, the mapping model worked. Core Data has updated the underlying schema of the SQLite store to reflect the changes in the v3 data model.

> **Note:** Again, you might want to make a copy of the v3 source code into a different folder to come back to later. Or if you're using source control, set a tag here so you can come back to this point. Again, you may also want to save a copy of the data store file and append the name with "v3" for this version of the application as you'll use this later on for more complex migrations.

A complex mapping model

The higher-ups have thought of a new feature for `UnCloudNotes`, so you know what that means. It's time to migrate the data model once again! This time, they've decided that supporting only image attachments isn't enough. They want future versions of the app to support videos, audio files or really add any kind of attachment that makes sense.

You make the decision to have a base entity called `Attachment` and a subclass called `ImageAttachment`. This will enable each attachment type to have its own useful information. Images could have attributes for caption, image size, compression level, file size, et cetera. Later, you can add more subclasses for other attachment types.

While new images will grab this information prior to saving, you'll need to extract that information from current images during the migration. You'll need to use either `CoreImage` or the `ImageIO` libraries. These are data transformations that Core Data definitely doesn't support out of the box, which makes a custom manual migration the proper tool for the job.

As usual, the first step in any data migration is to select the data model file in Xcode and select **Editor\Add Model Version…**. This time, create version 4 of the data model called `UnCloudNotesDataModel v4`. Don't forget to set the current version of the data model to v4 in the Xcode Inspector.

Open the v4 data model and add a new entity named `ImageAttachment`. Set the class to `ImageAttachment`, and the module to `UnCloudNotes`. Make the following changes to `ImageAttachment`:

1. Set the Parent Entity to `Attachment`.

2. Add a required String attribute named `caption`.

3. Add a required Float attribute named `width`.

4. Add a required Float attribute name `height`.

5. Add an optional Transformable attribute named `image`.

6. Set the Value Transformer Name to `ImageTransformer`, and set the Module value to **UnCloudNotes**.

Next, inside the `Attachment` entity:

7. Delete the `image` attribute.

8. If a newRelationship has been automatically created, delete it.

> **Note:** If a `newRelationship` has been created with the entity, delete it from `ImageAttachment`

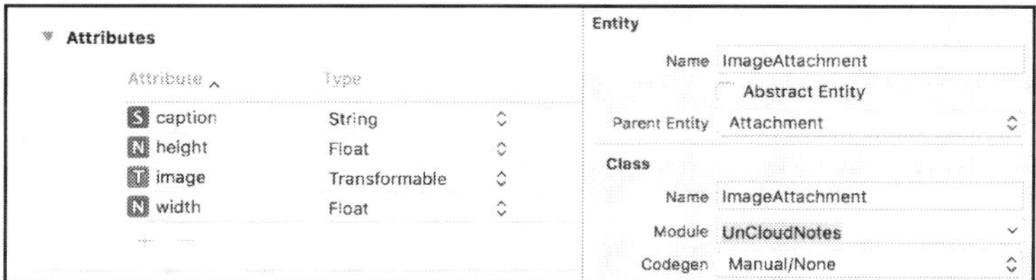

A parent entity is similar to having a parent class, which means `ImageAttachment` will inherit the attributes of `Attachment`. When you set up the managed object subclass later, you'll see this inheritance made explicit in the code.

Before you create the custom code for the mapping model, it'll be easier if you create the `ImageAttachment` source file now. Create a new Swift file called **ImageAttachment** and replace its contents with the following:

```swift
import UIKit
import CoreData

class ImageAttachment: Attachment {
  @NSManaged var image: UIImage?
  @NSManaged var width: Float
  @NSManaged var height: Float
  @NSManaged var caption: String
}
```

Next, open **Attachment.swift** and delete the `image` property. Since it's been moved to `ImageAttachment`, and removed from the `Attachment` entity in the v4 data model, it should be deleted from the code.

That should do it for the new data model. Once you've finished, your version 4 data model should look like this:

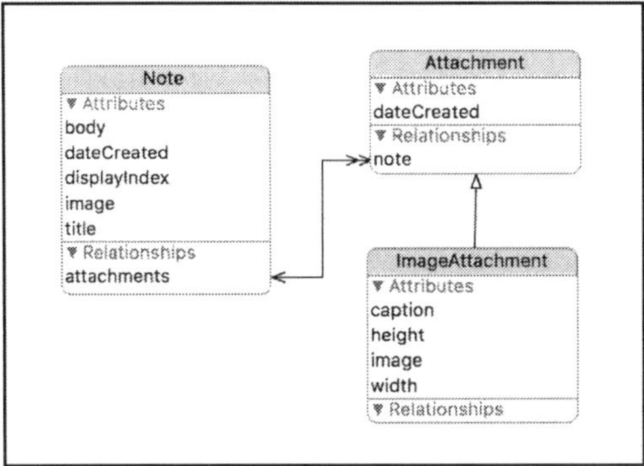

Mapping model

In the Xcode menu, choose **File\New File** and select the **iOS\Core Data\Mapping Model** template. Select version 3 as the source model and version 4 as the target. Name the file **UnCloudNotesMappingModel_v3_to_v4**.

Open the new mapping model in Xcode and you'll see Xcode has again helpfully filled in a few mappings for you.

Starting with the `NoteToNote` mapping, Xcode has directly copied the source entities from the source store to the target with no conversion or transformation. The default Xcode values for this simple data migration are good to go, as-is!

Select the `AttachmentToAttachment` mapping. Xcode has also detected some common attributes in the source and target entities and generated mappings. However, you want to convert `Attachment` entities to `ImageAttachment` entities. What Xcode has created here will map old `Attachment` entities to new `Attachment` entities, which isn't the goal of this migration. Delete this mapping.

Next, select the `ImageAttachment` mapping. This mapping has no source entity since it's a completely new entity. In the inspector, change the source entity to be `Attachment`. Now Xcode knows the source, it will fill in a few of the value expressions for you. Xcode will also rename the mapping to something a little more appropriate, `AttachmentToImageAttachment`.

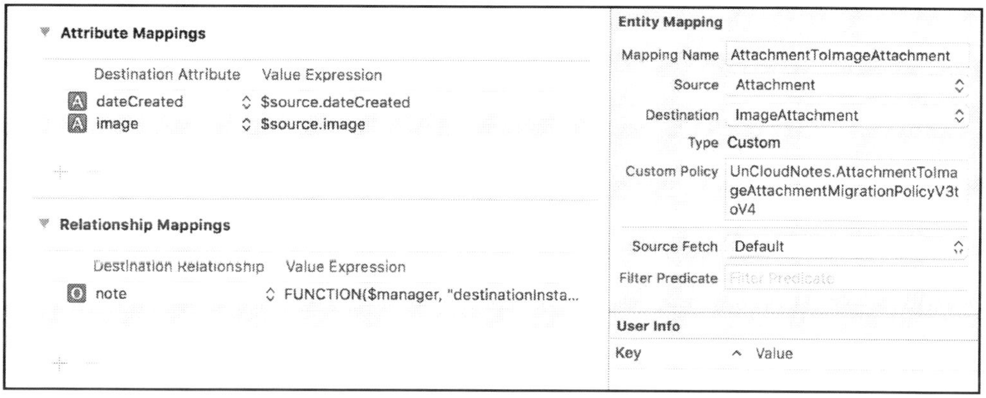

For the remaining, unfilled, attributes, you'll need to write some code. This is where you need image processing and custom code beyond simple FUNCTION expressions! But first, delete those extra mappings, *caption*, *height* and *width*. These values will be computed using a custom migration policy, which happens to be the next section!

Custom migration policies

To move beyond FUNCTION expressions in the mapping model, you can subclass `NSEntityMigrationPolicy` directly. This lets you write Swift code to handle the migration, instance by instance, so you can call on any framework or library available to the rest of your app.

Add a new Swift file to the project called **AttachmentToImageAttachmentMigrationPolicyV3toV4** and replace its contents with the following starter code:

```swift
import CoreData
import UIKit

let errorDomain = "Migration"

class AttachmentToImageAttachmentMigrationPolicyV3toV4:
  NSEntityMigrationPolicy {

}
```

This naming convention should look familiar to you; it's noting this is a custom migration policy and is for transforming data from `Attachments` in model version 3 to `ImageAttachments` in model version 4.

You'll want to connect this new mapping class to your newly created mapping file before you forget about it. Back in the **v3-to-v4 mapping model file**, select the **AttachmentToImageAttachment** entity mapping. In the `Entity Mapping Inspector`, fill in the **Custom Policy** field with the fully namespaced class name you just created (including the module): **UnCloudNotes.AttachmentToImageAttachmentMigrationPolicyV3toV4**. When you press Enter to confirm this change, the type above Custom Policy should change to read `Custom`.

When Core Data runs this migration, it will create an instance of your custom migration policy when it needs to perform a data migration for that specific set of data. That's your chance to run any custom transformation code to extract image information during migration! Now, it's time to add some custom logic to the custom entity mapping policy.

Open **AttachmentToImageAttachmentMigrationPolicyV3toV4.swift** and add the method to perform the migration:

```swift
override func createDestinationInstances(
  forSource sInstance: NSManagedObject,
  in mapping: NSEntityMapping,
  manager: NSMigrationManager) throws {

  // 1
  let description = NSEntityDescription.entity(
    forEntityName: "ImageAttachment",
    in: manager.destinationContext)
  let newAttachment = ImageAttachment(
    entity: description!,
    insertInto: manager.destinationContext)

  // 2
  func traversePropertyMappings(block:
    (NSPropertyMapping, String) -> ()) throws {
    if let attributeMappings = mapping.attributeMappings {
      for propertyMapping in attributeMappings {
        if let destinationName = propertyMapping.name {
          block(propertyMapping, destinationName)
        } else {
          // 3
          let message =
            "Attribute destination not configured properly"
          let userInfo =
            [NSLocalizedFailureReasonErrorKey: message]
          throw NSError(domain: errorDomain,
                        code: 0, userInfo: userInfo)
        }
      }
    } else {
      let message = "No Attribute Mappings found!"
      let userInfo = [NSLocalizedFailureReasonErrorKey: message]
      throw NSError(domain: errorDomain,
                    code: 0, userInfo: userInfo)
    }
  }
}
```

```swift
// 4
try traversePropertyMappings {
  propertyMapping, destinationName in
  if let valueExpression = propertyMapping.valueExpression {
    let context: NSMutableDictionary = ["source": sInstance]
    guard let destinationValue =
      valueExpression.expressionValue(with: sInstance,
                                      context: context) else {
        return
    }

    newAttachment.setValue(destinationValue,
                           forKey: destinationName)
  }
}

// 5
if let image = sInstance.value(forKey: "image") as? UIImage {
  newAttachment.setValue(image.size.width, forKey: "width")
  newAttachment.setValue(image.size.height, forKey: "height")
}

// 6
let body =
  sInstance.value(forKeyPath: "note.body") as? NSString ?? ""
newAttachment.setValue(body.substring(to: 80),
                       forKey: "caption")

// 7
  manager.associate(sourceInstance: sInstance,
                    withDestinationInstance: newAttachment,
                    for: mapping)
}
```

This method is an override of the default `NSEntityMigrationPolicy` implementation. It's what the migration manager uses to create instances of destination entities. An instance of the source object is the first parameter; when overridden, it's up to the developer to create the destination instance and associate it properly to the migration manager.

Here's what's going on, step by step:

1. First, you create an instance of the new destination object. The migration manager has two Core Data stacks — one to read from the source and one to write to the destination — so you need to be sure to use the destination context here. Now, you might notice that this section isn't using the new fancy short `ImageAttachment(context: NSManagedObjectContext)` initializer. Well, as it turns out, this migration will simply crash using the new syntax, because it depends on the model having been loaded and finalized, which hasn't happened halfway through a migration :[

2. Next, create a `traversePropertyMappings` function that performs the task of iterating over the property mappings if they are present in the migration. This function will control the traversal while the next section will perform the operation required for each property mapping

3. If, for some reason, the `attributeMappings` property on the `entityMapping` object doesn't return any mappings, this means your mappings file has been specified incorrectly. When this happens, the method will throw an error with some helpful information.

4. Even though it's a custom manual migration, most of the attribute migrations should be performed using the expressions you defined in the mapping model. To do this, use the traversal function from the previous step and apply the value expression to the source instance and set the result to the new destination object.

5. Next, try to get an instance of the image. If it exists, grab its width and height to populate the data in the new object.

6. For the caption, simply grab the note's body text and take the first 80 characters.

7. The migration manager needs to know the connection between the source object, the newly created destination object and the mapping. Failing to call this method at the end of a custom migration will result in missing data in the destination store.

That's it for the custom migration code! Core Data will pick up the mapping model when it detects a v3 data store on launch, and apply it to migrate to the new data model version. Since you added the custom `NSEntityMigrationPolicy` subclass and linked to it in the mapping model, Core Data will call through to your code automatically.

Finally, its time to go back to the main UI code and update the data model usage to take into account the new `ImageAttachment` entity. Open **AttachPhotoViewController.swift** and find `imagePickerController(_:didFinishPickingMediaWithInfo:)`. Change the line that sets up attachment so it uses `ImageAttachment` instead:

```swift
let attachment = ImageAttachment(context: context)
```

Next, open **Note.swift** and replace the `image` property with the following:

```swift
var image: UIImage? {
  let imageAttachment = latestAttachment as? ImageAttachment
  return imageAttachment?.image
}
```

Now all the code changes have been put in place, you need to update the main data model to use v4 as the main data model.

Select UnCloudNotesDataModel.xcdatamodeld in the project navigator. In the Identity pane, under *Model Version* select *UnCloudNotesDataModel v4*.

Build and run the app. The data should migrate properly. Again, your notes will be there, images and all, but you've now future-enabled UnCloudNotes to add video, audio and anything else!

Migrating non-sequential versions

Thus far, you've walked through a series of data migrations in order. You've migrated the data from version 1 to 2 to 3 to 4, in sequence. Inevitably, in the real world of App Store launches, a user might skip an update and need to go from version 2 to 4, for example. What happens then?

When Core Data performs a migration, its intention is to perform only a single migration. In this hypothetical scenario, Core Data would look for a mapping model that goes from version 2 to 4; if one didn't exist, Core Data would infer one, if you tell it to. Otherwise the migration will fail, and Core Data will report an error when attempting to attach the store to the persistent store coordinator.

How can you handle this scenario so your requested migration succeeds? You could provide multiple mapping models, but as your app grows, you'd need to provide an inordinate number of these: from v1 to v4, v1 to v3, v2 to v4, et cetera. You would spend more time on mapping models than on the app itself!

The solution to this scenario is to implement a fully custom migration sequence. You already know that the migration from version 2 to 3 works; to go from 2 to 4, it will work well if you manually migrate the store from 2 to 3 and from 3 to 4. This step-by-step migration means you'll prevent Core Data from looking for a direct 2 to 4 or even a 1 to 4 migration.

A self-migrating stack

To begin implementing this solution, you'll want to create a separate migration manager class. The responsibility of this class will be to provide a properly migrated Core Data stack, when asked. This class will have a stack property and will return an instance of CoreDataStack, as UnCloudNotes uses throughout, which has run through all the migrations necessary to be useful for the app.

First, create a new Swift file called `DataMigrationManager`. Open the file and replace its contents with the following:

```swift
import Foundation
import CoreData

class DataMigrationManager {
  let enableMigrations: Bool
  let modelName: String
  let storeName: String = "UnCloudNotesDataModel"
  var stack: CoreDataStack

  init(modelNamed: String, enableMigrations: Bool = false) {
    self.modelName = modelNamed
    self.enableMigrations = enableMigrations
  }
}
```

You'll notice that we're going to start this off looking like the current CoreDataStack initializer. That is intended to make this next step a little easier to understand.

Next, open **NotesListViewController.swift** and replace the stack lazy initialization code, as shown below:

```swift
fileprivate lazy var stack: CoreDataStack =
  CoreDataStack(modelName: "UnCloudNotesDataModel")
```

with:

```swift
fileprivate lazy var stack: CoreDataStack = {
  let manager = DataMigrationManager(
    modelNamed: "UnCloudNotesDataModel",
    enableMigrations: true)
  return manager.stack
}()
```

You'll use the `lazy` attribute to guarantee the stack is only `initialized` once. Second, initialization is actually handled by the `DataMigrationManager`, so the stack used will be the one returned from the `migration manager`. As mentioned, the signature of the new `DataMigrationManager` initializer is similar to the `CoreDataStack`. That's because you've got a large bit of migration code coming up, and its a good idea to separate the responsibility of migration from the responsibility of saving data.

> **Note:** The project won't build just yet as you've yet to initialize a value for the `stack` property in the `DataMigrationManager`. Rest assured, that's coming up soon.

Now to the harder part: How do you figure out if the store needs migrations? And if it does, how do you figure out where to start? In order to do a fully custom migration, you're going to need a little bit of support. First, finding out whether models match or not is not obvious. You'll also need a way to check a persistent store file for compatibility with a model. Let's get started with all the support functions first!

At the bottom of **DataMigrationManager.swift**, add an extension on `NSManagedObjectModel`:

```swift
extension NSManagedObjectModel {

  private class func modelURLs(
    in modelFolder: String) -> [URL] {

    return Bundle.main
      .urls(forResourcesWithExtension: "mom",
      subdirectory: "\(modelFolder).momd") ?? []
  }

  class func modelVersionsFor(
    modelNamed modelName: String) -> [NSManagedObjectModel] {

    return modelURLs(in: modelName)
      .flatMap(NSManagedObjectModel.init)
  }

  class func uncloudNotesModel(
    named modelName: String) -> NSManagedObjectModel {

    let model = modelURLs(in: "UnCloudNotesDataModel")
      .filter { $0.lastPathComponent == "\(modelName).mom" }
      .first
      .flatMap(NSManagedObjectModel.init)
    return model ?? NSManagedObjectModel()
  }
}
```

The first method returns all model versions for a given name. The second method returns a specific instance of `NSManagedObjectModel` named `UnCloudNotesDataModel`. Usually, Core Data will give you the most recent data model version, but this method will let you dig inside for a specific version.

> **Note:** When Xcode compiles your app into its app bundle, it will also compile your data models. The app bundle will have at its root a `.momd` folder that contains `.mom` files. **MOM**, or Managed Object Model, files are the compiled versions of `.xcdatamodel` files. You'll have a `.mom` for each data model version.

To use this method, add the following method inside the `NSManagedObjectModel` class extension:

```swift
class var version1: NSManagedObjectModel {
  return uncloudNotesModel(named: "UnCloudNotesDataModel")
}
```

This method returns the first version of the data model. That takes care of getting the model, but what about checking the version of a model? Add the following property to the class extension:

```swift
var isVersion1: Bool {
  return self == type(of: self).version1
}
```

The comparison operator for `NSManagedObjectModel` isn't very helpful for the purpose of properly checking model equality. To get the == comparison to work on two `NSManagedObjectModel` objects, add the following operator function to the file. You'll need to add this outside of the class extension, right in the global scope:

```swift
func == (firstModel: NSManagedObjectModel,
         otherModel: NSManagedObjectModel) -> Bool {
  return firstModel.entitiesByName == otherModel.entitiesByName
}
```

The idea here is simple: two `NSManagedObjectModel` objects are identical if they have the same collection of entities, with the same version hashes.

Now everything is set up, you can repeat the version and isVersion patter for the next 3 versions. Go ahead and add the following methods for versions 2 to 4 to the class extension:

```swift
class var version2: NSManagedObjectModel {
  return uncloudNotesModel(named: "UnCloudNotesDataModel v2")
}

var isVersion2: Bool {
  return self == type(of: self).version2
}

class var version3: NSManagedObjectModel {
  return uncloudNotesModel(named: "UnCloudNotesDataModel v3")
}

var isVersion3: Bool {
  return self == type(of: self).version3
}
```

```swift
class var version4: NSManagedObjectModel {
  return uncloudNotesModel(named: "UnCloudNotesDataModel v4")
}

var isVersion4: Bool {
  return self == type(of: self).version4
}
```

Now you have a way to compare model versions, you'll need a way to check that a
particular persistent store is compatible with a model version. Add these two helper
methods to the `DataMigrationManager` class:

```swift
private func store(at storeURL: URL,
    isCompatibleWithModel model: NSManagedObjectModel) -> Bool {

  let storeMetadata = metadataForStoreAtURL(storeURL: storeURL)

  return model.isConfiguration(
    withName: nil,
    compatibleWithStoreMetadata:storeMetadata)
}

private func metadataForStoreAtURL(storeURL: URL)
    -> [String: Any] {

  let metadata: [String: Any]
  do {
    metadata = try NSPersistentStoreCoordinator
    .metadataForPersistentStore(ofType: NSSQLiteStoreType,
                                at: storeURL, options: nil)
  } catch {
    metadata = [:]
    print("Error retrieving metadata for store at URL:
      \(storeURL): \(error)")
  }
  return metadata
}
```

The first method is a simple convenience wrapper to determine whether the persistent
store is compatible with a given model. The second method helps by safely retrieving the
metadata for the store.

Next, add the following computed properties to the `DataMigrationManager` class:

```swift
private var applicationSupportURL: URL {
  let path = NSSearchPathForDirectoriesInDomains(
        .applicationSupportDirectory,
        .userDomainMask, true)
        .first
  return URL(fileURLWithPath: path!)
```

```swift
}

private lazy var storeURL: URL = {
  let storeFileName = "\(self.storeName).sqlite"
  return URL(fileURLWithPath: storeFileName,
             relativeTo: self.applicationSupportURL)
}()

private var storeModel: NSManagedObjectModel? {
  return
    NSManagedObjectModel.modelVersionsFor(modelNamed: modelName)
    .filter {
        self.store(at: storeURL, isCompatibleWithModel: $0)
    }.first
}
```

These properties allow you to access the current store URL and model. As it turns out,
there is no method in the CoreData API to ask a store for its model version. Instead, the
easiest solution is brute force. Since you've already created helper methods to check if a
store is compatible with a particular model, you'll simply need to iterate through all the
available models until you find one that works with the store.

Next, you need your migration manager to remember the current model version. To do
this, you'll first create a general use method for getting models from a bundle, then you'll
simply use that general purpose method to look up the model.

First, add the following method to the `NSManagedObjectModel` class extension:

```swift
class func model(named modelName: String,
    in bundle: Bundle = .main) -> NSManagedObjectModel {

  return
    bundle
    .url(forResource: modelName, withExtension: "momd")
    .flatMap(NSManagedObjectModel.init)
      ?? NSManagedObjectModel()
}
```

This handy method is used to initialize a managed objet model using the top level folder.
Core Data will look for the current model version automatically and load that model
into an `NSManagedObjectModel` for use. It's important to note that this method will
only work with with Core Data models that have been versioned.

Next, add a property to the `DataMigrationManager` class, as follows:

```swift
private lazy var currentModel: NSManagedObjectModel =
    .model(named: self.modelName)
```

The `currentModel` property is lazy, so it loads only once since it should return the same thing every time. The .model is the shorthand way of calling the just-added-function that will look up the model from the top level `momd` folder.

Of course, if the model you have isn't the current model, that's the time to run the migration! Add the following starter method to the `DataMigrationManager` class (which you'll fill in later):

```
func performMigration() {
}
```

Next, replace the stack property definition you added earlier with the following:

```
var stack: CoreDataStack {
  guard enableMigrations,
        !store(at: storeURL,
          isCompatibleWithModel: currentModel)
    else { return CoreDataStack(modelName: modelName) }

  performMigration()
  return CoreDataStack(modelName: modelName)
}
```

In the end, the computed property will return a CoreDataStack instance. If the migration flag is set, then check if the store specified in the initialization is compatible with what Core Data determines to be the current version of the data model. If the store can't be loaded with the current model, it needs to be migrated. Otherwise, you can use a stack object with whatever version the model is currently set.

You now have a self-migrating Core Data stack that can always be guaranteed to be up to date with the latest model version! Build the project to make sure everything compiles. The next step is to add the custom migration logic.

The self-migrating stack

Now it's time to start building out the migration logic. Add the following method to the `DataMigrationManager` class:

```
private func migrateStoreAt(URL storeURL: URL,
  fromModel from: NSManagedObjectModel,
  toModel to: NSManagedObjectModel,
  mappingModel: NSMappingModel? = nil) {

  // 1
  let migrationManager =
    NSMigrationManager(sourceModel: from, destinationModel: to)

  // 2
```

```swift
  var migrationMappingModel: NSMappingModel
  if let mappingModel = mappingModel {
    migrationMappingModel = mappingModel
  } else {
    migrationMappingModel = try! NSMappingModel
    .inferredMappingModel(
        forSourceModel: from, destinationModel: to)
  }

  // 3
  let targetURL = storeURL.deletingLastPathComponent()
  let destinationName = storeURL.lastPathComponent + "~1"
  let destinationURL = targetURL
    .appendingPathComponent(destinationName)

  print("From Model: \(from.entityVersionHashesByName)")
  print("To Model: \(to.entityVersionHashesByName)")
  print("Migrating store \(storeURL) to \(destinationURL)")
  print("Mapping model: \(mappingModel)")

  // 4
  let success: Bool
  do {
    try migrationManager.migrateStore(from: storeURL,
          sourceType: NSSQLiteStoreType,
          options: nil,
          with: migrationMappingModel,
          toDestinationURL: destinationURL,
          destinationType: NSSQLiteStoreType,
          destinationOptions: nil)
    success = true
  } catch {
    success = false
    print("Migration failed: \(error)")
  }

  // 5
  if success {
    print("Migration Completed Successfully")

    let fileManager = FileManager.default
    do {
        try fileManager.removeItem(at: storeURL)
        try fileManager.moveItem(at: destinationURL,
                                 to: storeURL)
    } catch {
      print("Error migrating \(error)")
    }
  }
}
```

This method does all the heavy lifting. If you need to do a lightweight migration, you can pass `nil` or simply skip the final parameter.

Here's what's going on, step by step:

1. First, you create an instance of the migration manager.

2. If a mapping model was passed in to the method, use that. Otherwise, create an inferred mapping model.

3. Since migrations will create a second data store and migrate data, instance-by-instance, from the original to the new file, the destination URL must be a different file. Now, the example code in this section will create a `destinationURL` that is the same folder as the original and a file concatenated with "~1". The destination URL can be in a temp folder or anywhere your app has access to write files.

4. Here's where you put the migration manager to work! You've already set it up with the source and destination models, so you simply need to add the mapping model and the two URLs to the mix.

5. Given the result, you can print a success or error message to the console. In the success case, you perform a bit of cleanup, too. In this case, it's enough to remove the old store and replace it with the new store.

Now it's simply a matter of calling that method with the right parameters. Remember your empty implementation of `performMigration`? It's time to fill that in. Add the following lines to that method:

```swift
if !currentModel.isVersion4 {
  fatalError("Can only handle migrations to version 4!")
}
```

This code will only check that the current model is the most recent version of the model. This code bails out and kills the app if the current model is anything other than version 4. This is a little extreme — in your own apps, you might want to continue the migration anyway — but doing it this way will definitely remind you to think about migrations if you ever add another data model version to your app! Thankfully, even though this is the first check in the `perfromMigration` method, it should never be run as the next section stops after the last available migration has been applied.

The `performMigration` method can be improved to handle all known model versions. To do this, add the following below the previously added if-statement:

```swift
if let storeModel = self.storeModel {
  if storeModel.isVersion1 {
    let destinationModel = NSManagedObjectModel.version2
```

```
      migrateStoreAt(URL: storeURL,
             fromModel: storeModel,
               toModel: destinationModel)

      performMigration()
    } else if storeModel.isVersion2 {
      let destinationModel = NSManagedObjectModel.version3
      let mappingModel = NSMappingModel(from: nil,
                            forSourceModel: storeModel,
                          destinationModel: destinationModel)

      migrateStoreAt(URL: storeURL,
             fromModel: storeModel,
               toModel: destinationModel,
           mappingModel: mappingModel)

      performMigration()
    } else if storeModel.isVersion3 {
      let destinationModel = NSManagedObjectModel.version4
      let mappingModel = NSMappingModel(from: nil,
                            forSourceModel: storeModel,
                          destinationModel: destinationModel)

      migrateStoreAt(URL: storeURL,
             fromModel: storeModel,
               toModel: destinationModel,
           mappingModel: mappingModel)
    }
  }
```

The steps are similar, no matter which version you start from:

- Lightweight migrations use simple flags to 1) enable migrations, and 2) infer the mapping model. Since the `migrateStoreAt` method will infer a mapping model if one is missing, you've successfully replaced that functionality. By running `performMigration`, you've already enabled migrations.

- Set the destination model to the correct model version. Remember, you're only going "up" one version at a time, so from 1 to 2 and from 2 to 3.

- For version 2 and above, also load the mapping model.

- Finally, call `migrateStoreAt(URL:fromModel:toModel:mappingModel:)`, which you wrote at the start of this section.

What's nice about this solution is that the `DataMigrationManager` class, despite all the comparison support helper functions, is essentially using the mapping models and code that was already defined for each migration. This solution is manually applying each migration in sequence rather than letting Core Data try to do things automatically.

Note if you're starting from version 1 or 2, there's a recursive call to performMigration() at the end. This will trigger another run to continue the sequence; once you're at version 3 and run the migration to get to version 4. You will continue adding to this method as you add more data model versions to continue the automatic sequence of migrations.

Testing sequential migrations

Testing this type of migration can be a little complicated, since you need to go back in time and run previous versions of the app to generate data to migrate. If you saved copies of the app project along the way, great!

Otherwise, you'll find previous versions of the project in the resources bundled with the book.

First, make sure you make a copy of the project as it is right now — that's the final project!

Here are the general steps you'll need to take to test each migration:

1. Delete the app from the Simulator to clear out the data store.

2. Open version 2 of the app (so you can at least see some pictures!), and build and run.

3. Create some test notes.

4. Quit the app from Xcode and close the project.

5. Open the final version of the app, and build and run.

At this point, you should see some console output with the migration status. Note the migration will happen prior to the app presenting onscreen.

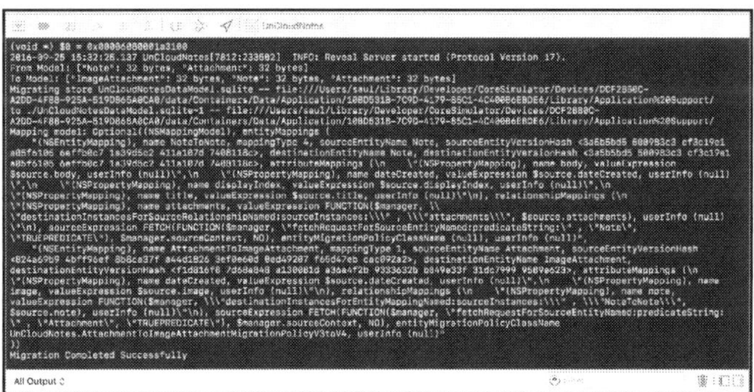

You now have an app that will successfully migrate between any combinations of old data versions to the latest version.

Where to go from here?

That was a whole lot of data migration! Migrations can be extremely tricky, as you've no doubt observed in the more complicated forms in this chapter.

Before you move on to the next chapter, I want to share a few words of advice from my experience using Core Data migrations.

First, when you decide a data migration is in order, make a reasonable effort to use the simplest migration possible. Migrations can be tricky to test, so you want them to be as simple as possible. As you've seen in this chapter, you can go a long way without the need for the most custom of migrations involving code.

Second, make sure to save some data store versions for testing future migrations. You'll thank yourself later. In some cases, real live data will be the only way to break a migration. Sometimes, it may be useful to ask a customer's permission to use their data store for testing a particular problem. Remember to use extreme care with customer data and properly secure, anonymize or encrypt the files when they aren't being used during testing.

Core Data migrations are one of the more powerful, and in many cases, useful, aspects of the Core Data framework. Now that you've seen the spectrum of Core Data migrations from lightweight all the way to fully custom manual migrations, you'll be able to tackle data even the most difficult model changes in your own apps.

Chapter 7: Unit Testing

By Aaron Douglas

Unit testing is the process of breaking down a project into small, testable pieces, or *units*, of software. Rather than test the "app creates a new record when you tap the button" scenario, you might break this down into testing smaller actions, such as the button touch-up event, creating the entity, and testing whether the save succeeded.

In this chapter, you'll learn how to use the **XCTest** framework in Xcode to test your Core Data apps. Unit testing Core Data apps isn't as straightforward as it could be, because most of the tests will depend on a valid Core Data stack. You might not want a mess of test data from the unit tests to interfere with your own manual testing done in the simulator or on a device, so you'll learn how to keep the test data separate.

Why should you care about unit testing your apps? There are lots of reasons:

- You can shake out the architecture and behavior of your app at a very early stage. You can test much of the app's functionality without needing to worry about the UI.

- You gain the confidence to add features or refactor your project without worrying about breaking things. If you have existing tests that pass, you can be confident that the tests will fail to warn you if you break something later.

- You can keep your team of multiple developers from falling over each other as each developer can make and test their changes independently of others.

- You can save time in testing. Instead of tapping through three different screens and entering test data in the fields, you can run a small test for any part of your app's code instead of manually working through the UI.

You'll get a good introduction to XCTest in this chapter, but you should have a basic understanding of it already to make the most from this chapter.

For more information, check out Apple's documentation (https://developer.apple.com/library/ios/documentation/DeveloperTools/Conceptual/testing_with_xcode/Introduction/Introduction.html) or our book *iOS 9 by Tutorials*, which includes a chapter on Testing and XCTest.

Getting started

The sample project you'll work with in this chapter, **CampgroundManager**, is a reservation system to track campground sites, the amenities for each site and the campers themselves.

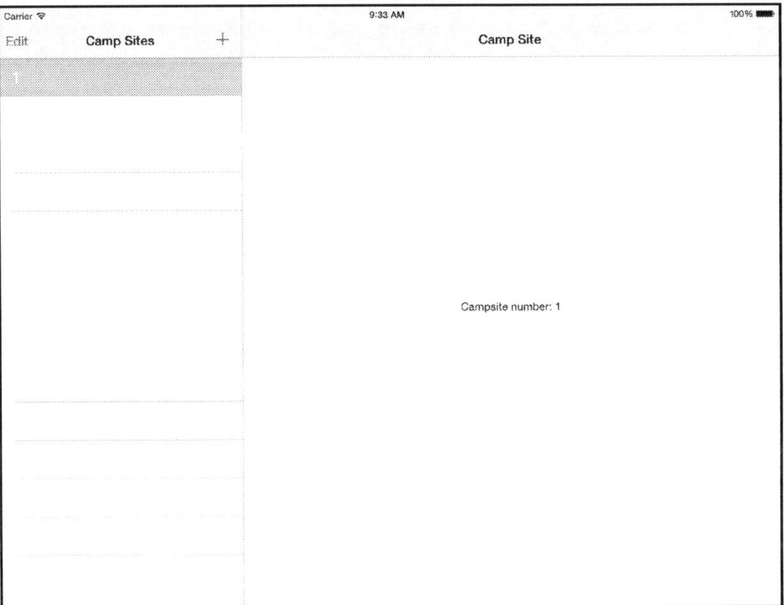

The app is a work in progress. The basic concept: a small campground could use this app to manage their campsites and reservations, including the schedule and payments. The user interface is extremely basic; it's functional but doesn't provide much value. That's OK — in this tutorial, you're never going to build and run the app!

The business logic for the app has been broken down into small pieces. You're going to write unit tests to help with the design. As you develop the unit tests and flesh out the business logic, it will be easy to see what work remains for the user interface.

The business logic is split into three distinct classes arranged by subject. There's one for campsites, one for campers and one for reservations. All classes have the suffix **Service**, and your tests will focus on these service classes.

Access control

By default, classes in Swift have the "internal" access level. That means you can only access them from within their own modules. Since the app and the tests are in separate targets and separate modules, you normally wouldn't be able to access the classes from the app in your tests.

There are three ways around this issue:

1. You can mark classes and methods in your app as `public` to make them visible from the tests.

2. You can add classes to the test target in the File Inspector so they will be compiled in, and accessible from, the tests.

3. You can add the Swift keyword `@testable` in front of any import in your unit test to gain access to everything imported in the class.

In the CampgroundManager sample project, the necessary classes and methods in the app target are already marked as `public`. That means you'll just need to `import` `CampgroundManager` from the tests and you'll be able to access whatever you need.

> **Note:** Using `@testable` would be the easiest approach, but its existence in the language is somewhat debatable. In theory, only public methods should be unit tested; anything not `public` isn't testable because there isn't a public interface or contract. Using `@testable` is definitely more acceptable than just blindly adding `public` to all of your classes and functions.

Core Data stack for testing

Since you'll be testing the Core Data parts of the app, the first order of business is getting the Core Data stack set up for testing.

Good unit tests follow the acronym **FIRST**:

*   Fast: If your tests take too long to run, you won't bother running them.

*   Isolated: Any test should function properly when run on its own or before or after any other test.

- **Repeatable**: You should get the same results every time you run the test against the same codebase.

- **Self-verifying**: The test itself should report success or failure; you shouldn't have to check the contents of a file or a console log.

- **Timely**: There's some benefit to writing the tests after you've already written the code, particularly if you're writing a new test to cover a new bug. Ideally, though, the tests come first to act as a specification for the functionality you're developing.

CampgroundManager uses Core Data to store data in a database file on disk. That doesn't sound very Isolated, since the data from one test may be written out to the database and could affect other tests. It doesn't sound very Repeatable, either, since data will build up in the database file each time you run a test. You could manually delete and recreate the database file before running each test, but that wouldn't be very Fast.

The solution is a modified Core Data stack that uses an **in-memory store** instead of an SQLite-backed store. This will be fast and provide a clean slate every time.

The `CoreDataStack` you've been using in most of this book can support multiple contexts, including a background root/parent context to which `NSPersistentStoreCoordinator` is connected. When you use `CoreDataStack` for a test, you want it to access the in-memory store instead of the SQLite database.

Create a new class that subclasses `CoreDataStack` so you can change the store:

1. Right-click **Services** under the **CampgroundManagerTests** group and click **New File**.

2. Select **Swift File** under **iOS\Source**. Click **Next**.

3. Name the file **TestCoreDataStack.swift**. Make sure only the **CampgroundManagerTests** target is selected.

4. Click **Create**.

5. Select **Don't Create** if prompted to add an Objective-C bridging header.

Replace the contents of the file with the following:

```swift
import CampgroundManager
import Foundation
import CoreData

class TestCoreDataStack: CoreDataStack {

  convenience init() {
    self.init(modelName: "CampgroundManager")
  }
```

```swift
  override init(modelName: String) {
    super.init(modelName: modelName)

    let persistentStoreDescription =
      NSPersistentStoreDescription()
    persistentStoreDescription.type = NSInMemoryStoreType

    let container = NSPersistentContainer(name: modelName)
    container.persistentStoreDescriptions =
      [persistentStoreDescription]

    container.loadPersistentStores {
      (storeDescription, error) in
      if let error = error as? NSError {
        fatalError(
          "Unresolved error \(error), \(error.userInfo)")
      }
    }

    self.storeContainer = container
  }
}
```

This class subclasses `CoreDataStack` and only overrides the default value of a single property: `storeContainer`. Since you are overriding the value in `init()`, the persistent container from `CoreDataStack` isn't used — or even instantiated. The persistent container in `TestCoreDataStack` uses an in-memory store only.

An in-memory store is never persisted to disk, which means you can instantiate the stack and write as much data you want in the test. When the test ends — *poof* — the in-memory store clears out automatically.

With the stack in place, it's time to create your first test!

Your first test

Unit tests work best when you design your app as a collection of small modules. Instead of throwing all of your business logic into one huge view controller, you create a class (or classes) to encapsulate that logic.

In most cases, you'll probably be adding unit tests to a partially-complete application. In the case of CampgroundManager, the `CamperService`, `CampSiteService` and `ReservationService` classes have already been created, but they aren't yet feature-complete. You'll test the simplest class, `CamperService`, first.

Begin by creating a new test class:

1. Right-click the **Services** group under the **CampgroundManagerTests** group and click **New File**.

2. Select **iOS\Source\Unit Test Case Class**. Click **Next**.

3. Name the class **CamperServiceTests**; subclass of **XCTestCase** should already be selected. Choose **Swift** for the language, then click **Next**.

4. Make sure the **CampgroundManagerTests** target checkbox is the only target selected. Click **Create**.

In **CamperServiceTests.swift**, import the app and Core Data frameworks into the test case, along with the other existing `import` statements:

```
import CampgroundManager
import CoreData
```

Add the following two properties to the class:

```
// MARK: Properties
var camperService: CamperService!
var coreDataStack: CoreDataStack!
```

These properties will hold references to the `CamperService` instance under test, and to the Core Data stack. The properties are implicitly unwrapped optionals, since they'll be initialized in `setUp` rather than in `init`.

Next, replace the implementation of `setUp` with the following:

```
override func setUp() {
  super.setUp()

  coreDataStack = TestCoreDataStack()
  camperService = CamperService(
    managedObjectContext: coreDataStack.mainContext,
    coreDataStack: coreDataStack)
}
```

`setUp` is called before each test runs. This is your chance to create any resources required by all unit tests in the class. In this case, you initialize the `camperService` and `coreDataStack` properties.

It's wise to reset your data after every test - your tests are **Isolated** and **Repeatable**, remember? Using the in-memory store and creating a new context in `setUp` accomplishes this reset for you.

Notice the `CoreDataStack` instance is actually a `TestCoreDataStack` instance. The `CamperService` initialization method takes the context it needs along with an instance of `CoreDataStack`, since the context save methods are part of that class. You can also use `setUp()` to insert standard test data into the context for use later.

Next, replace `tearDown` with the following implementation:

```
override func tearDown() {
  super.tearDown()

  camperService = nil
  coreDataStack = nil
}
```

`tearDown` is the opposite of `setUp`, and is called after each test executes. Here, the method will simply make all the properties `nil`, resetting `CoreDataStack` after every test.

There's only a single method on `CamperService` at this point: `addCamper(_:phonenumber:)`. Still in **CamperServiceTests.swift**, create a new method to test `addCamper`:

```
func testAddCamper() {
  let camper = camperService.addCamper("Bacon Lover",
    phoneNumber: "910-543-9000")

  XCTAssertNotNil(camper, "Camper should not be nil")
  XCTAssertTrue(camper?.fullName == "Bacon Lover")
  XCTAssertTrue(camper?.phoneNumber == "910-543-9000")
}
```

You create a camper with certain properties, then check to confirm that a camper exists with the properties you expect.

Remove the `testExample` and `testPerformanceExample` methods from the class.

It's a simple test, but it ensures that if any logic inside of `addCamper` is modified, the basic operation doesn't change. For example, if you add some new data validation logic to prevent bacon-loving people from reserving campgrounds, `addCamper` might return `nil`. This test would then fail, alerting you either that you made a mistake in the validation or that the test needs to be updated.

> **Note:** To round out this test case in a real development context, you would want to write unit tests for strange scenarios such as `nil` parameters, empty parameters, or duplicate camper namess.

Run the unit tests by clicking on the **Product** menu, then selecting **Test** (or type **Command+U**). You should see a green checkmark in Xcode:

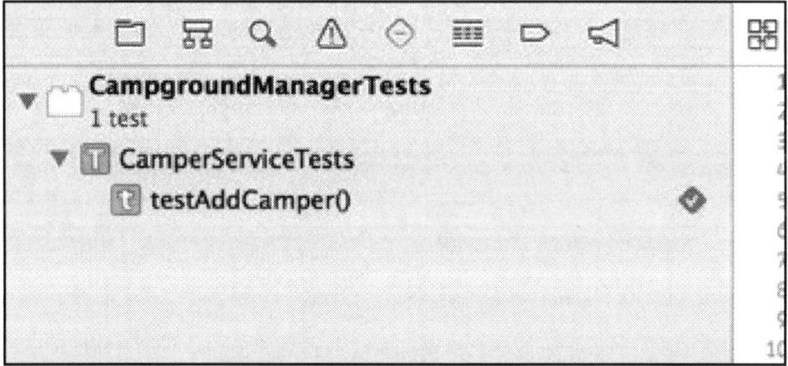

There's your first test! This type of testing is useful for leveraging your data models and checking that the attributes were stored correctly.

Also notice how the test serves as micro-documentation for people using the API. It's an example of how to call `addCamper` and describes the expected behavior. In this case, the method should return a valid object and not `nil`.

Notice this test creates the object and checks the attributes, but doesn't save anything to the store. This project uses a separate queue context so it can persist data in the background. However, the test runs straight through; this means you can't check for the save result with an `XCTAssert` as you can't be sure when the background operation has completed. Saving data is an important part of Core Data — so how can you test this part of the app?

Asynchronous tests

When using a single managed object context in Core Data, everything runs on the main UI thread. However, this project has a separate private queue context which acts as the root context, letting you save data on a background thread. The main context exposed by the Core Data stack is a child of this context.

Performing work on the correct thread for a given context is easy: You simply wrap the work in `performBlockAndWait()` or `performBlock()` to ensure it's executed on the thread associated with the context. `performBlockAndWait()` will wait to finish execution of the block before continuing, while `performBlock()` will immediately return and queue the execution on the context.

Testing `performBlock()` executions can be tricky since you need some way to send a signal about the test status to the outside world from inside the block. Luckily, there is a feature in `XCTestCase` called **expectations** that help with this.

The example below shows how you might use an expectation to wait for an asynchronous method to complete before finishing the test:

```
let expectation = expectation(withDescription: "Done!")

someService.callMethodWithCompletionHandler() {
  expectation.fulfill()
}

waitForExpectations(timeout: 2.0, handler: nil)
```

The key is that something must fulfill or trigger the expectation so the test moves forward. The wait method at the end takes a time parameter (in seconds) so that the test doesn't wait forever and can time out (and fail) in case the expectation is never fulfilled.

In the example provided, `fulfill()` is called explicitly in the completion handler passed in to the tested method. With Core Data save operations, it's easier to listen for the `NSManagedObjectContextDidSave` notification, since it happens in a place where you can't call `fulfill()` explicitly.

Add a new method to **CamperServiceTests.swift** to test that the root context is saved when you add a new camper:

```
func testRootContextIsSavedAfterAddingCamper() {
  //1
  let derivedContext = coreDataStack.newDerivedContext()
  camperService = CamperService(
    managedObjectContext: derivedContext,
    coreDataStack: coreDataStack)

  //2
  expectation(
    forNotification:
NSNotification.Name.NSManagedObjectContextDidSave.rawValue,
    object: coreDataStack.mainContext) {
      notification in
      return true
  }

  //3
  let camper = camperService.addCamper("Bacon Lover",
```

```
    phoneNumber: "910-543-9000")
  XCTAssertNotNil(camper)

  //4
  waitForExpectations(timeout: 2.0) { error in
    XCTAssertNil(error, "Save did not occur")
  }
}
```

Here's a breakdown of the code:

1. For this test, you create a background context to do the work. The `CamperService`
    instance is recreated using this context instead of the main context.

2. You create a text expectation linked to a notification. In this case, the expectation is
    linked to the `NSManagedObjectContextDidSave` notification from the root context
    of the Core Data stack. The handler for the notification is simple: it returns `true`
    since all you care about is that the notification is fired.

3. You add the camper, exactly the same as before.

4. The test waits up to two seconds for the expectation. If there are errors or the
    timeout passes, the `error` parameter for the handler block will contain a value.

Run the unit tests, and you should see a green checkmark next to this new method. It's
important to keep UI-blocking operations such as Core Data save actions off the main
thread so your app stays responsive. Test expectations are invaluable to make sure these
asynchronous operations are covered by unit tests.

You've added tests for existing features in the app; now it's time to add some features
yourself. Along with the tests too, of course. Or for even more fun — perhaps write the
tests first? :]

Tests first

An important function of CampgroundManager is its ability to reserve sites for campers.
Before it can accept reservations, the system has to know about all of the campsites at the
campground. `CampSiteService` was created to help with adding, deleting and finding
campsites.

Open `CampSiteService`, and you'll notice the only method implemented is
`addCampSite`. There are no unit tests for this method, so create a test case for the
service:

1. Right-click **Services** under the **CampgroundManagerTests** group and click **New
    File**.

2. Select **iOS\Source\Unit Test Case Class**. Click **Next**.

3. Name the class **CampSiteServiceTests**; subclass of **XCTestCase** should already be selected. Select **Swift** for the language, then click **Next**.

4. Make sure the **CampgroundManagerTests** target checkbox is the only target selected. Click **Create**.

Replace the contents of the file with the following:

```swift
import UIKit
import XCTest
import CampgroundManager
import CoreData

class CampSiteServiceTests: XCTestCase {

  // MARK: Properties
  var campSiteService: CampSiteService!
  var coreDataStack: CoreDataStack!

  override func setUp() {
    super.setUp()

    coreDataStack = TestCoreDataStack()
    campSiteService = CampSiteService(
      managedObjectContext: coreDataStack.mainContext,
      coreDataStack: coreDataStack)
  }

  override func tearDown() {
    super.tearDown()

    campSiteService = nil
    coreDataStack = nil
  }
}
```

This looks very similar to the previous test class. As your suite of tests expands and you notice common or repeated code, you can refactor your tests as well as your application code. You can feel safe doing this because the unit tests will fail if you mess anything up! :]

Add the following new method to test adding a campsite. This looks and works like the method for testing the creation of a new camper:

```swift
func testAddCampSite() {
  let campSite = campSiteService.addCampSite(1,
    electricity: true,
    water: true)
```

```
  XCTAssertTrue(campSite.siteNumber == 1,
    "Site number should be 1")
  XCTAssertTrue(campSite.electricity!.boolValue,
    "Site should have electricity")
  XCTAssertTrue(campSite.water!.boolValue,
    "Site should have water")
}
```

You also want to check that the context is saved during this method, so add the following method to test for that:

```
func testRootContextIsSavedAfterAddingCampsite() {
  let derivedContext = coreDataStack.newDerivedContext()

  campSiteService = CampSiteService(
    managedObjectContext: derivedContext,
    coreDataStack: coreDataStack)

  expectation(
    forNotification:
NSNotification.Name.NSManagedObjectContextDidSave.rawValue,
    object: coreDataStack.mainContext) {
      notification in
      return true
  }

  let campSite = campSiteService.addCampSite(1,
    electricity: true,
    water: true)
  XCTAssertNotNil(campSite)

  waitForExpectations(timeout: 2.0) { error in
    XCTAssertNil(error, "Save did not occur")
  }
}
```

This method should also look quite familiar to the ones you created earlier.

Run the unit tests; everything should pass. At this point, you should be feeling a bit paranoid. What if the tests are broken and they *always* pass? It's time to do some test-driven development and get the buzz that comes from turning red tests to green!

> **Note:** Test-Driven Development (TDD) is a way of developing an application by writing a test first, then incrementally implementing the feature until the test passes. The code is then refactored for the next feature or improvement. Covering TDD methodologies is beyond the scope of this chapter, but the steps you're covering here will help you use TDD if you do decide to follow it.

Add the following methods to **CampSiteServiceTests.swift** to test `getCampSite()`:

```swift
func testGetCampSiteWithMatchingSiteNumber() {
  _ = campSiteService.addCampSite(1,
    electricity: true,
    water: true)

  let campSite = campSiteService.getCampSite(1)
  XCTAssertNotNil(campSite, "A campsite should be returned")
}

func testGetCampSiteNoMatchingSiteNumber() {
  _ = campSiteService.addCampSite(1,
    electricity: true,
    water: true)

  let campSite = campSiteService.getCampSite(2)
  XCTAssertNil(campSite, "No campsite should be returned")
}
```

Both tests use the `addCampSite` method to create a new `CampSite`. You know this method works from your previous test, so there's no need to test it again. The actual tests cover retrieving the `CampSite` by ID and testing whether the result is `nil`.

Think about how more reliable it is to start every test with an empty database. If you weren't using the in-memory store, there could easily be a campsite matching the ID for the second test, which would then fail!

Run the unit tests. The test expecting a `CampSite` fails because you haven't implemented `getCampSite` yet.

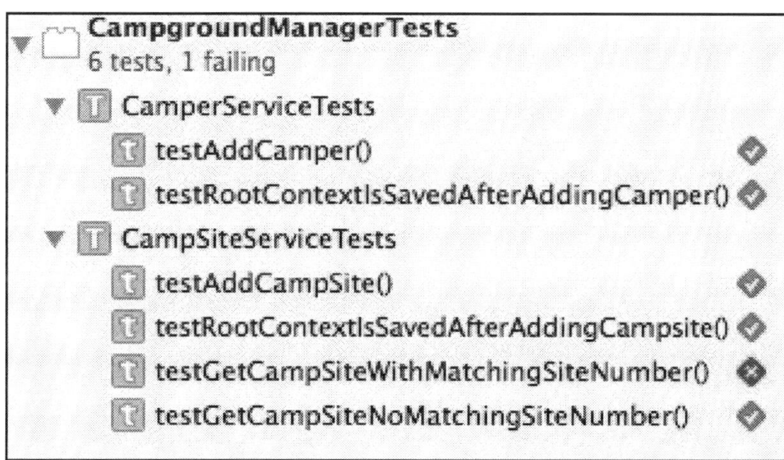

The other unit test — the one that expects no site — passes. This is an example of a false positive, because the method always returns `nil`. It's important that you add tests for multiple scenarios for each method to exercise as many code paths as possible.

Implement getCampSite in **CampSiteService.swift** with the following code:

```swift
public func getCampSite(_ siteNumber: NSNumber) -> CampSite? {
  let fetchRequest: NSFetchRequest<CampSite> =
    CampSite.fetchRequest()
  fetchRequest.predicate =
    Predicate(format: "siteNumber == %@",
      argumentArray: [siteNumber])
  let results: [CampSite]?
  do {
    results = try managedObjectContext.fetch(fetchRequest)
  } catch {
    return nil
  }

  return results?.first
}
```

Now rerun the unit tests and you should see green check marks. Ah, the sweet satisfaction of success! :]

> **Note:** The final project for this chapter included in the resources bundled with this book includes unit tests covering multiple scenarios for each method. You can browse through that code for even more examples.

Validation and refactoring

ReservationService will contain some fairly complex logic to figure out if a camper is able to reserve a site. The unit tests for ReservationService will require every service created so far to test its operation.

Create a new test class as you've done before:

1. Right-click **Services** under the **CampgroundManagerTests** group and click **New File.**

2. Select **iOS\Source\Unit Test Case Class.** Click **Next.**

3. Name the class **ReservationServiceTests**; subclass of **XCTestCase** should already be selected. Select **Swift** for the language. Click **Next.**

4. Make sure the **CampgroundManagerTests** target checkbox is the only target selected. Click **Create.**

Replace the contents of the file with the following:

```swift
import Foundation
import CoreData
import XCTest
import CampgroundManager

class ReservationServiceTests: XCTestCase {

  // MARK: Properties
  var campSiteService: CampSiteService!
  var camperService: CamperService!
  var reservationService: ReservationService!
  var coreDataStack: CoreDataStack!

  override func setUp() {
    super.setUp()
    coreDataStack = TestCoreDataStack()
    camperService = CamperService(
      managedObjectContext: coreDataStack.mainContext,
      coreDataStack: coreDataStack)
    campSiteService = CampSiteService(
      managedObjectContext: coreDataStack.mainContext,
      coreDataStack: coreDataStack)
    reservationService = ReservationService(
      managedObjectContext: coreDataStack.mainContext,
      coreDataStack: coreDataStack)
  }

  override func tearDown() {
    super.tearDown()

    camperService = nil
    campSiteService = nil
    reservationService = nil
    coreDataStack = nil
  }
}
```

This is a slightly longer version of the set up and tear down code you've used in the previous test case classes. Along with setting up the Core Data stack as usual, you're creating a fresh instance of each service in `setUp` for each test.

Add the following method to test creating a reservation:

```swift
func testReserveCampSitePositiveNumberOfDays() {
  let camper = camperService.addCamper("Johnny Appleseed",
    phoneNumber: "408-555-1234")!
  let campSite = campSiteService.addCampSite(15,
    electricity: false,
    water: false)
```

```
  let result = reservationService.reserveCampSite(campSite,
    camper: camper,
    date: Date(),
    numberOfNights: 5)

  XCTAssertNotNil(result.reservation,
    "Reservation should not be nil")
  XCTAssertNil(result.error,
    "No error should be present")
  XCTAssertTrue(result.reservation?.status == "Reserved",
    "Status should be Reserved")
}
```

The unit test creates a camper and campsite, both required to reserve a site. The new part here is that you're using the reservation service to reserve the campsite, linking the camper and campsite together with a date.

The unit test verifies that a `Reservation` object was created and an `NSError` object wasn't in the returned tuple. Looking at the `reserveCampSite` call, you've probably realized that the number of nights should be at least greater than zero. Add the following unit test to test that condition:

```
func testReserveCampSiteNegativeNumberOfDays() {
  let camper = camperService.addCamper("Johnny Appleseed",
    phoneNumber: "408-555-1234")!
  let campSite = campSiteService.addCampSite(15,
    electricity: false,
    water: false)

  let result = reservationService!.reserveCampSite(campSite,
    camper: camper,
    date: Date(),
    numberOfNights: -1)

  XCTAssertNotNil(result.reservation,
    "Reservation should not be nil")
  XCTAssertNotNil(result.error,
    "An error should be present")
  XCTAssertTrue(result.error?.userInfo["Problem"] as? String
    == "Invalid number of days",
    "Error problem should be present")
  XCTAssertTrue(result.reservation?.status == "Invalid",
    "Status should be Invalid")
}
```

Run the unit test, and you'll notice the test fails. Apparently whoever wrote `ReservationService` didn't think to check for this! It's a good thing you caught that bug here in a test before it made it out into the world — maybe booking a negative number of nights would cascade down to issuing a refund!

Tests are great places for probing your system and finding holes in its behavior. The test also serves as a quasi-specification; the tests indicate you're still expecting a valid, non-`nil` result, but one with the error condition set.

Open **ReservationService.swift** and add the check for `numberOfNights` to `reserveCampSite`. Replace the line `reservation.status = "Reserved"` with the following:

```
if numberOfNights <= 0 {
  reservation.status = "Invalid"
  registrationError = NSError(domain: "CampingManager",
    code: 5,
    userInfo: ["Problem": "Invalid number of days"])
} else {
  reservation.status = "Reserved"
}
```

Finally, change `registrationError` from a constant to a variable by replacing `let` with `var`.

Now rerun the tests and check that the negative number of days test passes. You can see how the process continues with refactoring when you want to add additional functionality or validation rules.

Whether you know the details of the code you're testing or you're treating it like a black box, you can write these kinds of tests against the API to see if it behaves as you expect. If it does, great! That means the test will ensure your code functions as expected. If not, you either need to change your test to match the code, or change the code to match the test.

Where to go from here?

You've probably heard many times that unit testing your work is key in maintaining a stable software product. While Core Data can help eliminate a lot of error-prone persistence code from your project, it can be a source of logic errors if used incorrectly.

Writing unit tests that can use Core Data will help stabilize your code before it even reaches your users. `XCTestExpectation` is a simple, yet powerful tool in your quest to test Core Data in an asynchronous manner. Use it wisely!

As a challenge, `CampSiteService` has a number of methods that are not implemented yet, marked with `TODO` comments. Using a TDD approach, write unit tests and then implement the methods to make the tests pass. If you get stuck, check out the `challenge` project included in the resources for this chapter for a sample solution.

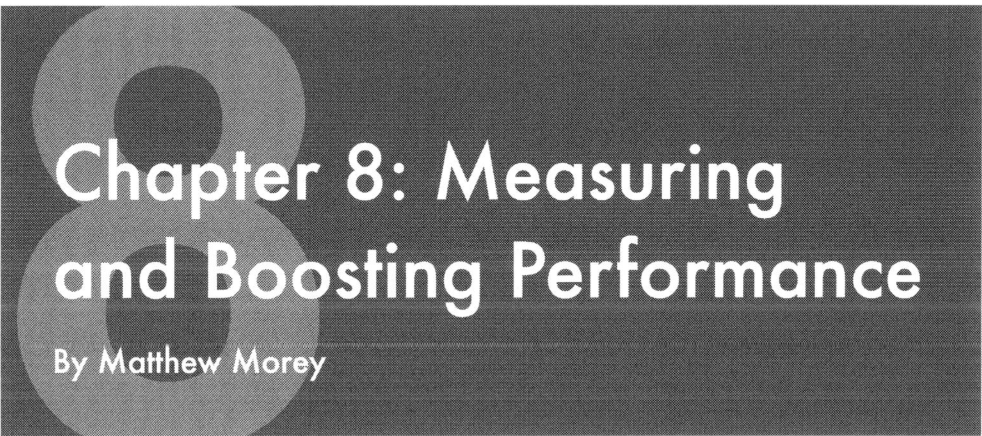

In many ways, it's a no-brainer: You should strive to optimize the performance of any app you develop. An app with poor performance will, at best, receive bad reviews and, at worst, become unresponsive and crash.

This is no less true of apps that use Core Data. Luckily, most implementations of Core Data are fast and light already, due to Core Data's built-in optimizations, such as faulting.

However, the flexibility that makes Core Data a great tool means you can use it in ways that negatively impact performance. From poor choices in setting up the data model to inefficient fetching and searching, there are many opportunities for Core Data to slow down your app.

You'll begin the chapter with an app that is a slow-working memory hog. By the end of the chapter, you'll have an app that is light and fast, and you'll know exactly where to look and what to do if you find yourself with your own heavy, sluggish app—and how to avoid that situation in the first place!

Getting started

As with most things, performance is a balance between memory and speed. Your app's Core Data model objects can exist in two places: in random access memory (RAM) or on disk. Accessing data in RAM is much faster than accessing data on disk, but devices have much less RAM than disk space.

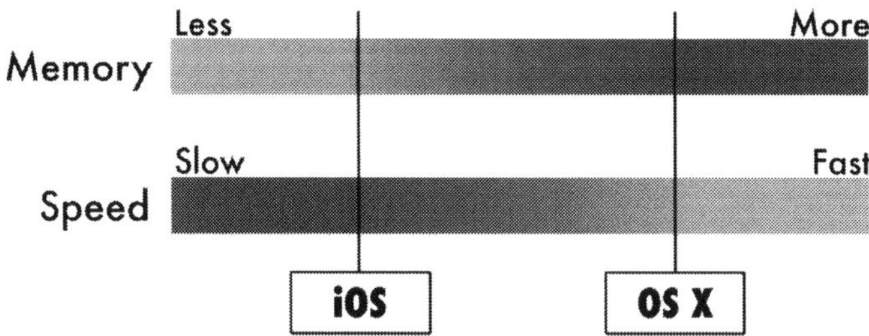

iOS devices, in particular, have less available RAM, which prevents you from loading tons of data into memory. With fewer model objects in RAM, your app's operations will be slower due to frequent slow disk access. As you load more model objects into RAM, your app will probably feel more responsive, but you can't starve out other apps or the OS will terminate your app!

The starter project

The starter project, EmployeeDirectory, is a tab bar-based app full of employee information. It's like the Contacts app, but for a single fictional company.

Open the EmployeeDirectory starter project for this chapter in Xcode and build and run it.

The app will take a long time to launch and once it does launch, it will feel sluggish and may even crash as you use it. Rest assured, this is by design!

> **Note:** It's possible the starter project may not even launch on your system. The app was architected to be as sluggish as possible while still able to run on most systems, so that the performance improvements you'll make will be easily noticeable. If the app refuses to work on your system, continue to follow along. The first set of changes you make should enable the app to work on even the slowest devices.

As you can see in the following screenshots, the first tab includes a table view and a custom cell with basic information, such as name and department, for all employees. Tap a cell to reveal more details for the selected employee, such as start date and remaining vacation days.

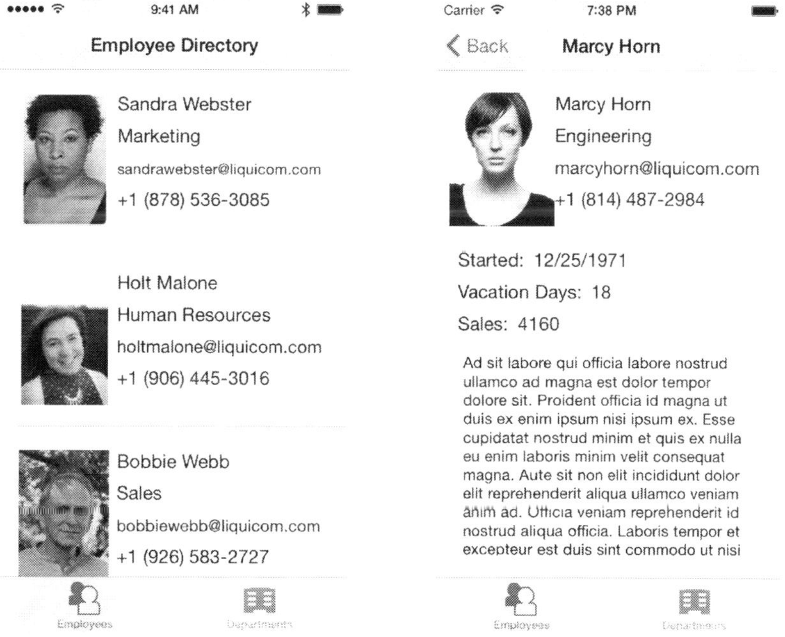

Tap the profile picture of the employee makes the picture full-screen; tap anywhere on the full-screen picture to dismiss that view.

The startup time of the app is quite long, and the scrolling performance of the initial employee list could use some work. The app also uses a lot of memory, which you'll measure yourself in the next section.

Measure, change, verify

Instead of guessing where your performance bottlenecks are, you can save yourself time and effort by first measuring your app's performance in targeted ways. Xcode provides tools just for this purpose.

Ideally, you should measure performance, make targeted changes and then measure again to validate your changes had the intended impact. You should repeat this measure–change–verify process as many times as needed until your app meets all of your performance requirements.

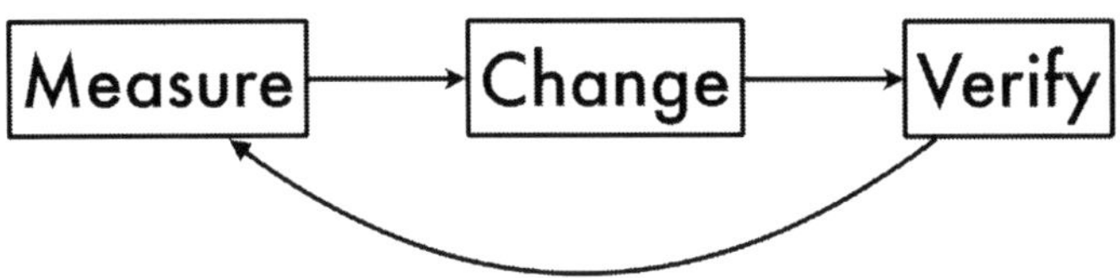

In this chapter, you'll do just that:

- You'll measure performance issues in the provided starter project using Gauges, Instruments and the XCTest framework.

- Next, you'll make changes to the code that will improve the performance of the app.

- Finally, you'll verify that the changes had the intended results by measuring again.

You'll then repeat this cycle until EmployeeDirectory performs like a Core Data champ!

Measuring the problem

Build, run, and wait for the app to launch. Once it does, use the **Memory Report** to view how much RAM the app is using.

To launch the Memory Report, first verify the app is running and then perform the following steps:

1. Click on the **Debug navigator** in the left navigator pane.

2. To get more information, expand the **running process** — in this case, **EmployeeDirectory** — by tapping on the arrow.

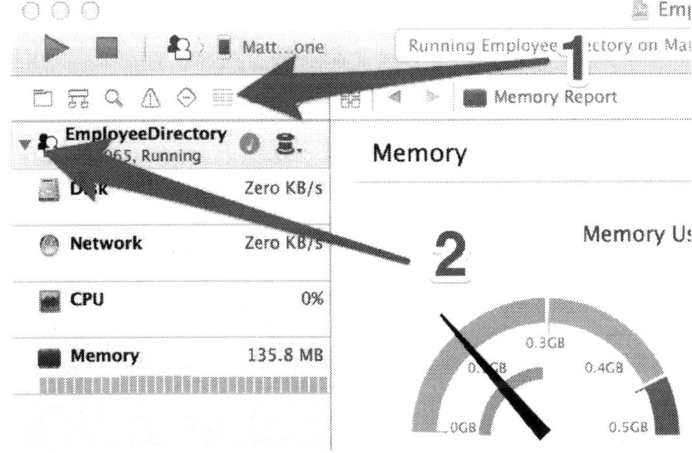

Now, click on the **Memory** row and look at the top half of the memory gauge:

The top half includes a **Memory Use** gauge showing the amount and percentage of memory your app is using. For EmployeeDirectory, you'll see about 135 MB of memory is in use, or about 10% of the available RAM on an iPhone 5, which is the least-performant device that will still run iOS 10.

The **Usage Comparison** pie chart depicts this chunk of memory as a fraction of the total available memory. It also shows the amount of RAM in use by other processes, as well as the amount of available free RAM, which in this case is 329.2 MB.

Now look at the bottom half of the Memory Report:

The bottom half consist of a chart that shows RAM usage over time. For EmployeeDirectory, you'll see two distinct areas.

1. Upon first launch, EmployeeDirectory performs an import operation before loading the primary employee list. Ignore these spikes in memory for now.

2. The next chunk of memory usage takes place after the import operation, when the employee list is visible. Once the app has fully loaded the list, you can see the memory usage is fairly stable.

> **Note:** If you use a device besides an iPhone 5, including the iOS Simulator, your memory gauge may not look exactly like these screenshots. The utilization percentages will be based off of the amount of available RAM on your test device, which may not match the RAM available on an iPhone 5.

The RAM usage is quite high, considering there are only 50 employee records in the app. The data model itself could be at fault here, so that's where you'll start your investigation.

Exploring the data source

In Xcode, open the project navigator and click on **EmployeeDirectory.xcdatamodeld** to view the data model.

The model for the starter project consists of an `Employee` entity with 11 attributes and a `Sale` entity with two attributes.

On the `Employee` entity, the `about`, `address`, `department`, `email`, `guid`, `name` and `phone` attributes are string types; `active` is a Boolean; `picture` is binary data; `startDate` is a date and `vacationDays` is an integer.

`Employee` has a *to-many* relationship with `Sale`, which contains an `amount` integer attribute and a `date` Date attribute.

On first launch, the app will import sample data from the bundled JSON file **seed.json**. Here's an excerpt of the JSON:

```json
{
  "guid": "769adb89-82ad-4b39-be41-d02b89de7b94",
  "active": true,
  "picture": "face10.jpg",
  "name": "Kasey Mcfarland",
  "vacationDays": 2,
  "department": "Marketing",
  "startDate": "1979-09-05",
  "email": "kaseymcfarland@liquicom.com",
  "phone": "+1 (909) 561-2981",
  "address": "201 Lancaster Avenue, West Virginia, 2583",
  "about": "Dolore reprehenderit ... voluptate consectetur.\r\n"
},
```

> **Note:** You can vary the amount and type of data the app imports from the **seed.json** file by modifying the `amountToImport` and `addSalesRecords` constants located at the top of **AppDelegate.swift**. For now, leave these constants set to their default values.

In terms of performance, the text showing the employee names, departments, email addresses and phone numbers is inconsequential compared to the size of the profile pictures, which are large enough to potentially impact the performance of the list.

Now that you've measured the problem and have a baseline for future comparisons, you'll make changes to the data model to reduce the amount of RAM in use.

Making changes to improve performance

The likely culprit for the high memory usage is the employee profile picture. Since the picture is stored as a binary data attribute, Core Data will allocate memory and load the entire picture when you access an employee record — even if you only need to access the employee's name or email address!

The solution here is to split out the picture into a separate, related record. In theory, you'll be able to access the employee record efficiently, and then take the hit for loading the picture only when you really need it.

To start, open the visual model editor by clicking on **EmployeeDirectory.xcdatamodeld**.

Start by creating an object, or entity, in your model. In the bottom toolbar, click the **Add Entity** plus (+) button to add a new entity.

Name the entity **EmployeePicture**. Then click the entity and make sure the third tab is selected in the Utilities section. Change the class to **EmployeePicture** and the Module to **EmployeeDirectory**.

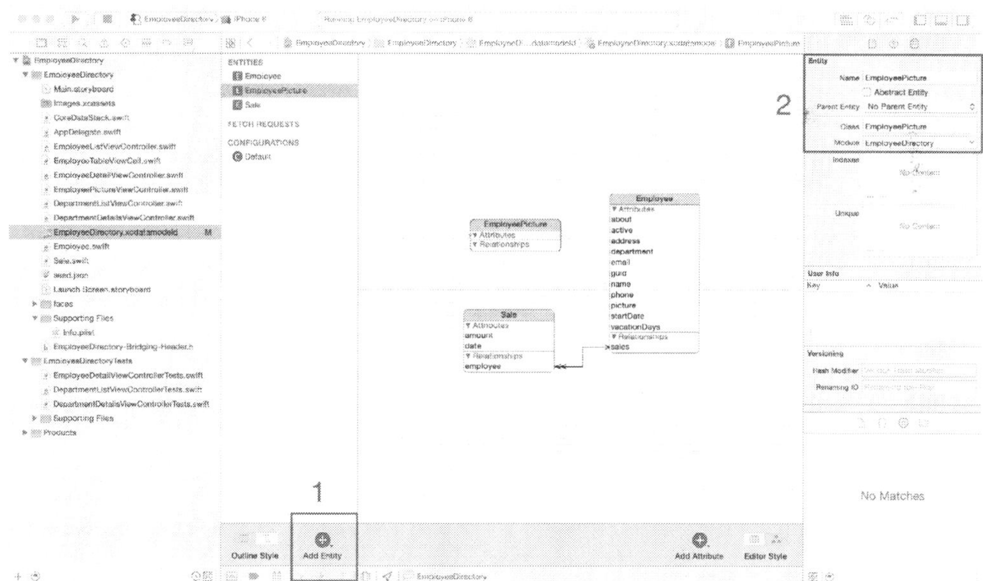

Make sure the **EmployeePicture** entity is selected by clicking on either the entity name in the left panel or the diagram for the entity in the diagram view.

Next, click and hold on the plus (+) button in the lower-right (next to the Editor Style segmented control) and then click **Add Attribute** from the popup. Name the new attribute **picture**.

Finally, in the data model inspector, change the **Attribute Type** to **Binary Data** and check the **Allows External** Storage option.

Your editor should look like this:

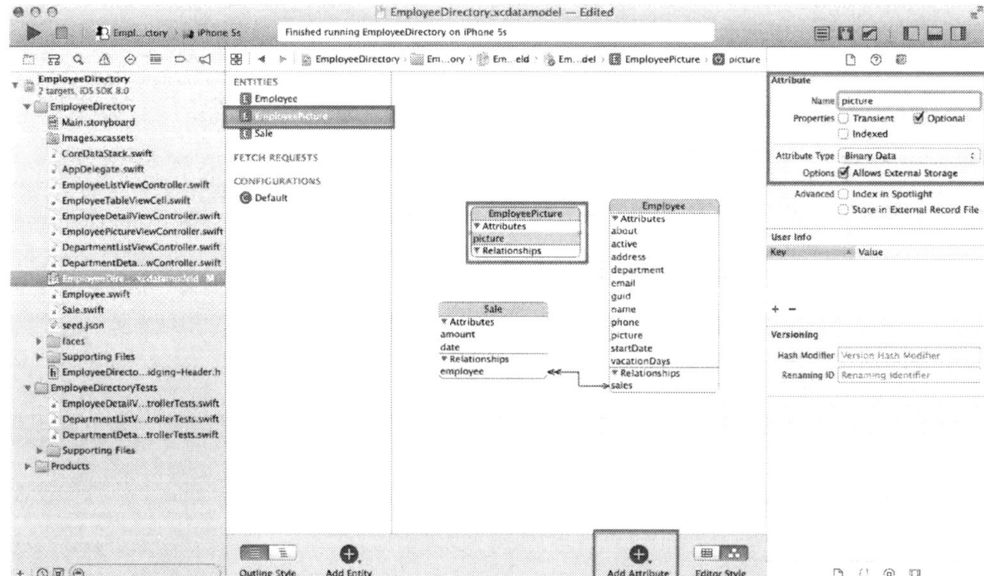

As previously mentioned, binary data attributes are usually stored right in the database. If you check the **Allows External Storage** option, Core Data automatically decides if it's better to save the data to disk as a separate file or leave it in the SQLite database.

Select the Employee entity and rename the **picture** attribute to **pictureThumbnail**. To do so, select the picture attribute in the diagram view and then edit the name in the data model inspector.

You've updated the model to store the original picture in a separate entity and a thumbnail version on the main Employee entity. The smaller thumbnail pictures won't require as much RAM when the app fetches Employee entities from Core Data. Once you've finished modifying the rest of the project, you'll get a chance to test this out and verify that the app is using less RAM than before.

You can link the two entities together with a relationship. That way, when the app needs the higher-quality, larger picture, it can still retrieve it via a relationship.

Select the **Employee** entity and click and hold the plus (+) button in the lower right. This time, select **Add Relationship**. Name the relationship **picture**, set the destination as **EmployeePicture** and finally, set the **Delete Rule** to **Cascade**.

Core Data relationships should always go both ways, so now add a corresponding relationship. Select the **EmployeePicture** entity and add a new relationship. Name the new relationship **employee**, set the **Destination** to **Employee** and finally, set the **Inverse** to **picture**.

Your model should now look like this:

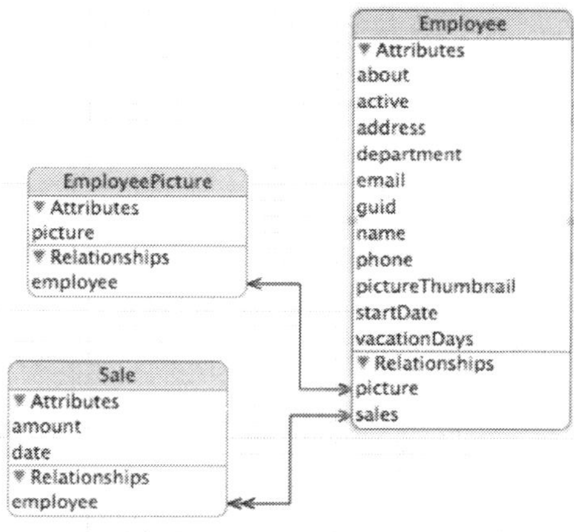

Now that you've finished making changes to the model, you need to create an NSManagedObject subclass for the new EmployeePicture entity. This subclass will let you access the new entity from code.

Right-click on the **EmployeeDirectory** group folder and select **New File**. Select the **Cocoa Touch Class** template and click **Next**. Name the class **EmployeePicture** and make it a subclass of **NSManagedObject**. Make sure that **Swift** is selected for the **Language**, click **Next** and finally click **Create**.

Select **EmployeePicture.swift** from the project navigator and replace the automatically generated code with the following code:

```swift
import Foundation
import CoreData

class EmployeePicture: NSManagedObject {
  @NSManaged var picture: Data
  @NSManaged var employee: EmployeeDirectory.Employee
}
```

This is a very simple class with just two properties. The first, **picture**, matches the single attribute on the **EmployeePicture** entity you just created in the visual data model editor. The second property, **employee**, matches the relationship you created on the **EmployeePicture** entity.

> **Note:** You could also have Xcode create the **EmployeePicture** class automatically. To add a new class this way, open **EmployeeDirectory.xcdatamodeld**, go to **Editor\Create NSManagedObject Subclass...**, select the data model and then select the **EmployeePicture** entity in the next two dialog boxes. Select **Swift** as the language option in the final box. If you're asked, say **No** to creating an Objective-C bridging header. Click **Create** to save the file.

Next, select the **Employee.swift** file from the project navigator and update the code to make use of the new **pictureThumbnail** attribute and **picture** relationship. Rename the picture variable to `pictureThumbnail` and add a new variable named `picture` of type `EmployeeDirectory.EmployeePicture`. Your file will now look like this:

```swift
import Foundation
import CoreData

class Employee: NSManagedObject {

  @NSManaged var startDate: Date
  @NSManaged var about: String
  @NSManaged var active: NSNumber
  @NSManaged var address: String
  @NSManaged var department: String
  @NSManaged var email: String
  @NSManaged var guid: String
  @NSManaged var name: String
  @NSManaged var phone: String
  @NSManaged var pictureThumbnail: Data
  @NSManaged var picture: EmployeeDirectory.EmployeePicture
  @NSManaged var vacationDays: NSNumber
  @NSManaged var sales : Set<Sale>

}
```

Next, you need to update the rest of the app to make use of the new entities and attributes.

Open **EmployeeListViewController.swift** and find the following lines of code in `tableView(_:cellForRowAt:)`. It should be easy to find, as it will have an error marker next to it!

```
cell.pictureImageView.image = UIImage(data: employee.picture)
```

This code sets the picture on the cell in the employee list. Now that the full picture is held in a separate entity, you should use the newly added `pictureThumbnail` attribute. Update the file to match the following code:

```
cell.pictureImageView.image =
  UIImage(data: employee.pictureThumbnail)
```

Now open **EmployeeDetailViewController.swift** and find the following code within `configureView()`. Again, it should be showing an error:

```
let image = UIImage(data: employee.picture)
headShotImageView.image = image
```

You'll need to update the picture that's set, just as you did in EmployeeListViewController.swift. Like the cell picture, the employee detail view will only have a small picture and therefore only needs the thumbnail version. Update the code to look like the following:

```
let image = UIImage(data: employee.pictureThumbnail)
headShotImageView.image = image
```

Open **EmployeePictureViewController.swift** and find the following code in `configureView()`:

```
employeePictureImageView.image =
  UIImage(data: employee.picture)
```

This time, you want to use the high-quality version of the picture, since the image will be shown full-screen. Update the file to use the **picture** relationship you created on the **Employee** entity to access the high-quality version of the picture:

```
employeePictureImageView.image =
  UIImage(data: employee.picture.picture)
```

There's one more thing to do before you build and run. Open **AppDelegate.swift** and find the following line of code in `importJSONSeedData(_:)`:

```
employee.picture = pictureData
```

Now that you have a separate entity for storing the high-quality picture, you need to update this line of code to set the `pictureThumbnail` attribute and the `picture` relationship.

Replace the line above with the following:

```
employee.pictureThumbnail =
  imageDataScaledToHeight(pictureData, height: 120)

let pictureObject =
  EmployeePicture(context: coreDataStack.mainContext)

pictureObject.picture = pictureData

employee.picture = pictureObject
```

First, you use `imageDataScaledToHeight` to set the `pictureThumbnail` to a smaller version of the original picture. Next, you create a new `EmployeePicture` entity. You set the `picture` attribute on the new `EmployeePicture` entity to the `pictureData` constant. Finally, you set the `picture` relationship on the `employee` entity to the newly-created `picture` entity.

> **Note:** `imageDataScaledToHeight` takes in image data, resizes it to the passed-in height and sets the quality to 80% before returning the new image data. If you have an app that needs pictures and retrieves data via a network call, you should make sure that the API doesn't already include smaller thumbnail versions of the pictures. There's a small performance cost associated with converting images on the fly like this.

Since you changed the model, delete the app from your testing device. Now build and run. Give it a go! You should see exactly what you saw before:

The app should work as before, and you might even notice a small performance difference because of the thumbnails. But the main reason for this change was to improve memory usage.

Verify the changes

Now that you've made all the necessary changes to the project, it's time to see if you actually improved the app.

While the app is running, use the **Memory Report** to view how much RAM the app is using. This time it's consumed only about 41 MB of RAM, or about 4% of the total available RAM of the iPhone 5.

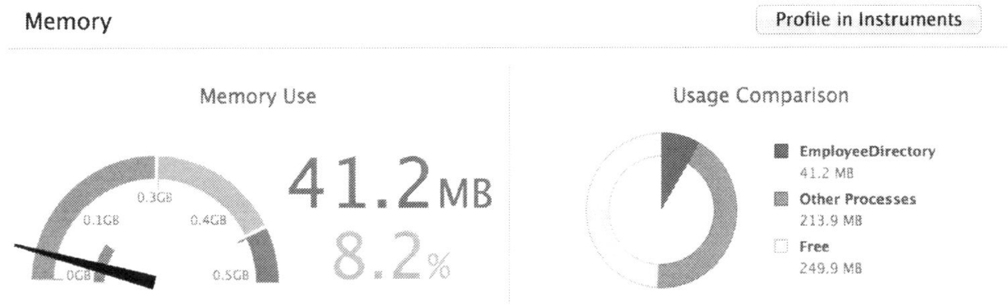

Now look at the bottom half of the report. Like last time, the initial spike is from the import operation and you can ignore it. The flat area is much lower this time.

Congratulations, you've reduced this app's RAM usage, simply by making adjustments to its data model!

First, you **measured** the app's performance using the Memory Report tool. Next, you made **changes** to the way Core Data stores and accesses the app's data. Finally, you **verified** that the changes improved the app's performance.

Fetching and performance

Core Data is the keeper of your app's data. Anytime you want to access the data, you have to retrieve it with a fetch request.

For example, when the app loads the employee list, it needs to perform a fetch. But each trip to the persistent store incurs overhead. You don't want to fetch more data than you need — just enough so that you aren't constantly going back to disk. Remember, disk access is much slower than RAM access.

For maximum performance, you need to strike a balance between the number of objects you fetch at any given time and the usefulness of having many records taking up valuable space in RAM.

The startup time of the app is a little slow, suggesting something is going on with the initial fetch.

Fetch batch size

Core Data fetch requests include the `fetchBatchSize` property, which makes it easy to fetch just enough data, but not too much. If you don't set a batch size, Core Data uses the default value of 0, which disables batching.

Setting a non-zero positive batch size lets you limit the amount of data returned to the batch size. As the app needs more data, Core Data automatically performs more batch operations. If you were to search the source code of the EmployeeDirectory app, you wouldn't see any calls to `fetchBatchSize`. That indicates another potential area for improvement!

Let's see if there are any places you could use a batch size to improve the app's performance.

Measuring the problem

You'll use the **Instruments** tool to analyze where the fetch operations are in your app.

First, select one of the iPhone simulator targets and then from Xcode's menu bar, select **Product** and then **Profile** (or press ⌘I). This will build the app and launch Instruments.

> **Note:** You can only use the Instruments Core Data template with the Simulator, as the template requires the DTrace tool which is not available on real iOS devices.

You'll be greeted by the following selection window:

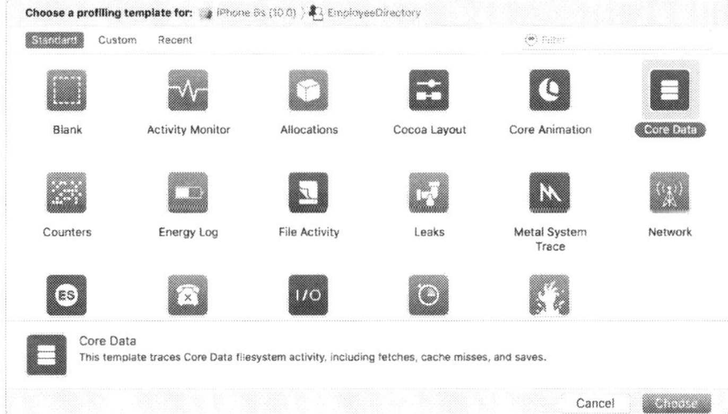

Select the **Core Data** template and click **Choose**. This will launch the Instruments window. If this is the first time you've launched Instruments, you might be asked for your password to authorize Instruments to analyze running processes — don't worry, it's safe to enter your password in this dialog.

Once Instruments has launched, click on the **Record** button in the top-left of the window.

Once EmployeeDirectory has launched, scroll up and down the employee list for about 20 seconds and then click on the **Stop** button that has appeared in place of the Record button.

Click on the **Fetches** tool. The Instruments window should now look like this:

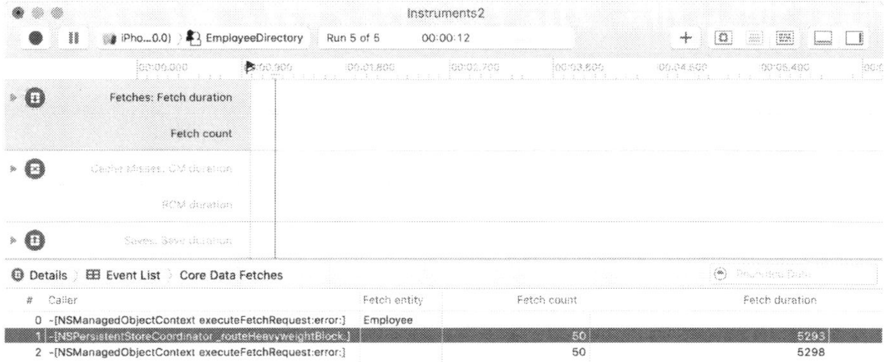

The default Core Data template includes the following tools to help you tune and monitor performance:

- **Fetches Instrument**: Captures fetch count and duration of fetch operations. This will help you balance the number of fetch requests versus the size of each request.

- **Cache Misses Instrument**: Captures information about fault events that result in cache misses. This can help diagnose performance in low-memory situations.

- **Saves Instrument**: Captures information on managed object context save events. Writing data out to disk can be a performance and battery hit, so this instrument can help you determine whether you should batch things into one big save rather than many small ones.

Since you clicked on the Fetches tool, the details section at the bottom of the Instruments window shows more information about each fetch that occurred.

Each of the three rows corresponds to the same line of code in the app. The first two rows are private Core Data calls that are generated by lines of code in the app, so you can ignore them.

Pay attention to the last row, though. This row includes the Objective-C versions of the **caller**, **fetch count** and **fetch duration** in microseconds.

EmployeeDirectory imports 50 employees. The fetch count shows 50, which means the app is fetching *all* employees from Core Data at the same time. That's not very efficient!

The Fetches tool corroborates your experience that the fetch is slow and is easily noticeable, as you can see it takes about 5,000 microseconds (5 seconds). The app has to complete this fetch before it makes the table view visible and ready for user interaction.

> **Note**: Depending on your Mac, the numbers onscreen (and the thickness of the bars) might not match those shown in these screenshots. Faster Macs will have quicker fetches. Don't worry — what's important is the change in time you'll see after you modify the project.

Changes to improve performance

Open **EmployeeListViewController.swift** and find the following line of code in `employeeFetchRequest(_:)`:

```swift
let fetchRequest: NSFetchRequest<Employee> =
  NSFetchRequest(entityName: "Employee")
```

This code creates a fetch request using the **Employee** entity. You haven't set a batch size, so it defaults to 0, which means no batching. Now set the batch size on the fetch request to 10, like so:

```swift
let fetchRequest: NSFetchRequest<Employee> =
  NSFetchRequest(entityName: "Employee")
fetchRequest.fetchBatchSize = 10
```

How do you come up with an optimal batch size? A good rule of thumb is to set the batch size to about double the number of items that appear onscreen at any given time. The employee list shows three to five employees onscreen at once, so 10 is a reasonable batch size.

Verify the changes

Now that you've made the necessary change to the project, it's once again time to see if you've actually improved the app.

To test this fix, first build and run the app and make sure it still works. Next launch Instruments again: from Xcode, select **Product** and then **Profile**, or press ⌘I) and repeat the steps you followed previously. Remember to scroll up and down the employee list for about **20 seconds** before clicking the **Stop** button in Instruments.

> **Note**: To use the latest code, make sure you launch the app from Xcode, which triggers a build, rather than just hitting the red button in Instruments.

This time, the Core Data Instrument should look like this:

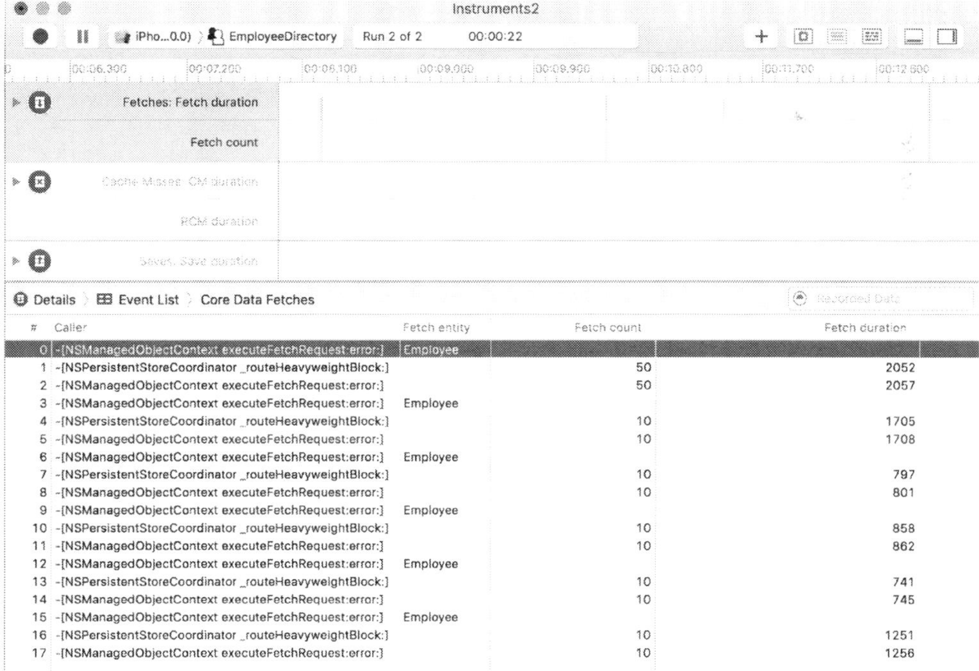

#	Caller	Fetch entity	Fetch count	Fetch duration
0	-[NSManagedObjectContext executeFetchRequest:error:]	Employee		
1	-[NSPersistentStoreCoordinator _routeHeavyweightBlock:]		50	2052
2	-[NSManagedObjectContext executeFetchRequest:error:]		50	2057
3	-[NSManagedObjectContext executeFetchRequest:error:]	Employee		
4	-[NSPersistentStoreCoordinator _routeHeavyweightBlock:]		10	1705
5	-[NSManagedObjectContext executeFetchRequest:error:]		10	1708
6	-[NSManagedObjectContext executeFetchRequest:error:]	Employee		
7	-[NSPersistentStoreCoordinator _routeHeavyweightBlock:]		10	797
8	-[NSManagedObjectContext executeFetchRequest:error:]		10	801
9	-[NSManagedObjectContext executeFetchRequest:error:]	Employee		
10	-[NSPersistentStoreCoordinator _routeHeavyweightBlock:]		10	858
11	-[NSManagedObjectContext executeFetchRequest:error:]		10	862
12	-[NSManagedObjectContext executeFetchRequest:error:]	Employee		
13	-[NSPersistentStoreCoordinator _routeHeavyweightBlock:]		10	741
14	-[NSManagedObjectContext executeFetchRequest:error:]		10	745
15	-[NSManagedObjectContext executeFetchRequest:error:]	Employee		
16	-[NSPersistentStoreCoordinator _routeHeavyweightBlock:]		10	1251
17	-[NSManagedObjectContext executeFetchRequest:error:]		10	1256

Now there are multiple fetches, and the initial fetch is faster!

Examine the detail section more closely.

#	Caller	Fetch entity	Fetch count	Fetch duration
0	-[NSManagedObjectContext executeFetchRequest:error:]	Employee		
1	-[NSPersistentStoreCoordinator _routeHeavyweightBlock:]		50	2052
2	-[NSManagedObjectContext executeFetchRequest:error:]		50	2057
3	-[NSManagedObjectContext executeFetchRequest:error:]	Employee		
4	-[NSPersistentStoreCoordinator _routeHeavyweightBlock:]		10	1705
5	-[NSManagedObjectContext executeFetchRequest:error:]		10	1708
6	-[NSManagedObjectContext executeFetchRequest:error:]	Employee		
7	-[NSPersistentStoreCoordinator _routeHeavyweightBlock:]		10	797
8	-[NSManagedObjectContext executeFetchRequest:error:]		10	801
9	-[NSManagedObjectContext executeFetchRequest:error:]	Employee		
10	-[NSPersistentStoreCoordinator _routeHeavyweightBlock:]		10	858
11	-[NSManagedObjectContext executeFetchRequest:error:]		10	862
12	-[NSManagedObjectContext executeFetchRequest:error:]	Employee		
13	-[NSPersistentStoreCoordinator _routeHeavyweightBlock:]		10	741
14	-[NSManagedObjectContext executeFetchRequest:error:]		10	745
15	-[NSManagedObjectContext executeFetchRequest:error:]	Employee		
16	-[NSPersistentStoreCoordinator _routeHeavyweightBlock:]		10	1251
17	-[NSManagedObjectContext executeFetchRequest:error:]		10	1256

Again, instead of a single fetch, you see multiple quicker fetches.

The first fetch looks similar to the original fetch, as it is fetching all 50 employees. This time, however, it's only fetching the count of the objects, instead of the full objects, which makes the fetch duration much shorter. Core Data does this automatically now that you've set a batch size on the request.

Looking at the results on my system, this fetch originally took over 5,000 microseconds, and now it only takes 2,000 microseconds.

After the first fetch, you can see numerous fetches in batches of 10. As you scroll through the employee list, new entities are fetched only when needed.

You've cut the time of the initial fetch down to almost a third of the original, and the subsequent fetches are much smaller and faster. Congratulations, you have increased the speed of your app again!

Advanced fetching

Fetch requests use predicates to limit the amount of data returned. As mentioned above, for optimal performance, you should limit the amount of data you fetch to the minimum needed: the more data you fetch, the longer the fetch will take.

> **Fetch Predicate Performance**: You can limit your fetch requests by using predicates. If your fetch request requires a compound predicate, you can make it more efficient by putting the more restrictive predicate first. This is especially true if your predicate contains string comparisons. For example, a predicate with a format of `"(active == YES) AND (name CONTAINS[cd] %@)"` would likely be more efficient than `"(name CONTAINS[cd] %@) AND (active == YES)"`. For

more predicate performance optimizations please consult Apple's Predicate Programming Guide: apple.co/2a1Rq2n.

Build and run EmployeeDirectory, and select the second tab labeled Departments. This tab shows a listing of departments and the number of employees in each department. Tap a department cell to see a list of the employees in the selected department.

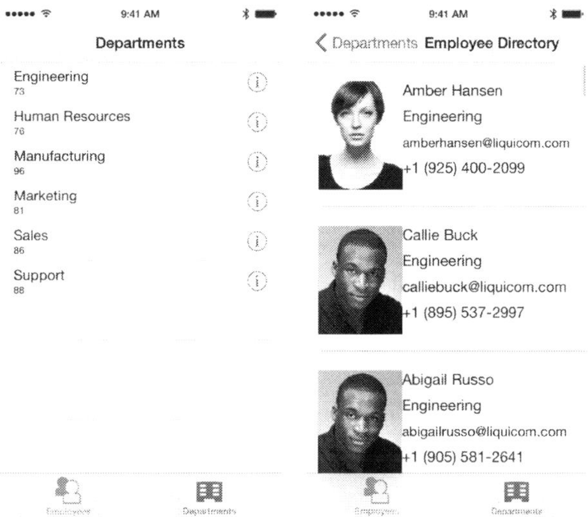

Tap the detail disclosure, also known as the information icon, in each department cell to show the total employees, active employees and a breakdown of employees' available vacations days.

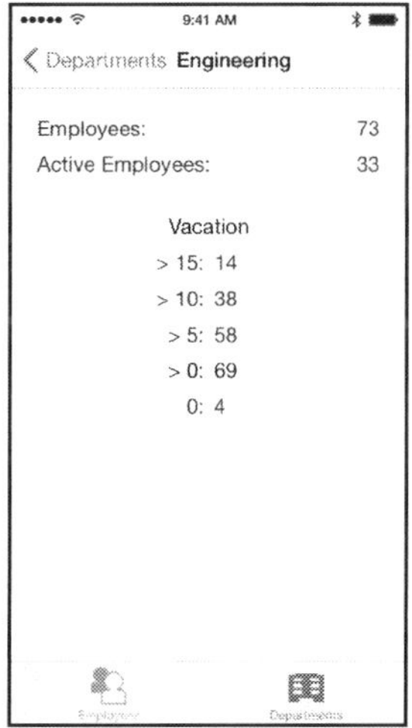

The first screen simply lists the departments and the number of employees per department. There's not too much data here, but there could still be performance issues lurking here. Let's find out.

Measure the problem

Instead of Instruments, you'll use the **XCTest** framework to measure the performance of the department list screen. XCTest is usually used for unit tests, but it also contains useful tools for testing performance.

> **Note:** For more information on unit tests and Core Data, check out Chapter 7, "Unit Testing".

First, familiarize yourself with how the app creates the department list screen. Open **DepartmentListViewController.swift** and find the following code in `totalEmployeesPerDepartment()`.

```swift
//1
let fetchRequest: NSFetchRequest<Employee> =
  NSFetchRequest(entityName: "Employee")
var fetchResults: [Employee] = []

do {
  fetchResults =
    try coreDataStack.mainContext.fetch(fetchRequest)
} catch let error as NSError {
  print("ERROR: \(error.localizedDescription)")
  return [[String: String]]()
}

//2
var uniqueDepartments: [String: Int] = [:]
for employee in fetchResults {

  if let employeeDepartmentCount =
    uniqueDepartments[employee.department] {
      uniqueDepartments[employee.department] =
        employeeDepartmentCount + 1
  } else {
    uniqueDepartments[employee.department] = 1
  }
}

//3
var results: [[String: String]] = []
for (department, headCount) in uniqueDepartments {
  let departmentDictionary: [String: String] =
```

```
    ["department": department,
     "headCount": String(headCount)]

  results.append(departmentDictionary)
}

return results
```

This code does the following:

1. It creates a fetch request with the Employee entity and then fetches all employees.

2. It iterates though the employees and builds a dictionary, where the key is the department name and the value is the number of employees in that department.

3. It builds an array of dictionaries with the required information for the department list screen.

Now to measure the performance of this code.

Open **DepartmentListViewControllerTests.swift** (notice the Tests suffix in the filename) and add the following method:

```
func testTotalEmployeesPerDepartment() {
  measureMetrics([XCTPerformanceMetric_WallClockTime],
              automaticallyStartMeasuring: false) {

    let departmentList = DepartmentListViewController()
    departmentList.coreDataStack =
      CoreDataStack(modelName: "EmployeeDirectory")
    self.startMeasuring()
    _ = departmentList.totalEmployeesPerDepartment()
    self.stopMeasuring()
  }
}
```

This function uses `measureMetrics` to see how long code takes to execute.

You have to set up a new Core Data stack each time so that your results don't get skewed by Core Data's excellent caching abilities, which would make subsequent test runs really fast!

Inside the block, you first create a `DepartmentListViewController` and give it a `CoreDataStack`. Then, you call `totalEmployeesPerDepartment` to retrieve the number of employees per department.

Now you need to run this test. From Xcode's menu bar, select **Product** and then **Test**, or press ⌘U. This will build the app and run the tests.

Once the tests have finished running, Xcode will look like this:

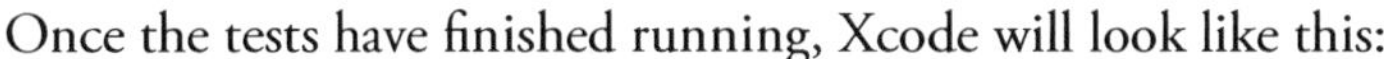

Notice two new things:

1. There's a green checkmark next to `testTotalEmployeesPerDepartment`. That means the test ran and passed.

2. There's a message on the right side with the amount of time the test took.

On the low-spec iPhone 5 test device used for the above screenshot, the test took 0.192 seconds to perform the `totalEmployeesPerDepartment` operation. These results might seem good, but there is still room for improvement.

> **Note:** These screenshots were generated with an iPhone 5. You might get somewhat different test results, depending on your test device. Don't worry — what's important is the change in time you'll see after you modify the project.

Changes to improve performance

The current implementation of `totalEmployeesPerDepartment` uses a fetch request to iterate through all employee records. Remember the very first optimization in this chapter, where you split out the full-size photo into a separate entity? There's a similar issue here: Core Data loads the entire employee record, but all you really need is a count of employees by department.

It would be more efficient to somehow group the records by department and count them. You don't need details like employee names and photo thumbnails!

Open **DepartmentListViewController.swift** and add the following code to the class below the `totalEmployeesPerDepartment()` method:

```
func totalEmployeesPerDepartmentFast() -> [[String: String]] {
  //1
  let expressionDescription = NSExpressionDescription()
  expressionDescription.name = "headCount"

  //2
  expressionDescription.expression =
    NSExpression(forFunction: "count:",
                  arguments: [NSExpression(forKeyPath:
"department")])

  //3
  let fetchRequest: NSFetchRequest<NSDictionary> =
    NSFetchRequest(entityName: "Employee")
  fetchRequest.propertiesToFetch =
    ["department", expressionDescription]
  fetchRequest.propertiesToGroupBy = ["department"]
  fetchRequest.resultType = .dictionaryResultType

  //4
  var fetchResults: [NSDictionary] = []
  do {
    fetchResults =
      try coreDataStack.mainContext.fetch(fetchRequest)
  } catch let error as NSError {
    print("ERROR: \(error.localizedDescription)")
    return [[String: String]]()
  }
  return fetchResults as! [[String: String]]
}
```

This code still uses a fetch request to populate the department list screen, but it takes advantage of an `NSExpression`. Here's how it works:

1. First, you create an `NSExpressionDescription` and name it `headCount`.

2. Next, you then create an `NSExpression` with the `count:` function for the `department` attribute.

3. Then you create a fetch request with the `Employee` entity. This time, the fetch request should only fetch the minimum required properties by using `propertiesToFetch`; you only need the department attribute and the calculated property the expression created earlier. The fetch request also groups the results by the `department` attribute. You're not interested in the managed object, so the fetch request return type is `DictionaryResultType`. This will return an array of dictionaries, each containing a department name and an employee count — just what you need!

4. Finally, you execute the fetch request.

Find the following line of code in `viewDidLoad()`:

```
items = totalEmployeesPerDepartment()
```

This line of code uses the old and slow function to populate the department list screen. Replace it by calling the function you just created:

```
items = totalEmployeesPerDepartmentFast()
```

Now the app populates the table view data source for the department list screen with the faster, NSExpression-backed fetch request.

> **Note**: NSExpression is a powerful API, yet it is seldom used, at least directly. When you create predicates with comparison operations, you may not know it, but you're actually using expressions. There are many pre-built statistical and arithmetical expressions available in NSExpression, including `average`, `sum`, `count`, `min`, `max`, `median`, `mode` and `stddev`. Consult the NSExpression documentation for a comprehensive overview.

Verify the changes

Now that you've made all the necessary changes to the project, it's once again time to see if you've improved the app's performance.

Open **DepartmentListViewControllerTests.swift** and add a new function to test the `totalEmployeesPerDepartmentFast` function you just created.

```swift
func testTotalEmployeesPerDepartmentFast() {
  measureMetrics([XCTPerformanceMetric_WallClockTime],
                  automaticallyStartMeasuring: false) {

    let departmentList = DepartmentListViewController()
    departmentList.coreDataStack =
      CoreDataStack(modelName: "EmployeeDirectory")
    self.startMeasuring()
    _ = departmentList.totalEmployeesPerDepartmentFast()
    self.stopMeasuring()
  }
}
```

As before, this test uses `measureMetrics` to see how long a particular function is taking, in this case `totalEmployeesPerDepartmentFast`.

Now you need to run this test. From Xcode's menu bar, select **Product** and then **Test**, or press ⌘U. This will build the app and run the tests.

Once the tests have finished running, Xcode will look like this:

```swift
func testTotalEmployeesPerDepartment() {
    measureMetrics([XCTPerformanceMetric_WallClockTime],
                   automaticallyStartMeasuring: false) {

        let departmentList = DepartmentListViewController()
        departmentList.coreDataStack = CoreDataStack(modelName: "EmployeeDirectory")
        self.startMeasuring()
        _ = departmentList.totalEmployeesPerDepartment()
        self.stopMeasuring()
    }
}

func testTotalEmployeesPerDepartmentFast() {
    measureMetrics([XCTPerformanceMetric_WallClockTime],
                   automaticallyStartMeasuring: false) {

        let departmentList = DepartmentListViewController()
        departmentList.coreDataStack = CoreDataStack(modelName: "EmployeeDirectory")
        self.startMeasuring()
        _ = departmentList.totalEmployeesPerDepartmentFast()
        self.stopMeasuring()
    }
}
```

This time, you'll see two messages with total execution time, one next to each test function.

> **Note:** If you don't see the time messages, you can view the details of each individual test run in the logs generated during the test. From Xcode's menu bar, select **View, Debug Area**, and then **Show Debug Area**.

As you can see, the new function, `totalEmployeesPerDepartmentFast`, took approximately 0.003 seconds to complete. That's much faster than the 0.005 seconds used by the original function, `totalEmployeesPerDepartment`. You've increased the speed of this fetch by about 40%!

Fetching counts

As you've already seen, your app doesn't always need all information from your Core Data objects; some screens simply need the counts of objects that have certain attributes.

For example, the employee detail screen shows the total number of sales an employee has made since they've been with the company.

For the purposes of this app, you don't care about the content of each individual sale —
for example, the date of the sale or the name of the purchaser — only how many sales
there are in total.

Measure the problem

You'll use XCTest again to measure the performance of the employee detail screen.

Open **EmployeeDetailViewController.swift** and find `salesCountForEmployee(_:)`.

```swift
func salesCountForEmployee(_ employee:Employee) -> String {

  let fetchRequest: NSFetchRequest<Sale> =
    NSFetchRequest(entityName: "Sale")
  let predicate =
    Predicate(format: "employee == %@", employee)
  fetchRequest.predicate = predicate

  let context = employee.managedObjectContext!
  do {
    let results = try context.fetch(fetchRequest)
    return "\(results.count)"
  } catch let error as NSError {
    print("Error: \(error.localizedDescription)")
    return "0"
  }
}
```

This code fetches all sales for a given employee and then returns the count of the returned array.

Fetching the full sale object just to see how many sales exist for a given employee is probably wasteful. This might be another opportunity to boost performance!

Let's measure the problem before attempting to fix it.

Open **EmployeeDetailViewControllerTests.swift** and find `testCountSales()`.

```swift
func testCountSales() {
  measureMetrics([XCTPerformanceMetric_WallClockTime],
                 automaticallyStartMeasuring: false) {

    let employee = self.getEmployee()
    let employeeDetails = EmployeeDetailViewController()
    self.startMeasuring()
    _ = employeeDetails.salesCountForEmployee(employee)
    self.stopMeasuring()
  }
}
```

Like the previous example, this function is using `measureMetrics` to see how long a single function takes to run. The test gets an employee from a convenience method, creates an `EmployeeDetailViewController`, begins measuring and then calls the method in question.

From Xcode's menu bar, select **Product** and then **Test**, or press ⌘U. This will build the app and run the test.

Once the test has finished running, you'll see a time next to this test method, as before.

The performance is not too bad — but there is still some room for improvement.

Changes to improve performance

In the previous example, you used NSExpression to group the data and provide a count of employees by department instead of returning the actual records themselves. You'll do the same thing here.

Open **EmployeeDetailViewController.swift** and add the following code to the class below the `salesCountForEmployee(_:)` method.

```swift
func salesCountForEmployeeFast(_ employee: Employee) -> String {

  let fetchRequest: NSFetchRequest<Sale> =
    NSFetchRequest(entityName: "Sale")

  let predicate =
    Predicate(format: "employee == %@", employee)
  fetchRequest.predicate = predicate

  let context = employee.managedObjectContext!

  do {
    let results = try context.count(for: fetchRequest)
    return "\(results)"
  } catch let error as NSError {
    print("Error: \(error.localizedDescription)")
    return "0"
  }
}
```

This code is very similar to the function you reviewed in the last section. The primary difference is that instead of calling `execute(_:)`, you now call `count(for:)`.

Find the following line of code in `configureView()`:

```swift
salesCountLabel.text = salesCountForEmployee(employee)
```

This line of code uses the old sales count function to populate the label on the department details screen. Replace it by calling the function you just created:

```swift
salesCountLabel.text = salesCountForEmployeeFast(employee)
```

Verify the changes

Now that you've made the necessary changes to the project, it's once again time to see if you've improved the app.

Open **EmployeeDetailViewControllerTests.swift** and add a new function to test the `salesCountForEmployeeFast` function you just created.

```swift
func testCountSalesFast() {
  measureMetrics([XCTPerformanceMetric_WallClockTime],
                  automaticallyStartMeasuring: false) {

    let employee = self.getEmployee()
    let employeeDetails = EmployeeDetailViewController()
    self.startMeasuring()
    _ = employeeDetails.salesCountForEmployeeFast(employee)
    self.stopMeasuring()
  }
}
```

This test is identical to the previous one, except it uses the new and, with any luck, faster function. From Xcode's menu bar, select **Product** and then **Test**, or press ⌘U. This will build the app and run the test.

Looks great — another performance improvement under your belt!

Using relationships

The code above is fast, but the faster method still seems like a lot of work. You have to create a fetch request, create a predicate, get a reference to the context, execute the fetch request and get the results out.

The Employee entity has a `sales` property, which holds a `Set` containing objects of type `Sale`. Open **EmployeeDetailViewController.swift** and add the following new method below the `salesCountForEmployeeFast(_:)` method:

```swift
func salesCountForEmployeeSimple(_ employee: Employee) -> String
{
  return "\(employee.sales.count)"
}
```

That looks better. By using the sales relationship on the Employee entity, the code is much simpler — and easier to comprehend.

Update the view controller and tests to use this method instead, following the same pattern as above. Check out the change in performance now:

> **Challenge**: Using the techniques you just learned, try to improve the performance of the `DepartmentDetailsViewController` class. Don't forget to write tests to measure the before and after execution times. As a hint, there are many methods that provide counts, rather than the full records — these can probably be optimized somehow to avoid loading the contents of the records.

Where to go from here?

If you followed this chapter all the way through, you've turned a slow, memory hog of an app into a light and fast app. You can find the final project in the folder for this chapter.

When optimizing the sample app's performance, you followed the measure–change–verify process to avoid unnecessary work. You learned how to use the Memory Report, Instruments and XCTest tools to take measurements.

Along the way, you learned how to improve your data model by putting large BLOBs in separate entities and by letting Core Data decide if data should be stored externally. You also learned how to improve fetching performance by setting batch sizes and taking advantage of the NSExpression API.

As with most things, performance is a balance between memory and speed. When using Core Data in your apps, always keep this balance in mind. With the measurement tools and some of the techniques in this book, you're well on the way to measuring, improving and verifying performance in your own apps!

Chapter 9: Multiple Managed Object Contexts

By Matthew Morey

A managed object context is an in-memory scratchpad for working with your managed objects. In Chapter 3, "The Core Data Stack", you learned how the managed object context fits in with the other classes in the Core Data stack.

Most apps need just a single managed object context. The default configuration in most Core Data apps is a single managed object context associated with the main queue. Multiple managed object contexts make your apps harder to debug; it's not something you'd use in every app, in every situation.

That being said, certain situations do warrant the use of more than one managed object context. For example, long-running tasks, such as exporting data, will block the main thread of apps that use only a single main-queue managed object context and cause the UI to stutter.

In other situations, such as when edits are being made to user data, it's helpful to treat a managed object context as a set of changes that the app can discard if it no longer needs them. Using child contexts makes this possible.

In this chapter, you'll learn about multiple managed object contexts by taking a journaling app for surfers and improving it in several ways by adding multiple contexts.

> **Note:** If common Core Data phrases such as managed object subclass and persistent store coordinator don't ring any bells, or if you're unsure what a Core Data stack is supposed to do, you may want to read or reread the first three chapters of this book before proceeding. This chapter covers advanced topics and assumes you already know the basics.

Getting started

This chapter's starter project is a simple journal app for surfers. After each surf session, a surfer can use the app to create a new journal entry that records marine parameters, such as swell height or period, and rate the session from 1 to 5. Dude, if you're not fond of hanging ten and getting barreled, no worries, brah. Just replace the surfing terminology with your favorite hobby of choice!

Introducing SurfJournal

Go to this chapter's files and find the **SurfJournal** starter project. Open the project, then build and run the app.

On startup, the application lists all previous surf session journal entries. Tapping a row brings up the detail view of a surf session with the ability to make edits.

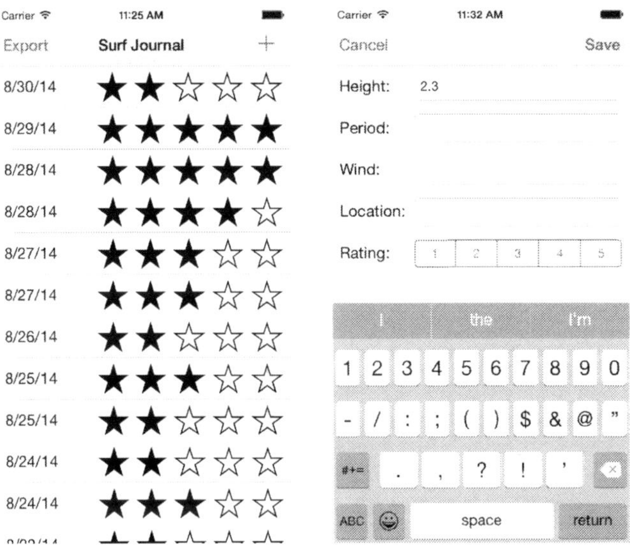

As you can see, the sample app works and has data. Tapping the Export button on the top-left exports the data to a comma-separated values (CSV) file. Tapping the plus (+) button on the top-right adds a new journal entry. Tapping a row in the list opens the entry in edit mode, where you can change or view the details of a surf session.

Although the sample project appears simple, it actually does a lot and will serve as a good base to add multi-context support. First, let's make sure you have a good understanding of the various classes in the project.

Open the project navigator and take a look at the full list of files in the starter project:

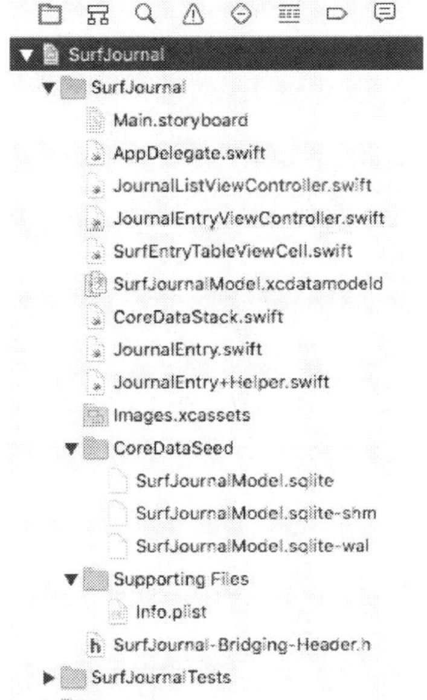

Before jumping into the code, take a brief moment to go over what each class does for you out of the box. If you've completed the earlier chapters, you should find most of these classes familiar:

- **AppDelegate**: On first launch, the app delegate creates the Core Data stack and sets the `coreDataStack` property on the primary view controller `JournalListViewController`.

- **CoreDataStack**: As in previous chapters, this object contains the cadre of Core Data objects known as the **stack**. Unlike in previous chapters, this time the stack installs a database that already has data in it on first launch. No need to worry about this just yet; you'll see how it works shortly.

- **JournalListViewController**: The sample project is a one-page, table-based application. This file represents that table. If you're curious about its UI elements, head over to **Main.storyboard**. There's a table view controller embedded in a navigation controller and a single prototype cell of type **SurfEntryTableViewCell**.

- **JournalEntryViewController**: This class handles creating and editing surf journal entries. You can see its UI in **Main.storyboard**.

- **JournalEntry**: This class represents a surf journal entry. It's an `NSManagedObject` subclass with six properties for attributes: `date`, `height`, `location`, `period`, `rating` and `wind`. If you're curious about this class's entity definition, check out **SurfJournalModel.xcdatamodel**.

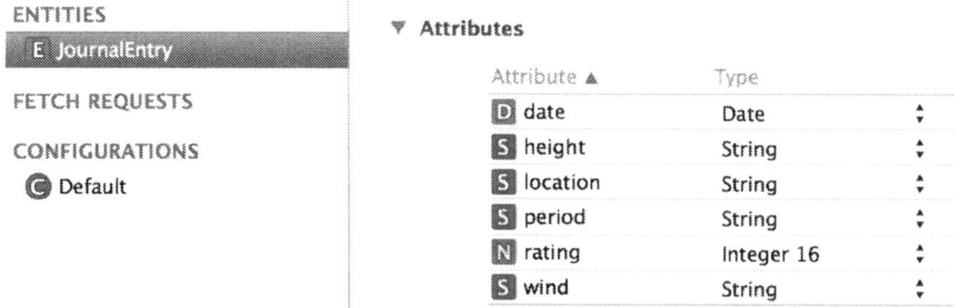

- **JournalEntry+Helper**: This is an extension to the `JournalEntry` object. It includes the CSV export method `csv()` and the `stringForDate()` helper method. These methods are implemented in the extension to avoid being destroyed when you make changes to the Core Data model.

There was already a significant amount of data when you first launched the app. While the projects in some of the previous chapters import seed data from a JSON file, this sample project comes with a seeded Core Data database.

The Core Data stack

Open **CoreDataStack.swift** and find the following code in `seedCoreDataContainerIfFirstLaunch()`:

```swift
// 1
let previouslyLaunched =
  UserDefaults.standard.bool(forKey: "previouslyLaunched")
if !previouslyLaunched {
  UserDefaults.standard.set(true, forKey: "previouslyLaunched")

  // Default directory where the CoreDataStack will store its
files
  let directory = NSPersistentContainer.defaultDirectoryURL()
  let url =
    directory.appendingPathComponent(modelName + ".sqlite")

  // 2: Copying the SQLite file
  let seededDatabaseURL =
    Bundle.main.urlForResource(modelName,
      withExtension: "sqlite")!
  _ = try? FileManager.default.removeItem(at: url)
  do {
    try FileManager.default.copyItem(at: seededDatabaseURL,
```

```
                                            to: url)
} catch let nserror as NSError {
  fatalError("Error: \(nserror.localizedDescription)")
}
```

As you can see, this chapter's version of **CoreDataStack.swift** is a little different:

1. You first check UserDefaults for the previouslyLaunched boolean value. If the current execution is indeed the app's first launch, the Bool will be **false**, making the if statement true. On first launch, the first thing you do is set previouslyLaunched to true so the seeding operation never happens again.

2. You then copy the SQLite seed file **SurfJournalModel.sqlite**, included with the app bundle, to the directory returned by the Core Data-provided method NSPersistentContainer.defaultDirectoryURL().

Now view the rest of seedCoreDataContainerIfFirstLaunch():

```
// 3: Copying the SHM file
let seededSHMURL = Bundle.main.urlForResource(modelName,
  withExtension: "sqlite-shm")!
let shmURL = directory.appendingPathComponent(
  modelName + ".sqlite-shm")
_ = try? FileManager.default.removeItem(at: shmURL)
do {
  try FileManager.default.copyItem(at: seededSHMURL,
                                    to: shmURL)
} catch let nserror as NSError {
  fatalError("Error: \(nserror.localizedDescription)")
}

// 4: Copying the WAL file
let seededWALURL = Bundle.main.urlForResource(modelName,
  withExtension: "sqlite-wal")!
let walURL = directory.appendingPathComponent(
  modelName + ".sqlite-wal")
_ = try? FileManager.default.removeItem(at: walURL)
do {
  try FileManager.default.copyItem(at: seededWALURL,
                                    to: walURL)
} catch let nserror as NSError {
  fatalError("Error: \(nserror.localizedDescription)")
}

  print("Seeded Core Data")
}
```

3. Once the copy of **SurfJournalModel.sqlite** has succeeded, you then copy over the support file **SurfJournalModel.sqlite-shm**.

4. Finally, you copy over the remaining support file **SurfJournalModel.sqlite-wal**.

The only reason **SurfJournalModel.sqlite**, **SurfJournalModel.sqlite-shm** or **SurfJournalModel.sqlite-wal** would fail to copy on first launch is if something really bad happened, such as disk corruption from cosmic radiation. In that case the device, including any apps, would likely also fail. If the files fail to copy, there's no point in continuing, so the `catch` blocks call `fatalError`.

> **Note:** Developers often frown upon using `abort` and `fatalError`, as it confuses users by causing the app to quit suddenly and without explanation. This is one scenario where `fatalError` is acceptable, since the app needs Core Data to work. If an app requires Core Data and Core Data isn't working, there's no point in letting the app continue on, only to fail sometime later in a non-deterministic way.
>
> Calling `fatalError`, at the very least, generates a stack trace, which can be helpful when trying to fix the problem. If your app has support for remote logging or crash reporting, you should log any relevant information that might be helpful for debugging before calling `fatalError`.

To support concurrent reads and writes, the persistent SQLite store in this sample app uses SHM (shared memory file) and WAL (write-ahead logging) files. You don't need to know how these extra files work, but you *do* need to be aware of their existence, and that you need to copy them over when seeding the database. If you fail to copy over these files, the app will work, but it might be missing data.

Now that you know something about beginning with a seeded database, you'll start learning about multiple managed object contexts by working on a temporary private context.

Doing work in the background

If you haven't done so already, tap the Export button at the top-left and then immediately try to scroll the list of surf session journal entries. Notice anything? The export operation takes several seconds, and it prevents the UI from responding to touch events such as scrolling.

The UI is blocked during the export operation because both the export operation and UI are using the main queue to perform their work. This is the default behavior.

The traditional way to fix this is to use Grand Central Dispatch to run the export operation on a background queue. However, Core Data managed object contexts are not thread-safe. That means you can't just dispatch to a background queue and use the same Core Data stack.

The solution is simple: use a private background queue rather than the main queue for the export operation. This will keep the main queue free for the UI to use.

But before you jump in and fix the problem, you need to understand how the export operation works.

Exporting data

Start by viewing how the app creates the CSV strings for the `JournalEntry` entity. Open **JournalEntry+Helper.swift** and find `csv()`:

```swift
func csv() -> String {
  let coalescedHeight = height ?? ""
  let coalescedPeriod = period ?? ""
  let coalescedWind = wind ?? ""
  let coalescedLocation = location ?? ""
  let coalescedRating: String
  if let rating = rating?.int32Value {
    coalescedRating = String(rating)
  } else {
    coalescedRating = ""
  }

  return "\(stringForDate()),\(coalescedHeight),
    \(coalescedPeriod), \(coalescedWind),
    \(coalescedLocation),\(coalescedRating)\n"
}
```

As you can see, `JournalEntry` returns a comma-separated string of the entity's attributes. Because the `JournalEntry` attributes are allowed to be `nil`, the function uses the nil coalescing operator (`??`) to export an empty string instead of an unhelpful debug message that the attribute is `nil`.

Note: The nil coalescing operator (`??`) unwraps an optional if it contains a value; otherwise it returns a default value. For example, the following: `let coalescedHeight = height != nil ? height! : ""` can be shortened using the nil coalescing operator to: `let coalescedHeight = height ?? ""`.

That's how the app creates the CSV strings for an individual journal entry, but how does the app save the CSV file to disk? Open **JournalListViewController.swift** and find the following code in `exportCSVFile()`:

```swift
// 1
let context = coreDataStack.mainContext
var results: [JournalEntry] = []
do {
  results = try context.fetch(self.surfJournalFetchRequest())
} catch let error as NSError {
  print("ERROR: \(error.localizedDescription)")
}


// 2
let exportFilePath = NSTemporaryDirectory() + "export.csv"
let exportFileURL = URL(fileURLWithPath: exportFilePath)
FileManager.default.createFile(atPath: exportFilePath,
  contents: Data(), attributes: nil)
```

Going through the CSV export code step-by-step:

1. First, retrieve all `JournalEntry` entities by executing a fetch request.

    The fetch request is the same one used by the fetched results controller. Therefore you reuse the `surfJournalFetchRequest` method to create the requst to avoid duplication.

2. Next, create the URL for the exported CSV file by appending the file name ("export.csv") to the output of the `NSTemporaryDirectory` method.

    The path returned by `NSTemporaryDirectory` is a unique directory for temporary file storage. This a good place for files that can easily be generated again and don't need to be backed up by iTunes or to iCloud.

    After creating the export URL, call `createFileAtPath(_:contents:attributes:)` to create the empty file where you'll store the exported data. If a file already exists at the specified file path, this method will remove it first.

Once the app has the empty file, it can write the CSV data to disk:

```swift
// 3
let fileHandle: FileHandle?
do {
  fileHandle = try FileHandle(forWritingTo: exportFileURL)
} catch let error as NSError {
  print("ERROR: \(error.localizedDescription)")
  fileHandle = nil
}
```

```swift
if let fileHandle = fileHandle {
  // 4
  for journalEntry in results {
    fileHandle.seekToEndOfFile()
    guard let csvData = journalEntry
      .csv()
      .data(using: .utf8, allowLossyConversion: false) else {
        continue
    }

    fileHandle.write(csvData)
  }

  // 5
  fileHandle.closeFile()

  print("Export Path: \(exportFilePath)")
  self.navigationItem.leftBarButtonItem =
    self.exportBarButtonItem()
  self.showExportFinishedAlertView(exportFilePath)
} else {
  self.navigationItem.leftBarButtonItem =
    self.exportBarButtonItem()
}
```

Here's how the file-handling works:

3. First, the app needs to create a file handler for writing, which is simply an object that handles the low-level disk operations necessary for writing data. To create a file handler for writing, use the `FileHandle(forWritingTo:)` initializer.

4. Next, iterate over all `JournalEntry` entities.

   During each iteration, you attempt to create a UTF8-encoded string using `csv()` on `JournalEntry` and `data(using:allowLossyConversion:)` on `String`.

   If it's successful, you write the UTF8 string to disk using the file handler `write()` method.

5. Finally, close the export file-writing file handler, since it's no longer needed.

Once the app has written all the data to disk, it shows an alert dialog with the exported file path.

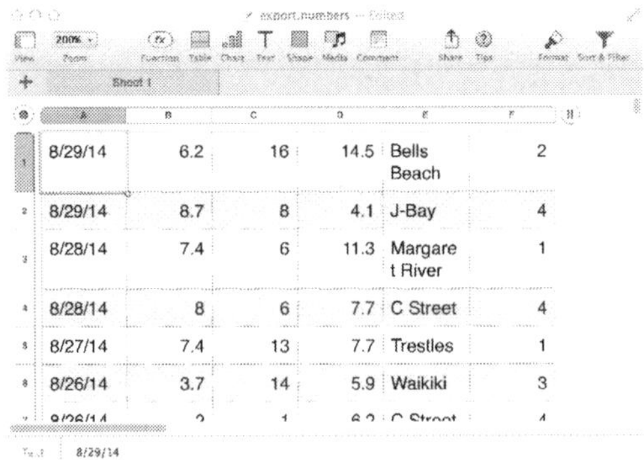

> **Note:** This alert view with the export path is fine for learning purposes, but for a real app, you'll need to provide the user with a way to retrieve the exported CSV file, for example by using `UIActivityViewController`.

To open the exported CSV file, use Excel, Numbers or your favorite text editor to navigate to and open the file specified in the alert dialog. If you open the file in Numbers you will see the following:

Now that you've seen how the app currently exports data, it's time to make some improvements.

Exporting in the background

You want the UI to continue working while the export is happening. To fix the UI problem, you'll perform the export operation on a private background context instead of on the main context.

Open **JournalListViewController.swift** and find the following code in `exportCSVFile()`:

```
// 1
let context = coreDataStack.mainContext
var results: [JournalEntry] = []
do {
  results = try context.fetch(self.surfJournalFetchRequest())
} catch let error as NSError {
  print("ERROR: \(error.localizedDescription)")
}
```

As you saw earlier, this code retrieves all of the journal entries by calling `fetch()` on the managed object context.

Next, replace the above code with the following:

```
// 1
coreDataStack.storeContainer.performBackgroundTask {
  (context) in

  var results: [JournalEntry] = []
  do {
    results = try context.fetch(self.surfJournalFetchRequest())
  } catch let error as NSError {
    print("ERROR: \(error.localizedDescription)")
  }
```

Instead of using the main managed object context also used by the UI, you're now calling `performBackgroundTask(_:)` method. This creates and executes the code block on that private context.

The private context created by `performBackgroundTask(_:)` is on a private queue, which doesn't block the main UI queue. You could also manually create a new temporary private context with a concurrency type of `PrivateQueueConcurrencyType` instead of using `performBackgroundTask(_:)`.

> **Note:** There are three concurrency types a managed object context can use:
>
> **ConfinementConcurrencyType** specifies that the context will use the thread confinement pattern and that the developer will be responsible for managing all

thread access. You should consider this type deprecated and never use it, as the next two types cover all use cases.

PrivateQueueConcurrencyType specifies the context will be associated with a private dispatch queue instead of the main queue. This is the type of queue you just used to move the export operation off of the main queue so it would no longer interfere with the UI.

MainQueueConcurrencyType, the default type, specifies that the context will be associated with the main queue. This type is what the main context (`coreDataStack.mainContext`) uses. Any UI operation, such as creating the fetched results controller for the table view, must use a context of this type.

Next, find the following code in the same method:

```
print("Export Path: \(exportFilePath)")
self.navigationItem.leftBarButtonItem =
  self.exportBarButtonItem()
self.showExportFinishedAlertView(exportFilePath)
} else {
self.navigationItem.leftBarButtonItem =
  self.exportBarButtonItem()
}
```

Replace the code with the following:

```
print("Export Path: \(exportFilePath)")
// 6
DispatchQueue.main.async {
  self.navigationItem.leftBarButtonItem =
    self.exportBarButtonItem()
  self.showExportFinishedAlertView(exportFilePath)
}
} else {
DispatchQueue.main.async {
  self.navigationItem.leftBarButtonItem =
    self.exportBarButtonItem()
}
}
} // 7 Closing brace for performBackgroundTask
```

To finish off the task:

6. You should always perform all operations related to the UI on the main queue, such as showing an alert view when the export operation is finished; otherwise, unpredictable things might happen. Use `DispatchQueue.main.async` to show the final alert view message on the main queue.

7. Finally, add a closing curly brace to close the block you opened earlier in step 1 via the `performBackgroundTask(_:)` call.

Now that you've moved the export operation to a new context with a private queue, build and run to see if it works!

You should see exactly what you saw before:

Tap the Export button in the top left, and immediately try to scroll the list of surf session journal entries. Notice anything different this time? The export operation still takes several seconds to complete, but the table view continues to scroll during this time. The export operation is no longer blocking the UI.

Cowabunga, dude! Gnarly job making the UI more responsive.

You've just witnessed how doing work on a private background queue can improve a user's experience with your app. Now you'll expand on the use of multiple contexts by examining a child context.

Editing on a scratchpad

Right now, SurfJournal uses the main context (`coreDataStack.mainContext`) when creating a new journal entry or or viewing an existing one. There's nothing wrong with this approach; the starter project works as-is.

For journaling-style apps like this one, you can simplify the app architecture by thinking of edits or new entries as a set of changes, like a scratch pad. As the user edits the journal entry, you update the attributes of the managed object. Once the changes are complete, you either save them or throw them away, depending on what the user wants to do.

You can think of child managed object contexts as temporary scratch pads that you can either discard completely, or save and send the changes to the parent context.

But what *is* a child context, technically?

All managed object contexts have a parent store from which you can retrieve and change data in the form of managed objects, such as the `JournalEntry` objects in this project. Typically, the parent store is a persistent store coordinator, which is the case for the main context provided by the `CoreDataStack` class. Alternatively, you can set the parent store for a given context to another managed object context, making it a child context.

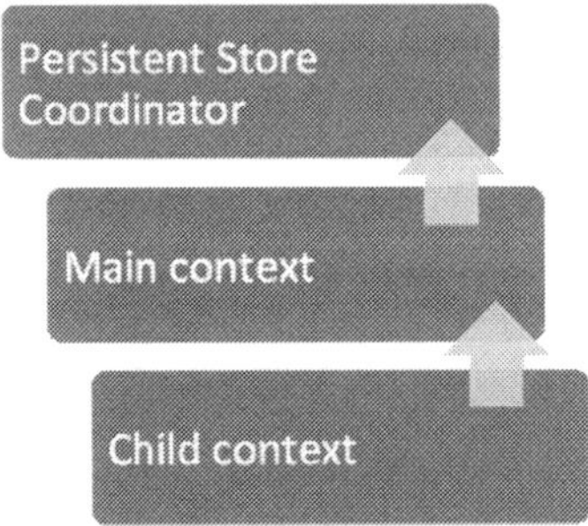

When you save a child context, the changes only go to the parent context. Changes to the parent context won't be sent to the persistent store coordinator until the parent context is saved.

Before you jump in and add a child context, you need to understand how the current viewing and editing operation works.

Viewing and editing

The first part of the operation requires segueing from the main list view to the journal detail view. Open **JournalListViewController.swift** and find `prepareForSegue(for:sender:)`:

```swift
// 1
if segue.identifier == "SegueListToDetail" {

  // 2
  guard let navigationController =
    segue.destination as? UINavigationController,
    let detailViewController =
      navigationController.topViewController
        as? JournalEntryViewController,
    let indexPath = tableView.indexPathForSelectedRow else {
```

```
      fatalError("Application storyboard mis-configuration")
  }

  // 3
  let surfJournalEntry =
    fetchedResultsController.object(at: indexPath)

  //4
  detailViewController.journalEntry = surfJournalEntry
  detailViewController.context =
    surfJournalEntry.managedObjectContext
  detailViewController.delegate = self
```

Taking the segue code step-by-step:

1. There are two segues: **SegueListToDetail** and **SegueListToDetailAdd**. The first, shown in the previous code block, runs when the user taps on a row in the table view to view or edit a previous journal entry.

2. Next, you get a reference to the `JournalEntryViewController` that the user is going to end up seeing. It's presented inside a navigation controller so there's some unpacking to do. This code also verifies there's a selected index path in the table view.

3. Then you get the `JournalEntry` selected by the user, using the fetched results controller's `object(at:)` method.

4. Finally, you set all required variables on the `JournalEntryViewController` instance. The `surfJournalEntry` variable corresponds to the `JournalEntry` entity resolved in step 3. The context variable is the managed object context to be used for any operation; for now, it just uses the main context. The `JournalListViewController` sets itself as the delegate of the `JournalEntryViewController` so it can be informed when the user has completed the edit operation.

SegueListToDetailAdd is similar to **SegueListToDetail**, except the app creates a new `JournalEntry` entity instead of retrieving an existing one. The app executes **SegueListToDetailAdd** when the user taps the plus (+) button on the top-right to create a new journal entry.

Now you know how both segues work, switch to **JournalEntryViewController.swift** and look at the `JournalEntryDelegate` protocol at the top of the file:

```
protocol JournalEntryDelegate {
  func didFinish(viewController: JournalEntryViewController,
    didSave: Bool)
}
```

The `JournalEntryDelegate` protocol is very short and consists of only one method: `didFinish(viewController:didSave:)`. This method, which the protocol requires the delegate to implement, indicates if the user is done editing or viewing a journal entry and whether any changes should be saved.

To understand how `didFinish(viewController:didSave:)` works, switch back to **JournalListViewController.swift** and find that method:

```swift
func didFinish(viewController: JournalEntryViewController,
                      didSave: Bool) {

  // 1
  guard didSave,
    let context = viewController.context,
    context.hasChanges else {
      dismiss(animated: true)
      return
  }

  // 2
  context.perform {
    do {
      try context.save()
    } catch let error as NSError {
      fatalError("Error: \(error.localizedDescription)")
    }

    // 3
    self.coreDataStack.saveContext()
  }

  // 4
  dismiss(animated: true)
}
```

Taking each numbered comment in turn:

1. First, use a `guard` statement to check the `didSave` parameter. This will be `true` if the user taps the Save button instead of the Cancel button, so the app should save the user's data. The `guard` statement also uses the `hasChanges` property to check if anything's changed; if nothing has changed, there's no need to waste time doing more work.

2. Next, save the `JournalEntryViewController` context inside of a `perform(_:)` closure. The code sets this context to the main context; in this case it's a bit redundant since there's only one context, but this doesn't change the behavior.

   Once you add a child context to the workflow later on, the `JournalEntryViewController` context will be different from the main context, making this code necessary.

If the save fails, call `fatalError` to abort the app with the relevant error information.

3. Next, save the main context via `saveContext`, defined in **CoreDataStack.swift**, persisting any edits to disk.

4. Finally, dismiss the `JournalEntryViewController`.

> **Note:** If a managed object context is of type `MainQueueConcurrencyType`, you don't *have* to wrap code in `perform(_:)`, but it doesn't hurt to use it.

> If you don't know what type the context will be, as is the case in `didFinish(viewController:didSave:)`, it's safest to use `perform(_:)` so it will work with both parent and child contexts.

There's a problem with the above implementation — have you spotted it?

When the app adds a new journal entry, it creates a new object and adds it to the managed object context. If the user taps the Cancel button, the app won't save the context, but the new object will still be present. If the user then adds and saves another entry, the canceled object will *still* be present! You won't see it in the UI unless you've got the patience to scroll all the way to the end, but it will show up at the bottom of the CSV export.

You could solve this problem by deleting the object when the user cancels the view controller. But what if the changes were complex, involved multiple objects, or required you to alter properties of an object as part of the editing workflow? Using a child context will help you manage these complex situations with ease.

Using child contexts for sets of edits

Now that you know how the app currently edits and creates `JournalEntry` entities, you'll modify the implementation to use a child managed object context as a temporary scratch pad.

It's easy to do — you simply need to modify the segues. Open **JournalListViewController.swift** and find the following code for **SegueListToDetail** in `prepareForSegue(for:sender:)`:

```
detailViewController.journalEntry = surfJournalEntry
detailViewController.context =
  surfJournalEntry.managedObjectContext
```

```
detailViewController.delegate = self
```

Next, replace that code with the following:

```
// 1
let childContext =
  NSManagedObjectContext(
    concurrencyType: .mainQueueConcurrencyType)
childContext.parent = coreDataStack.mainContext

// 2
let childEntry =
  childContext.object(with: surfJournalEntry.objectID)
    as? JournalEntry

// 3
detailViewController.journalEntry = childEntry
detailViewController.context = childContext
detailViewController.delegate = self
```

Here's the play-by-play:

1. First, you create a new managed object context named `childContext` with a
    `MainQueueConcurrencyType`. Here you set a parent context instead of a persistent
    store coordinator as you would normally do when creating a managed object context.
    Here, you set `parent` to `mainContext` of your `CoreDataStack`.

2. Next, you retrieve the relevant journal entry using the child context's
    `object(with:)` method. You must use `object(with:)` to retrieve the journal entry
    because managed objects are specific to the context that created them. However,
    `objectID` values are not specific to a single context, so you can use them when you
    need to access objects in multiple contexts.

3. Finally, you set all required variables on the `JournalEntryViewController`
    instance. This time, you use `childEntry` and `childContext` instead of the original
    `surfJournalEntry` and `surfJournalEntry.managedObjectContext`.

> **Note:** You might be wondering why you need to pass *both* the managed object
> and the managed object context to the `detailViewController`, since managed
> objects already have a context variable. This is because managed objects only have
> a weak reference to the context. If you don't pass the context, ARC will remove
> the context from memory (since nothing else is retaining it) and the app will not
> behave as you expect.

Build and run your app; it should work exactly as before. In this case, no visible changes to the app are a good thing; the user can still tap on a row to view and edit a surf session journal entry.

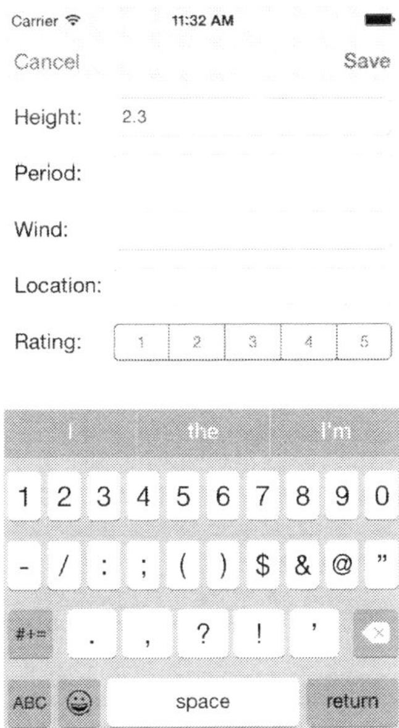

By using a child context as a container for the journal edits, you've reduced the complexity of your app's architecture. With the edits on a separate context, canceling or saving managed object changes is trivial.

Nice work, dude! You're no longer a kook when it comes to multiple managed object contexts. Bodacious!

Where to go from here?

If you followed this chapter all the way through, you've turned an app with a single managed object context into an app with multiple contexts. You can find the final project in the folder for this chapter.

You improved UI responsiveness by performing the export operation on a private background managed object context, and you improved the app's architecture by creating a child context and using it like a scratch pad.

But best of all, you learned how to talk like a surfer. That's a good day's work! :]

Challenge

With your newfound knowledge, try to update **SegueListToDetailAdd** to use a child context when adding a new journal entry.

Just like before, you'll need to create a child context that has the main context as its parent. You'll also need to remember to create the new entry on the correct context.

If you get stuck, check out the project with the challenge solution in the folder for this chapter — but give it your best shot first!

We hope this book has helped you get up to speed with Core Data and Swift! You're well on your way to developing your own high-performance apps with well-designed models and unit tests.

As you've seen, you can use Core Data to model all kinds of data — from names and addresses to images and the relationships in between. We encourage you to find where Core Data and its object graph-based persistence can work for you and give it a try.

If you have any questions or comments as you continue to use Core Data, please stop by our forums at http://www.raywenderlich.com/forums.

Thank you again for purchasing this book. Your continued support is what makes the tutorials, books, videos and other things we do at raywenderlich.com possible — we truly appreciate it!

Wishing you speed, stability and smooth migrations in all your Core Data adventures,

– Pietro, Saul, Aaron, Matthew, Rich, Darren and Chris

The *Core Data by Tutorials* team

Made in the USA
Middletown, DE
18 July 2017